15

L'anglais de la presse

Jérôme Lepioufle
Éloi Le Divenach

BELIN
8, rue Férou - 75278 Paris cedex 06
www.editions-belin.com

 ISSN 1159-7135 ISBN 978-2-7011-3933-3

Table des matières

Avant-propos

Cette nouvelle édition de *L'anglais de la presse (English in the News)* consacrée au vocabulaire anglais de l'actualité s'inscrit dans la continuité des trois versions précédentes tout en y intégrant de nombreuses modifications et innovations.
Nous avons en effet profité de cette nouvelle édition pour effectuer une mise à jour approfondie du vocabulaire en constante évolution. Ainsi, certains mots sortis de l'usage ont disparu. De nombreux autres, nouvellement apparus ou récemment poussés sur le devant de la scène, avec bien souvent de nouvelles acceptions, ont quant à eux été inclus. Des thèmes dont l'importance n'a cessé de croître font maintenant l'objet de parties à part entière dans divers chapitres. Figurent dans ces catégories des sujets comme : *Renewable Energy (The Environment), Globalisation (The Economy I), E-Commerce (The Economy II), Cloning and Genetics (Medicine), Crashes (Space)*. Le chapitre 23 (*Sport*) a lui été totalement remanié pour une lisibilité accrue.

Nouvelles rubriques, suppressions, déplacements et ajouts de vocabulaire, cette nouvelle édition de *L'anglais de la presse* bénéficie donc d'un enrichissement lexical considérable.

Chaque chapitre de vocabulaire est complété d'un ou deux nouveaux articles, selon leur longueur, (à l'exception du chapitre 24) tirés des meilleurs quotidiens et hebdomadaires britanniques. Ils sont suivis d'exercices qui permettent de pratiquer le vocabulaire acquis et de se familiariser avec la presse anglophone. De courtes dépêches de presse suivent ces textes didactisés et permettent de rebrasser le vocabulaire spécifique de chaque chapitre. L'utilisateur trouvera en fin d'ouvrage un corrigé. Celui-ci joue un rôle de guide sémantique, de test d'évaluation, de source d'information et il incite l'utilisateur à la recherche personnelle.

Le court descriptif et la mention du site Internet de chacun des organes de presse utilisés dans cette édition doivent permettre aux utilisateurs de resituer chacune de ces sources dans le paysage médiatique et d'encourager la consultation périodique d'articles de presse grâce à l'Internet.

Par ailleurs, notre souci d'accompagner au mieux le lecteur dans sa compréhension de la presse anglo-saxonne nous a conduit à élaborer une aide méthodologique visant à éclaircir le sens des titres des articles qui constituent une difficulté que même les anglophones éprouvent parfois en lisant rapidement les titres.
Ainsi conçu, le livre permet l'acquisition systématique et graduée du vocabulaire de l'actualité. Pour tous ceux qui s'efforcent d'entretenir ou de perfectionner leur anglais, soit par un travail individuel, soit dans le cadre de cours de langues, *L'anglais de la presse* devrait constituer un outil précieux.

Il s'adresse tout particulièrement aux étudiants de premier cycle de l'enseignement supérieur désireux d'acquérir une connaissance du vocabulaire anglais de l'actualité.

Conseils d'utilisation

Aux nouveaux utilisateurs, nous croyons utile de rappeler que, pour faciliter l'utilisation de l'ouvrage, le vocabulaire a été divisé en deux parties : le *Vocabulaire à haute fréquence* et le *Vocabulaire complémentaire,* séparées par un ensemble d'expressions et de locutions idiomatiques.

Nous conseillons de commencer par le *Vocabulaire à haute fréquence* choisi dans un chapitre quelconque du livre, en fractionnant l'étude de ce vocabulaire selon les possibilités ou les disponibilités de chacun et de jeter un coup d'œil rapide au *Vocabulaire complémentaire* avant d'étudier les articles situés en fin de chapitre et de faire les exercices qui les accompagnent ; certains de ces exercices sont spécialement conçus pour obtenir une lecture attentive et précise. Enfin, vérifier le travail en le confrontant au corrigé situé à la fin de l'ouvrage. L'étude du *Vocabulaire complémentaire* peut ensuite être modulée selon l'objectif plus ou moins avancé poursuivi par l'utilisateur.

La lecture des journaux et des magazines, la compréhension des informations des média audio-visuels ainsi que l'expression orale et écrite seront sensiblement améliorées par une utilisation de *L'anglais de la presse.*

Afin d'enrichir le travail de préparation, nous suggérons que l'étudiant, pour chaque exercice du type QCM ou « vrai/faux » justifie sa réponse en se référant à l'article de journal concerné. Nous suggérons également l'entraînement à l'écoute de courts bulletins d'information, en se greffant sur l'actualité du moment, de préférence enregistrés. Cet exercice de compréhension et d'expression complétera de façon très profitable les exercices proposés dans *L'anglais dans la presse.*

Abréviations utilisées dans l'ouvrage

EU	The European Union
UK	the United Kingdom
sb.	somebody
sth.	something
US	The United States
UE	l'Union Européenne
qch.	quelque chose
qn.	quelqu'un
fam.	familier

Signes phonétiques

Sons voyelles

about	[ə]	bird	[ɜː]
bag	[æ]	clock	[ɒ]
car	[ɑː]	four	[ɔː]
head	[e]	put	[ʊ]
seat	[iː]	moon	[uː]
sit	[ɪ]	bus	[ʌ]

Sons diphtongues

make	[eɪ]	toy	[ɔɪ]
so	[əʊ]	near	[ɪə]
five	[aɪ]	chair	[ɛə]
now	[aʊ]	pure	[ʊə]

Sons triphtongues

player	[eɪə]	power	[aʊə]
fire	[aɪə]	slower	[əʊə]

Sons consonnes

book	[b]	narrow	[n]
cap	[k]	part	[p]
down	[d]	river	[r]
four	[f]	simple	[s]
go	[g]	top	[t]
hat	[h]	very	[v]
Jim	[dʒ]	west	[w]
list	[l]	yes	[j]
mist	[m]	zoo	[z]
measure	[ʒ]	shop	[ʃ]
chicken	[tʃ]	long	[ŋ]
think	[θ]	this	[ð]

Les titres des journaux

Alors que les titres de la presse française sont en général très détaillés et explicites, les titres de journaux de langue anglaise sont souvent difficiles à comprendre, voire abscons. Le titre ne prend tout son sens qu'après lecture de l'article. On conseillera donc au lecteur de ne s'intéresser en détail au titre qu'après une lecture attentive du texte. La difficulté de compréhension de ces titres est due aux règles spécifiques et au système grammatical particulier qui les régissent et dont voici les grands principes.

1. Les titres ne sont pas de vraies phrases et peuvent parfois se limiter à une succession d'adjectifs et de noms. Il faut alors rétablir le lien logique qui les unit :

HSBC in pact with union on Asia jobs *(The Daily Telegraph,* page 58)
« Asia jobs » = *jobs in Asia.* Notez aussi que on est souvent utilisé comme un raccourci de *concerning* ou *over,* et *in* est un raccourci de *involved in.*

Teacher in head scarf charge *(The Guardian,* page 127)
« head scarf charge » = *a charge concerning (the wearing of) a head scarf*

2. On opère une ellipse quasi-systématique des articles définis et indéfinis dans les titres d'articles.

UN postpones global human cloning ban *(New Scientist,* page 84)
Skier survives blizzard ordeal *(The Observer,* page 227)

3. La construction des titres d'articles répond à un système de conjugaison très simplifié dû à l'élision systématique de l'auxiliaire *be.* Les formes verbales complexes sont ainsi extrêmement rares *(has plunged, is starting...)* et seule la construction du présent simple est utilisée *(plunges, starts...)* :

Eurotunnel plunges £1.3bn into red *(The Daily Telegraph,* page 42)
« plunges » = *has plunged*

Kerry starts campaigns with attack on Bush *(The Times,* page 101)
« starts » = *is starting*

Une terminaison *-ed* ne sera donc pas un prétérit mais une forme passive :

"At least 50" killed in Iraq car bomb attack *(AP,* page 187)
« killed » – *have been killed*

L'expression du futur s'effectue au moyen d'un infinitif, contraction de la structure *be to* après ellipse de *be* :

Bombardier to axe 1,362 jobs in UK *(The Daily Telegraph,* page 80)
« to axe » = *is to axe/is going to axe/intends to axe...*

Children to study atheism at school *(The Observer,* page 124)
« to study » = *are to study/will have to study...*

Il est parfois difficile d'identifier le verbe, s'il y en a un :

French drug rival moves for Aventis (*The Daily Telegraph*, page 44)
Si *« moves »* est bien ici un verbe, *moves* est également un substantif très utilisé dans les titres de journaux d'où un risque d'erreur d'interprétation, même pour des anglophones.

4. Enfin, le titre est souvent l'occasion pour l'auteur de montrer sa culture, son érudition ou son humour par des références littéraires, cinématographiques, etc. ou des jeux de mots :

Opportunity knocks in latest Mars Landing (*The Guardian*, page 91)
« Opportunity knocks » est une référence non seulement au proverbe « opportunity seldom knocks twice » mais aussi à un jeu télévisé très célèbre des années 60-70 qui s'appelait *« Opportunity knocks »*.

On voit donc bien que le caractère apparemment sibyllin du titre répond en fait à un nombre de règles et principes répertoriés et que ce n'est souvent qu'après la lecture de l'article qu'il prend tout son sens.

1 THE ENVIRONMENT

L'ENVIRONNEMENT

Vocabulaire à haute fréquence

General background	**Contexte général**
to pollute [pə'lu:t]	polluer
pollution	la pollution
environment [ɪn'vaɪərənmənt]	l'environnement
an environmentalist [ɪnˌvaɪərən'mentəlɪst]	un défenseur de l'environnement
nature conservation	la protection de la nature
a conservationist	un protecteur de la nature
to discharge	décharger, déverser
to dump	rejeter, déposer
to get rid of, to dispose of	se débarrasser de
to phase out	abandonner progressivement
disposal	la destruction, l'élimination
waste, rubbish, refuse ['refju:s], trash, garbage *(US)*	les déchets, les ordures
litter	les détritus
a tip, a dump	une décharge, un dépôt
to escape	s'échapper
to leak	fuir, s'échapper
a leak, a leakage	une fuite, une coulée
a sewer ['sju:ə]	un égout
sewage	les eaux usées
a sewage farm/plant	une station d'épuration
a sewage system	un réseau d'assainissement
to treat	traiter

treatment	le traitement
a standard	une norme
to recycle	recycler
recyclable	recyclable
biodegradable	biodégradable
the greenhouse effect	l'effet de serre
greenhouse gas	gaz à effet de serre
global warming	le réchauffement planétaire
climate change	le changement climatique
biodiversity	la biodiversité

Industry and car pollution — La pollution industrielle et automobile

chemistry ['kemɪstrɪ]	la chimie
a chemical	un produit chimique
a gas	un gaz, une vapeur
exhaust fumes	les gaz d'échappement
to release	libérer, dégager
a release	un dégagement, une émanation
an emission	une émission, un rejet
a particle	une particule
nitrogen ['naɪtrədʒən]	l'azote
mercury	le mercure
lead [led]	le plomb
lead-free, unleaded	sans plomb
acid rain	la pluie acide
the ozone layer	la couche d'ozone
the ozone hole	le trou dans la couche d'ozone

Farm pollution — La pollution agricole

a pesticide	un pesticide
an insecticide	un insecticide
to spread	épandre
a fertiliser	un engrais
manure [mə'njʊə]	le fumier
nitrates ['naɪtreɪts]	les nitrates
to spray	pulvériser
a spray	une pulvérisation
a crop	une récolte
intensive	intensif
factory farming	l'élevage hors-sol
organic farming	l'agriculture biologique
GM (genetically modified) food/crops	aliments/cultures transgéniques
GM labelling	l'étiquetage OGM

Oil pollution	**La pollution pétrolière**
crude oil	le pétrole brut
an oil tanker	un pétrolier
a cargo	une cargaison
a tank	une cuve
the hull	la coque
single hulled/double hulled	à simple/double coque
to spill	(se) déverser
a spill	un déversement
a black tide, an oil spill	une marée noire
a slick	une nappe
a detergent [dɪ'tɜːdʒənt]	un détersif
marine life	le milieu marin
to soil, to foul [faʊl]	salir, souiller
to clean up	nettoyer
relief workers, salvage workers	les secouristes

Nuclear pollution	**La pollution nucléaire**
a power plant/station	une centrale
fuel	le combustible
enriched uranium	l'uranium enrichi
to cool	refroidir
a cooling system	un système de refroidissement
a breakdown	une panne
a fault	un défaut, une anomalie
faulty	défectueux
radiation [ˌreɪdɪ'eɪʃn]	les radiations
radioactivity	la radioactivité
radioactive	radioactif
radioactive discharges	des rejets radioactifs
a level	un niveau, une teneur
a fall-out	une retombée
dust	la poussière
to process	traiter
to reprocess	retraiter
material	des matières
to bury	enfouir
burying	l'enfouissement
to store	stocker
storage	le stockage

Renewable energy	**Les énergies renouvelables**
fossil fuel	l'énergie fossile
clean/green energy	l'énergie propre
to tap	exploiter
wind power	l'énergie éolienne

a wind turbine, a wind mill	une éolienne
a windfarm	une ferme éolienne
water power	l'énergie hydraulique
a dam, a barrage	un barrage
solar power	l'énergie solaire
solar cells, photo-voltaic cells	des cellules photovoltaïques
solar panels	des panneaux solaires
a fuel cell	une pile à combustible

Consequences — Les conséquences

to sustain	faire durer, maintenir
sustainable	durable, pérenne
sustainable development	développement durable
a hazard	un risque
to affect, to hit	toucher, atteindre
to do harm to sth.	faire du mal à qch.
harmful	nuisible
safe, harmless	sans danger, inoffensif
noxious	nocif
to endanger	mettre en danger
to threaten ['θretn]	menacer
a threat	une menace
to poison	empoisonner
toxic, poisonous	toxique, empoisonné
a dose	une dose
a trace, a residue	une trace, un résidu
drinking water	l'eau potable
underground waters	les nappes souterraines
water supply	l'alimentation en eau
the food chain	la chaîne alimentaire
to damage	endommager
damage	les dégâts
to destroy	détruire
destruction	la destruction
a disaster	un désastre
a catastrophe [kə'tæstrəfɪ]	une catastrophe
to contaminate	contaminer
a contamination	une contamination
to compensate	indemniser
compensation	une indemnité

Expressions

to deplete the ozone layer	appauvrir la couche d'ozone
dumping at sea	les décharges en mer
to break down a slick	réduire une nappe

the balance of nature	l'équilibre de la nature
environmentally friendly	respecte l'environnement
the "polluter pays" principle	le principe du pollueur-payeur

Vocabulaire complémentaire

General background	Contexte général
the rainforest	la forêt tropicale
deforestation/reforestation	déboisement/reboisement
carbon sink	puits à carbone
a pollutant	un polluant
ecology ['ɪkɒlədʒɪ]	l'écologie
an ecologist	un écologiste
ecological [i:kə'lɒdʒɪkl]	écologique
an ecosystem	un écosystème
a dustbin, a trash can *(US)*	une poubelle
a dustman	un éboueur
a landfill site	un site d'enfouissement
strewn/littered with	jonché de
a bottle bank	un conteneur de collecte du verre

Industry and car pollution	La pollution industrielle et automobile
an effluent	un effluent
carbon	le carbone
chlorofluorocarbons *(CFCs)*	les chlorofluorocarbones
a propellant	un propulseur
an aerosol	un aérosol
a substitute	un produit de substitution
an alternative	un produit de remplacement
depletion	l'appauvrissement
a monoxide	un monoxyde
carbon dioxide	le gaz carbonique
catalytic	catalytique
asbestos	l'amiante
dioxin	la dioxine

Farm pollution	La pollution agricole
the precautionary principe	le principe de précaution
a weedkiller	un désherbant
a herbicide	un herbicide
weeds	les mauvaises herbes
a fungicide	un fongicide
to apply	appliquer, mettre (sur)

an application	une application, un usage
slurry	le lisier
fish farming	l'élevage piscicole
a battery	une batterie (élevage)
animal feed	les aliments pour animaux
a hormone	une hormone
a preservative	un produit conservateur
a substance	une substance

Oil and nuclear pollution — La pollution pétrolière et nucléaire

to flush, to swill tanks	dégazer
hydrocarbons	les hydrocarbures
the hold	la soute
an oil rig	une plate-forme de forage
to drill	forer
offshore	au large
to drift	dériver
ashore	vers la côte
a containment boom, a floating boom	un barrage flottant
a skimmer vessel	une barge de récupération
spent fuel	le combustible usé
to decommission	désaffecter
a reprocessing plant	une usine de retraitement
leukaemia [luːˈkiːmɪə]	la leucémie
caesium [ˈsiːzɪəm]	le césium
iodine [ˈaɪədaɪn, ˈaɪədiːn]	l'iode
a containment structure	une enceinte de confinement
the core	le cœur
a fast breeder	un surgénérateur
plutonium	le plutonium
to expose to	mettre en contact avec
exposure	l'exposition, la mise en contact

Consequences — Les conséquences

sustainability	la pérennité, la durabilité
to cull	éliminer, abattre
a cull	une élimination, un abattage
to concentrate	concentrer
a concentration	une concentration
to build up	accumuler
a build-up	une accumulation
a living tissue [ˈtɪʃuː]	un tissu vivant
cancer	le cancer
a carcinogen [kɑːˈsɪnədʒn]	un produit cancérigène

carcinogenic	cancérigène
wildlife	la faune et la flore
habitat	le biotope
long-term	à longue échéance
threatened species	les espèces menacées
endangered species	les espèces en voie de disparition
to wipe out species	détruire/anéantir des espèces
extinct	disparu
a strain	une souche (d'espèce)
resistant	insensible, résistant

Ozone hole to start shrinking and will close in 50 years, say scientists

by Kathy Marks in Sydney

The hole in the ozone layer over Antarctica is about to start shrinking and will close by 2050, Australian researchers say. Government scientists at Cape Grim in Tasmania said scientific data showed the level of ozone-depleting chlorine in the atmosphere was declining because of the ban on the use of chlorofluorocarbons (CFCs) in fridges and air conditioners, agreed under the Montreal Protocol in 1987.

Dr Paul Fraser, the chief atmospheric research scientist with the Commonwealth Scientific and Industrial Research Organisation, said: "This is big news. We have been waiting for this. We think the trend is definite now. It is very significant."

Dr Fraser said that after the ban was adopted, the atmospheric level of chlorine continued to rise, peaking in 2000. "That was simply due to old refrigerators and old air-conditioners in cars," he says.

Since then, the level had stabilised and was now declining, albeit slowly, Dr Fraser said. He predicted that the hole in the ozone layer would contract steadily from about 2005 and disappear by mid-century, although the ozone would be vulnerable for a decade.

Under the Montreal Protocol, developing countries committed themselves to halving consumption and production of CFCs by 2005 and achieving an 85 per cent cut by 2007. The hole in the ozone layer, which protects Earth from the Sun's ultraviolet rays, was first detected nearly 30 years ago. It was then three times the size of Australia, itself covering nearly 3 million square miles.

In a reference to the international dissent over the Kyoto Protocol on greenhouse gas emissions, Dr Fraser said: "I think this shows global protocols can work."

Earlier this month, Russia said it would ratify Kyoto, meaning that enough big carbon dioxide producers had signed up for it to take effect without America, which has refused to support it.

The Independent, 18 September 2002

1 Choose the right explanation for each of the following words underlined in the text.

1. to shrink
A. to become smaller
B. to become bigger
C. to stabilise

2. to peak
A. to choose
B. to remove
C. to reach the highest value

3. a dissent
A. a reasonable behaviour
B. a disagreement
C. a movement from a higher to a lower level

2 Say whether the following statements are true (T) or false (F).

1. The hole in the ozone layer has begun to close and will be totally closed by 2050.
2. Chlorine is detrimental to the ozone layer.
3. From now on the level of chlorine is set to decrease.
4. The 1987 ban on the use of CFCs agreed in the Montreal Protocol had an immediate effect.
5. The hole in the ozone layer will have already contracted between now and 2005.
6. 30 years ago the size of the hole in the ozone layer was approximately 3 million square miles.
7. Although America still refuses to sign the Kyoto Protocol, Dr Fraser thinks it could work.

3 There are several words in the text ending with the suffix "–ic" (scien__ti__fic, atmos__phe__ric...). When you find the suffixes "–ic" or "-ical" in adjectives or "-ically" in adverbs, the stress on the word is on the last but one syllable. Look at the examples below.

scien**ti**fic atmos**pher**ic

Underline the stressed syllable in the following words.

organic	carcinogenic
chemical	historically
ecological	biological
catalytic	philosophically

4 Fill in the eight lines across the grid with translations of the corresponding French words. This will give you the answer to number 9 in column D.

1. les déchets
2. durable
3. engrais
4. le plomb
5. une nappe
6. nocif
7. nuisible
8. épandre
9. la faune et la flore

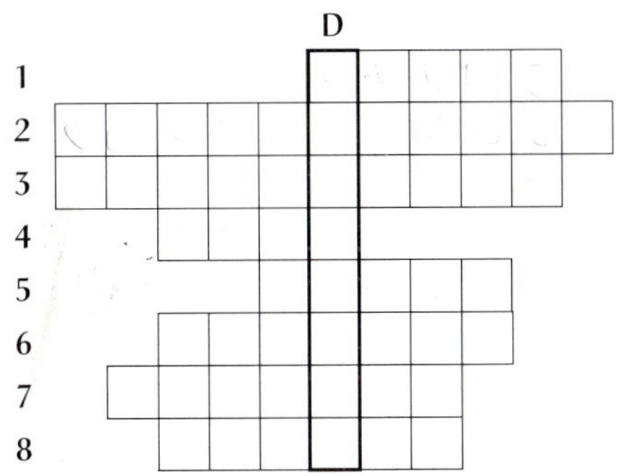

'Pristine' Amazonian rainforests are changing

by Bob Holmes

Changes to apparently pristine parts of the Amazonian rainforests have been revealed by a survey of trees. Tall, fast-growing trees are doing better than those that grow slowly. The changes – possibly the result of increasing levels of carbon dioxide in the atmosphere – threaten to reduce the Amazon basin's crucial ability to store excess CO2.

The discovery comes from a study of 18 undisturbed plots in the heart of the Brazilian Amazon that researchers have been monitoring since the 1980s. Tropical ecologist Bill Laurance, of the Smithsonian Tropical Research Institute in Balboa, Panama, and his colleagues combed through census records of the plots to see how their trees have changed over time.

Of 115 tree genera, they found that two became significantly more common and 14 became significantly rarer over the 15 years of the study. The winners tended to be tall, relatively fast-growing canopy trees, while the losers tended to be slower-growing trees that live their whole lives in the dim depths of the forest below the canopy.

Laurance and his colleagues could find no past anomalies in rainfall that might explain this pattern of change. Nor is it due to some peculiarity of their research techniques - a second, independent set of study plots nearby showed similar changes.

Dense wood

Instead, Laurance speculates that rising levels of CO2 in the atmosphere may be to blame. More CO2 means faster photosynthesis. Faster growth, in turn, favours those trees that already grow the fastest.

"It's very difficult to predict what the long-term effects of these changes will be," says Laurance. However, because under-storey trees grow slowly, they produce denser wood, which in turn means that the carbon content of each tree is greater.

If the forest composition shifts away from these trees toward faster-growing genera with lighter wood, the forest will be less able to take up CO2.

Many ecologists think the Amazon rainforest is one of the major "carbon sinks" that keep atmospheric CO2 from rising more quickly than it already has.

If anything were to interfere with that, says Oliver Phillips, a tropical forest ecologist at the University of Leeds, UK, "that's bad news".

Journal reference: Nature (vol 428, p 171)
New Scientist, 10 March 2004

1 Choose the right explanation for each of the following words underlined in the article.

1. pristine
A. virgin
B. exploited
C. endangered

2. a survey
A. a cut
B. a threat
C. a study

3. to comb
A. to search very carefully
B. to combine
C. to walk

4. a census
A. an official censoring of books, films, plays…
B. an official count and statistical survey of a population
C. a period of a hundred year

5. genera (sing. genus)
A. ideas having general application
B. taxonomic groups containing one or more species
C. normal periods of time between successive generations

6. rainfall
A. an amount of rain
B. a shower
C. a deluge

7. under-storey
A. which is at a higher level
B. which grows very fast
C. which is at a lower level

8. a carbon sink
A. an area of forest which releases CO_2 therefore contributing to global warming
B. an area of forest which exhausts CO_2 therefore increasing global warming
C. an area of forest which absorbs CO_2 therefore reducing global warning

2 Say whether the following statements are true (T) or false (F)

1. Changes to the natural pattern of rainforests have been caused by human activities in the forests.
2. Two types of tall, relatively fast-growing trees have become more common in the Amazonian rainforests over the past 15 years.
3. Droughts seem to be at the origin of the changes observed by Laurance and his colleagues.
4. Laurance's experimental protocol seems to be reliable.
5. The more CO_2 there is, the faster tall trees grow.
6. The more fast-growing trees there are, the more CO_2 tropical forests recycle.
7. The disappearance of slow-growing trees would lead to a greater ability of the forest to take up CO_2.
8. If the evolution showed by Laurance's survey of trees continues in the future, atmospheric CO_2 could rise more quickly than it is currently doing.

3 The first word in each list is taken from the article. Which of the other three should not be associated with it?

1. pristine, undisturbed, untapped, untested
2. to threaten, to trouble, to menace, to jeopardise
3. to monitor, to check, to train, to survey

4 Irregular plural forms. In the article we read "Of 115 genera […]." "Genera" is the plural of the word "genus" – a class of plants or animals – and may be considered

"irregular" because it uses the original Latin plural. Find the plural forms of the following words.

1. child
2. mouse
3. life
4. phenomenon
5. knife
6. leaf
7. criterion
8. thief
9. woman
10. man
11. fungus
12. foot
13. wife
14. half
15. calf
16. tooth
17. sheep
18. bacterium

THE ECONOMY I

2

L'ÉCONOMIE

Vocabulaire à haute fréquence

Variations and assessment	Variations et évaluation
to go up, to rise	monter
a rise in prices	une hausse des prix
inflation	l'inflation
inflationary	inflationniste
to be down/up	être à la baisse/à la hausse
to drop, to fall, to come down	baisser, diminuer
a fall/drop in prices	une baisse des prix
expensive, dear	cher
to cost	coûter
the cost	le coût
costly	coûteux
cheap	bon marché
worth	la valeur
to be worth	valoir
a profit	un bénéfice
profit	le profit
profitable, economic	rentable
a benefit	un avantage, une allocation, une prestation
to gain	gagner
a gain	un gain, une plus-value
a loss	une perte
loss-making, unprofitable, uneconomic	non rentable
economical	économique, économe
to survey	étudier
a survey	une étude, une enquête

a price index	un indice des prix
consumer confidence	le niveau de confiance des consommateurs
to assess, to estimate	évaluer
an assessment, an estimate	une évaluation
to value	évaluer, apprécier
the face value	la valeur nominale
a figure	un chiffre
a billion	un milliard
to exceed	dépasser
a trend	une tendance
a downtrend	une tendance à la baisse
to grow	croître
growth	la croissance
a rate	un taux
to expand	(se) développer
expansion	l'expansion
to thrive, to prosper	prospérer
thriving, prosperous	prospère
prosperity	la prospérité
a boom	une vague de prospérité
to decline	décliner
a decline	un déclin, une baisse
a crisis	une crise
a recession	une récession
to improve	(s')améliorer
an improvement	une amélioration
to recover	reprendre, se rétablir
recovery	la reprise, le rétablissement

Measures	**Les mesures**
a policy	une politique
to increase, to raise	augmenter
an increase	une augmentation
to bring down	abaisser, diminuer
to reduce, to cut back	réduire
a reduction, a cut-back	une réduction
to curb	juguler, maîtriser
a curb	un frein
austerity	l'austérité
to restrict	restreindre
a restriction	une restriction
to devalue	dévaluer
a devaluation	une dévaluation
to subsidise	subventionner
a subsidy	une subvention
to boost	doper, relancer
a boost	une relance

Taxes / Les impôts

to tax	taxer, imposer
taxation	l'imposition, la taxation
income tax	l'impôt sur le revenu
a taxpayer	un contribuable
the community charge	les impôts locaux
to collect	lever, recouvrer
collection	le recouvrement
a tax collector	un percepteur, un receveur

Money / L'argent

cash	les espèces, le numéraire
a banknote, a bill *(US)*	un billet de banque
a coin	une pièce
currency	les devises, la monnaie
to earn	gagner
earnings	les gains
to spend	dépenser
spending	les dépenses
expenses	les dépenses, les frais
to owe money	devoir de l'argent
to save	économiser
savings	l'épargne, les économies
to invest	investir
an investment	un investissement
an investor	un investisseur
a sum	une somme
an amount	un montant
to amount to	s'élever à, revenir à

Production / La production

to produce	produire
a product	un produit
production, output	la production
productivity	la productivité
farm produce	les produits agricoles
to manufacture	fabriquer
a manufactured product	un produit fabriqué
goods, wares	les marchandises
a warehouse	un entrepôt
a commodity	une marchandise primaire
supply	l'offre
demand	la demande
to consume	consommer
a consumer	un consommateur
consumption	la consommation
a grade	une catégorie

Trade and the EU	Le commerce et l'UE
business	les affaires
a customer	un client
to sell retail	vendre au détail
a sale	une vente
to buy wholesale	acheter en gros
to purchase	acheter, acquérir
a purchase	un achat, une acquisition
to order	commander
an order	une commande
to supply/provide sb. with sth.	fournir qch. à qn.
to charge	faire payer
a charge	les frais, un prix à payer
an invoice	une facture
a bill, a check *(US)*	une note, une addition
to bargain	marchander, négocier
a bargain	une (bonne) affaire
a (clearance) sale	les ventes de soldes
an auction	une vente aux enchères
to trade	faire du commerce
a market	un marché
to advertise	faire de la publicité
advertising	la publicité
an advertisement [əd'vɜːtɪsmənt]	une publicité
an adman	un publicitaire
to import [ɪm'pɔːt]	importer
an import ['ɪmpɔːt]	une importation
to export [eks'pɔːt]	exporter
an export ['ekspɔːt]	une exportation
home trade	le commerce intérieur
foreign/overseas trade	le commerce exterieur
to share	partager
a share	une part
a trade gap/deficit	un déficit commercial
a budget deficit	un déficit budgétaire
a deficit	un déficit
a surplus	un excédent
an outlet	un débouché, un point de vente
to compete with sb.	concurrencer qn.
competition	la concurrence
competitive	compétitif
competitiveness	la compétitivité
to protect	protéger
protectionism	le protectionnisme
a protectionist	un protectionniste
customs	la douane
a duty	un droit

to join sth.	adhérer à qch.
a summit	un sommet
a directive	une directive
a single market	un marché unique
the eurozone	la zone Euro
a single currency	une monnaie unique
the euro	l'Euro
the enlargement process	le processus d'élargissement
to veto sth.	opposer son veto à qch.
a veto	un veto
the qualified majority	la majorité qualifiée
the stability pact	le pacte de stabilité
an opt-out (clause)	une clause d'exemption

Globalisation / La mondialisation

to globalise	mondialiser
the World Trade Organisation (WTO)	L'Organisation Mondiale du Commerce (OMC)
the World Bank	la Banque Mondiale
the International Monetary Fund (IMF)	le Fonds Monétaire International (FMI)
free trade	le libre-échange
a free trade area/zone	une zone de libre-échange, une zone franche
a free trader	un libre-échangiste
a trade dispute/agreement	un désaccord/accord commercial
a trade war	une guerre commerciale
economic retaliation	des représailles économiques
a tariff	un tarif douanier
a barrier	une barrière
a quota	un quota
a global trade summit	un sommet du commerce mondial
an alternative summit	un contre sommet
the anti/alter-globalisation movement	le mouvement alter-mondialiste
an anti/alter-globalisation activist/campaigner	un alter-mondialiste

Expressions

it's worth trying	cela mérite d'être essayé
it sells well	cela se vend bien
to sustain/suffer a loss	subir une perte
to recoup one's losses	récupérer ses pertes
to plough back profits	réinvestir les bénéfices
to get value for money	en avoir pour son argent
to hit the jackpot	gagner le pactole
to earn one's living	gagner sa vie

the standard of living	le niveau de vie
the cost of living	le coût de la vie
the poverty line	le seuil de pauvreté
to fetch a high price	atteindre un prix élevé
to sell at a premium	(se) vendre au-dessus du cours
to foot the bill	payer la note, régler l'addition
to pick up the tab	payer l'addition
the retail price index	l'indice des prix de détail
the consumer price index	l'indice des prix à la consommation
the consumer sentiment index	l'indice de confiance des consommateurs
a package of measures	un ensemble de mesures
to kickstart the economy	faire démarrer l'économie
pay as you earn (PAYE)	le prélèvement à la source
value added tax (VAT)	la taxe à la valeur ajoutée (TVA)
to put out to tender	lancer un appel d'offres
to drive a hard bargain	ne pas faire de cadeau, être dur en affaires
to cut corners	rogner sur les coûts
the Gross National Product (GNP)	le produit national brut (PNB)
the Gross Domestic Product (GDP)	le produit intérieur brut (PIB)
the Balance of Trade	la balance commerciale
the Balance of Payments	la balance des paiements
a current account deficit	un déficit de la balance des paiements courants
a European Member of Parliament (MEP, Euro MP)	un député européen

Vocabulaire complémentaire

Variations and assessment / Variations et évaluation

a profit margin	une marge bénéficiaire
cost effective	rentable, d'un bon rapport coût-performance
dirt cheap	très bon marché
to stagnate	stagner
stagnation	la stagnation
an upwards/downwards move	un mouvement à la hausse/baisse
to slacken, to slow down	ralentir
a slack, a slow-down	un ralentissement
to dip	fléchir, baisser
a dip	un fléchissement
to slump	baisser brutalement
a slump	une chute brutale, un marasme
to plummet	dégringoler
to collapse	s'effondrer
a collapse	un effondrement
a recession	une récession

to look up, to pick up	se redresser
an upturn, an upswing, a pick-up	un redressement
a downturn, a downswing	un fléchissement
a muted return	une reprise timide
to flourish	prospérer
flourishing	florissant, prospère
to overheat	surchauffer
to soar, to surge	s'envoler
to shoot up	monter en flèche
to revive	se rétablir
a revival	une rétablissement
to make up for sth.	compenser qch.
to offset	contrebalancer, compenser
in real terms	en argent constant
a spin-off	une retombée
an analyst	un analyste, conjoncturiste
a pundit	un expert
a prospect	une perspective
to forecast	prévoir
a forecast, an outlook	une prévision

Measures and taxes — Les mesures et les impôts

the Budget	le budget
public expenditure	les dépenses publiques
monetary	monétaire
deflation	la déflation
deflationary	déflationniste
to levy	percevoir, prélever
a levy	un prélèvement, une taxe
a fee	un droit, une redevance
to squeeze	comprimer
a squeeze	une compression, une rigueur
to bite	faire de l'effet
to nationalise	nationaliser
nationalisation	la nationalisation
to privatise	privatiser
privatisation	la privatisation
regulation	la réglementation
deregulation	la déréglementation
an incentive	une mesure d'incitation
to stimulate	stimuler
to grant	accorder
a grant	une aide financière
to finance, to fund	financer
funds	les fonds
to slash	réduire radicalement
a slash	une réduction radicale

to jack up	relever (les prix)
to hike prices *(US)*	relever les prix
a price hike *(US)*	une augmentation des prix
to index	indexer
index-linked	indexé
a tax haven	un paradis fiscal
tax relief	un dégrèvement fiscal
a tax allowance	un abattement fiscal
a tax break	une réduction d'impôt
tax evasion	la fraude fiscale
to cap taxes	fixer un plafond à l'impôt
revenue	les rentrées fiscales
to put up taxes	augmenter les impôts
the tax burden	le poids des impôts
inheritance tax	les droits de succession

Money — L'argent

a hard currency	une devise forte
currency depreciation	la dépréciation monétaire
to waste	gaspiller
waste, wastage	le gaspillage
to squander	dilapider, gaspiller
to skimp	lésiner, économiser
thrift	l'épargne
thrifty	économe
a spendthrift	un panier percé
extravagant, profligate	dépensier, prodigue
extravagance, profligacy	la prodigalité
amortisation	amortissement
a windfall	une aubaine, un pactole
a godsend	un don du ciel, une manne
a money-spinner	une mine d'or, un filon

Production — La production

just-in-time production, zero stock production	la production à flux tendu
the production line	la chaîne de production
a shortage	une pénurie
a shortfall	une insuffisance, un manque
a glut	un engorgement
to contract	s'engager par contrat
a contract	un contrat
a contractor	un entrepreneur
an entrepreneur	un chef d'entreprise
enterprise	l'esprit d'entreprise
to subcontract	sous-traiter

a subcontractor	un sous-traitant
a tender	une soumission
to exhaust	épuiser
exhaustion	l'épuisement
a brand	une marque commerciale
a make	une marque, une fabrication
to target	cibler
a target	une cible
custom-made	fait sur commande

Trade and the EU — Le commerce et l'UE

a niche	un créneau, un marché
a shopper	un client de magasin
a patron	un client fidèle
a punter	un chaland
a good buy	un bon achat
barter	le troc
to haggle	marchander
to shop around	comparer les prix
to refund	restituer de l'argent
a refund	une restitution d'argent
a discount	une remise
a rebate	un rabais
into the bargain	par-dessus le marché
hard sell	l'agressivité de vente
a hoarding, a billboard *(US)*	un panneau publicitaire
to undercut, to undersell	vendre moins cher que
to net	empocher, engranger
proceeds	le produit, les recettes
consumer goods	les biens de consommation
capital goods	les biens d'équipement
business premises	les locaux commerciaux
mail-order	l'achat par correspondance
a middleman	un intermédiaire
to insure	assurer
insurance	l'assurance
to underwrite	souscrire
a policy	une police
a premium	une cotisation, une prime
a claim	une demande d'indemnisation
invisibles	les exportations et les importations invisibles
an imbalance	un déséquilibre
to corner	accaparer
to fix prices	s'entendre sur les prix
price-fixing	l'entente illicite
to rig	truquer

a loophole — un vide juridique
a contribution — une contribution, une cotisation
a commissioner — un commissaire
subsidiarity — la subsidiarité
set-aside land — les terres incultes, gelées

Anti-globalisation march brings Mumbai to a standstill

Jeremy Lennard and agencies

Tens of thousands of activists brought the Mumbai traffic to a standstill today as they marched through the streets of India's financial capital to mark the end of the World Social Forum – the world's biggest anti-globalisation gathering.

The march was led by protesters carrying a huge black banner that read: "Stop the killings. Stop the lying." Others waved red and white flags and showed the thumbs-down sign while shouting: "George Bush, no, no. George Bush, terrorist." The march brought to an end six days of colourful protests and intense discussions about global economic policy, the war in Iraq and racial and caste oppression, among other issues.

Some 100,000 people, from 132 countries, attended the forum, timed as a counterpoint to the World Economic Forum, which opens today in Davos, Switzerland. The alternative gathering is intended to highlight the paradox of big businesses thriving alongside widespread human despair.

Coca-Cola and Pepsi were barred from the refreshment stands in favour of locally produced sugar-cane juice and lemonade, while the forum's information needs and those of its media entourage were met with the free Linux operating system rather than Microsoft Windows.

Organisers called it a huge success in mobilising opinion, widening the global network of civil society groups – especially in Asia and Africa – and raising awareness of, and opposition to, the perceived trinity of global injustice: the World Bank, the International Monetary Fund and the World Trade Organization. "There was an identification of common economic struggles," said Kent Klandt of Black Rock City, Nevada, in the US. "It is crucially important for first world activists to be in the third world."

The agenda of the gathering appeared to have shifted from its central focus on trade and the inequities of global capitalism to splinter into a long list of regional causes. But, whatever its focus, the World Social Forum seems to be gaining momentum. About 50,000 people attended the WTO protest in Seattle in 1999, while at the three previous World Social Forum gatherings in Brazil, participation was put at 20,000 in 2001, 55,000 in 2002 and 100,000 in 2003. [...]

Two Nobel laureates – the Iranian human rights worker and winner of this year's peace prize, Shirin Ebadi, and Joseph Stiglitz, the former World Bank director and past winner of the economics prize, were among the main speakers, as was the former Irish president, Mary Robinson. José Bové, the French farmer who led the demolition of a half-built McDonald's outlet, and the Indian novelist Arundhati Roy also gave keynote speeches.

Although left-leaning activists formed the overwhelming majority, participants were wide-ranging in their ideas, beliefs and origins: villagers from Kenya, European aid workers, Hiroshima survivors and tribe members from remote corners of south Asia. "The celebrations and demonstrations are important to show that we are not isolated in our own little regions," said Serg Nuss, 29, from Girona in Catalonia.

The forum is expected to move back to its Brazilian base next year.

The Guardian, 21 January 2004

1 Read the first three paragraphs of the text and find words which mean the same as the following words.

1. a campaigner
2. to demonstrate
3. world
4. to stress
5. companies
6. to prosper

2 Read the following three paragraphs and find words which mean the contrary to the following.

1. to the detriment of
2. tiny, very small
3. failure
4. to narrow
5. equalities
6. next

3 Say whether the following statements are true (T) or false (F).

1. Tens of thousands of anti-globalisation campaigners have gathered in India's capital.
2. The World Social Forum was timed to run concurrently with the World Economic Forum in Davos.
3. Microsoft Windows was discarded in favour of Linux operating systems.

4. The World Bank, the IMF and the WTO offer great economic opportunities to developing countries according to anti-globalisation groups.
5. Discussions about trade, global economic policy and the war in Iraq have overshadowed regional causes.
6. The World Social Forum seems to be gathering impetus.
7. World Social Forum attendance increased fivefold between 2001 and 2003.
8. The 2005 World Social Forum will be probably held in Porto Allegre.

4 Find the correct definition (A-E) for each organisation (1-5).

1. the World Social Forum
2. the World Economic Forum
3. the World Bank
4. the International Monetary Fund (IMF)
5. the World Trade Organization (WTO)

A. An international cooperative organisation established to assist economic development by the advance of loans guaranteed by member governments.
B. An international body concerned with promoting and regulating trade between its member states.
C. The annual meeting of business people, politicians and campaigners to discuss global issues.
D. An alternative meeting to the yearly gathering of world political and business leaders in Davos.
E. An international financial institution for the promotion of international trade by increasing the exchange stability of the major currencies.

5 Which of the words in each list does not have the same meaning as the first word ?

1. to participate in, to take part in, to march, to attend
2. global, world, international, regional
3. to highlight, to undermine, to emphasize, to underline
4. discussion, talk, agenda, debate

Brussels approves airline merger

by Anita Arthur

Air France and KLM on Wednesday received conditional clearance from the European Commission on their merger which would create the world's largest airline by turnover and third biggest by traffic volume.

To secure regulatory clearance, the French and Dutch carriers have agreed to give up 94 single airport take-off and landing slots per day.

The Commission said this would enable rival airlines to start services on routes where competition would have been eliminated or significantly reduced by the merged carrier. It said the concessions will preserve choice and competitive prices for European travellers.

The merger also requires approval by the US Department of Justice. KLM filed for US approval on January 12 and the DoJ has 30 days to make an initial response or extend its inquiry by an additional 30 days.

The Financial Times, 11 February 2004

3

THE ECONOMY II

L'ÉCONOMIE II

Vocabulaire à haute fréquence

Real estate	Les biens immobiliers
to own	posséder
ownership	la propriété
property	les biens
a landlord	un propriétaire immobilier
a tenant	un locataire
to let	donner en location
to rent	prendre en location
rent	le loyer
a flat, an apartment *(US)*	un appartement
an estate agent, a realtor *(US)*	agent immobilier
housing	le logement
a council house	une HLM

Wealth and poverty	La richesse et la pauvreté
rich, wealthy	riche
well-off	aisé, bien nanti
poor	pauvre
the poverty line	le seuil de pauvreté
hard up, broke	fauché
a need	un besoin
the needy	les nécessiteux
misery	la misère
hardship	les difficultés matérielles
to beg	mendier

a beggar	un mendiant
destitute	sans ressources, démuni
destitution	l'indigence
deprived	déshérité
deprivation	le dénuement
underprivileged	défavorisé
to assist	assister, aider
assistance, welfare	l'assistance, l'aide
the welfare system	l'aide sociale
the welfare state	l'État providence

Banking — Les banques

a bank	une banque
an account	un compte
a balance	un solde
a cheque book	un carnet de chèques
to draw money	tirer de l'argent
a credit card	une carte de crédit
a draft	un retrait
to overdraw	tirer à découvert
an overdraft	un découvert
to borrow	emprunter
to lend	prêter
a loan	un prêt, un emprunt
a mortgage ['mɔːgɪdʒ]	un prêt immobilier
a debt	une dette
a debtor	un débiteur
credit	le crédit
a creditor	un créancier
to pay back, to repay	rembourser
a payment	un paiement, versement
repayment	le remboursement
to settle	régler
a settlement	un règlement
overdue	en retard, échu
interest	l'intérêt
the exchange rate	le taux de change

Businesses — Les entreprises

to set up	(s')établir
to establish	fonder
a firm, a business	une firme, une affaire
a multinational	une multinationale
to manage, to run	diriger, gérer
management	la direction, la gestion
a partner	un associé
a partnership	une société de personnes

a company, a corporation *(US)*	une société commerciale
a joint-stock company	une société par actions
the head office, the headquarters	le siège social
capital	le capital
a stake, a holding	une participation au capital
a chairman, a president *(US)*	un président
a chief executive officer (CEO)	un président directeur général
a managing director	un directeur général
a chief executive	un président délégué
a director	un administrateur
a board of directors	un conseil d'administration
an executive	un cadre
an annual report	un rapport d'activité
a general meeting	une assemblée générale
an agenda	un ordre du jour
turnover	le chiffre d'affaires
a dividend	un dividende
to bid for	faire une offre pour
a bid	une offre d'achat
to take over	racheter, prendre le contrôle de
a takeover	un rachat, une prise de contrôle
a takeover bid	une offre publique d'achat

Ailing companies / Les sociétés en difficulté

running costs	les frais de fonctionnement
overheads, fixed costs	les frais généraux
cost savings	les économies sur les frais
cost cutting	la réduction des frais
assets	l'actif
liabilities	le passif
cash flow	le flux de liquidités
a lame duck	un canard boiteux
to prop up	soutenir, étayer
to bail out	renflouer
mismanagement	la mauvaise gestion
indebted companies	les sociétés endettées
insolvent	non solvable
insolvency	insolvabilité
to fail, to go bust, to go bankrupt, to go under, to collapse	faire faillite
a failure, a bankruptcy	une faillite
a receiver	un administrateur judiciaire
to wind up, to liquidate	liquider
liquidation	la liquidation

The Stock Exchange / La Bourse des valeurs

stock, securities	les valeurs, les titres

a share	une action
a bond	une obligation
a shareholder	un actionnaire
to subscribe	souscrire
a deal	une transaction
a dealer	un opérateur
a bearer	un porteur
a stockbroker	un agent de change
a trader	un négociateur en bourse
brokerage	le courtage
to quote	coter
a quotation	une cote, un cours
to close	clôturer
close [kləʊz]	la clôture
to open up	ouvrir en hausse
to close down	clôturer en baisse
to yield	rapporter
a yield	un rapport

Market fluctuations — Les fluctuations du marché

the lead of the market	l'orientation du marché
steady, stationary	stable
firm	ferme
dull	inactif, maussade
volatile	nerveux, fébrile
to gain/lose ground	gagner/perdre du terrain
to slide, to slip	baisser
a slide, a slip	une baisse
to crumble	s'effriter
to fall back	se replier
a fall-back	un repli
a crash	un krach
to rally	se raffermir
a rally	un raffermissement
to level off	se stabiliser
to ease	se détendre
buoyant ['bɔɪənt]	soutenu, bien orienté
brisk	actif, animé

E-commerce — Le commerce électronique

broadband/highspeed internet	l'Internet à haut débit
the Internet	l'Internet
to be online	être en ligne
to buy online	acheter en ligne
online shopping	les achats en ligne
a mobile operator	un opérateur de téléphonie mobile

wireless	sans fil
information and communication technology (IT)	les technologies d'information et de communication (NTIC)
the digital divide	le fossé/l'écart numérique
to close/to bridge the gap	combler le fossé
coverage	la couverture

Expressions

to go on welfare	s'inscrire à l'aide sociale
to feel the pinch	sentir les effets de la rigueur
to tighten one's belt	se serrer la ceinture
to tighten one's purse strings	resserrer les cordons de la bourse
to make ends meet	joindre les deux bouts
a balance of account	un solde de compte
a statement of account	un relevé de compte
to be in the red	être à découvert, en déficit
to be in the black	être créditeur
to break even	équilibrer les comptes
to dabble on the Stock Exchange	boursicoter
an all-time high	un record à la hausse
an all-time low	un record à la baisse
the Securities and Investment Board *(UK)*, the Securities and Exchange Commission *(US)*	l'Autorité des marchés financiers (AMF)
misuse of corporate funds	détournement de fonds privés
to mount a take over bid	lancer une OPA
to drive out of business	contraindre à la fermeture
to go out of business	cesser son activité
to go to the wall	aller à sa perte
to file for bankrutcy, to file under chapter 11 *(US)*	déposer son bilan
to go belly up *(US)*	faire faillite
to go into administration	être mis en redressement judiciaire
to be placed into receivership, to go into liquidation	entrer en liquidation

Vocabulaire complémentaire

Wealth, poverty and housing	**La richesse, la pauvreté et le logement**
affluent	fortuné
affluence	l'abondance, l'opulence
means	les moyens
means testing	l'évaluation des ressources

purchasing power	le pouvoir d'achat
a breadwinner	un soutien de famille
down and out	sans le sou
National Insurance	la Sécurité sociale
social security	l'aide sociale
food stamps *(US)*	les bons de nourriture
a bread line, a soup kitchen	une soupe populaire, un resto du cœur
to lease	prendre, donner en location
a lease	un bail
a housing estate	un lotissement
a council estate	une cité HLM
a slum	un taudis
homeless	sans logis
to sleep rough	dormir dehors
housing benefit	l'allocation de logement
child benefit	les allocations familiales
planning permission	le permis de construire
town planning	l'urbanisme
a property developer	un promoteur immobilier
to repossess	saisir pour non-paiement
repossession	saisie pour non-paiement
to evict	expulser
eviction	expulsion

Banking	**Les banques**
the base rate	le taux de base
the discount rate	le taux d'escompte
the lending rate	le taux de l'argent
a flat rate	un taux uniforme
a merchant bank	une banque d'affaires
a building society	une mutuelle d'épargne-logement
a bounced cheque	un chèque refusé
a dud/rubber cheque	un chèque sans provision
to default	ne pas honorer, se dérober
a cash point	un distributeur de billets
a card receipt	un ticket de carte bancaire
a pin card	une carte à code
credit card fraud	l'escroquerie à la carte bancaire
a chip	une puce
direct debit	le prélèvement direct
a quid *(fam. UK)*	une livre sterling
a buck *(fam. US)*	un dollar
to loan	prêter
a loan shark	un usurier
a bad debt	une créance impayée
arrears [ə'rɪəz]	les arriérés
money supply	la masse monétaire

Businesses	Les entreprises
a concern	une entreprise, une firme
to undertake	entreprendre
an undertaking	une opération entreprise
a limited partnership	une société en commandite
a private company	une société à responsabilité limitée
a public company	une société anonyme
a parent company	une société mère
a sister company	une société du même groupe
a holding company	une société de portefeuille, un holding
an offshoot	une branche
a subsidiary	une filiale
a joint venture	une société commune
a front company	une société écran
a deputy chairman, a vice-president *(US)*	un vice président
a non-executive director	un administrateur extérieur à la société
working capital	les fonds de roulement
returns, proceeds	les recettes, les rentrées
corporate tax	l'impôt sur les sociétés
pre-tax profits	les bénéfices avant impôt
a profit warning	un avertissement à la baisse sur les bénéfices
a balance sheet	un bilan comptable
provisions	les provisions
the bottom line	le résultat final
an auditor	un commissaire aux comptes
consultancy	le conseil
to issue shares	émettre des actions
a share issue	une émission d'actions
a rights issue	une émission de droits d'attribution
a golden share	une action à droit particulier
to allot	attribuer
an allotment	une attribution
to float	lancer (une société, des actions)
a flotation	une émission financière
a high flier	une personne de haut vol
a yuppie	un jeune cadre dynamique
a tycoon, a magnate	un magnat
a fat cat	un nanti, un nabab
a pay-off	une indemnité de départ
a golden handshake	une indemnité en or

Companies as targets	Les sociétés pour cible
to amalgamate, to merge	fusionner
an amalgamation, a merger	une fusion
a management buy-out	un rachat par les cadres
a leveraged buy-out	un rachat avec emprunt
a war chest	un trésor de guerre
a bidder	un repreneur
a predator	un rapace boursier
a raider	un assaillant
a raid	une attaque, un assaut
a white knight	un chevalier blanc
a (friendly) suitor	un repreneur amical
a sweetener	une douceur, une sucrette
an insider	un initié
insider dealing/trading	le délit d'initié
a watchdog	un organisme de surveillance

The Stock Exchange	La Bourse des valeurs
a stock market	une place boursière
a portfolio	un portefeuille (valeurs)
equities	les actions ordinaires
gilt-edged securities	les valeurs sans risque (obligations d'État)
blue chips	les actions des grandes sociétés
junk bonds	obligations de pacotille
a bull	un spéculateur à la hausse
a bear	un spéculateur à la baisse
the spot market	le marché au comptant
the futures market	le marché à terme
to hedge	se couvrir (risque)
the Mercantile Exchange	la Bourse des marchandises

Eurotunnel plunges £1.3bn into red

by Alistair Osborne, Associate City Editor

Eurotunnel yesterday called for the complete restructuring of the cross-Channel rail industry as it crashed £1.33 billion into the red at the full-year.

The debt-laden Channel Tunnel operator, which faces a looming cash crisis in 2006, confirmed it was in talks with the UK and French governments to "address the structural problems" faced by the industry.

Eurotunnel proposed to "significantly reduce" its charges to customers such as Eurostar and freight operator EWS in return for the industry's assistance in refinancing its business.

Richard Shirrefs, chief executive, said it had cost the private sector £10 billion to build the tunnel, while taxpayers on both sides of the Channel had «directly or indirectly» spent £15 billion on related infrastructure, such as the Channel Tunnel Rail Link.

Despite the investment, Mr Shirrefs said: "Traffic growth for Eurostar and rail freight is strangled by high tunnel access charges and we have too much debt to reduce them unilaterally. Taxpayers are not getting the benefit they should for their money and Eurotunnel's shareholders have seen a substantial loss on their investment."

The crisis talks have been triggered by Eurotunnel's requirement in 2006 to begin making capital repayments on its £6.4 billion debt. It is currently in no position to do so, yesterday revealing its £315m of cash flow was not enough to cover a £318m interest bill. The shares fell 4p to 34.75p.

In addition, from November 2006, Eurotunnel will stop receiving a minimum payment from rail customers, mainly Eurostar, which last year accounted for £77m of its £232m rail revenues.

Mr Shirrefs said his proposals would "align the incentives of the cross-Channel operators", adding: "We can put a sizeable amount of money on the table in the form of reduced access charges." In return, he wanted a deal to enable Eurotunnel to buy back debt, trading at an average 50p in the pound, so reducing interest payments. "We are not, I will admit, being hugely descriptive on how that will work," he conceded.

City analysts and other cross-Channel operators were left puzzled. One train operator said "it's pretty woolly". Eurostar said: "The current structure is not holding back our growth in passengers."

Analysts said Eurotunnel could try some form of securitisation, by raising cash against future revenues from track charges. A Department of Transport spokesman said: "The Government has made it absolutely clear we will not put any public money into Eurotunnel."

Technically, this may not rule out some form of restructuring involving the assets of government-backed companies, such as London & Continental Railways, or the use of government guarantees.

Eurotunnel has hired Merrill Lynch, Dresdner Kleinwort Wasserstein and SocGen to work on its proposals, while Citigroup is advising the UK Government.

Eurotunnel's plans were revealed alongside a 5pc fall in full-year operating revenues to £566m and an 18pc drop in operating profits to £170m. The underlying loss of £148m swelled to £1.33billion after a £1.3 billion asset writedown due to less traffic than expected.

The Daily Telegraph, 10 February 2004

1 Match the following words (1-6) underlined in the article with their corresponding definitions (A-F).

1. debt-laden
2. to loom
3. to strangle
4. to trigger
5. woolly
6. to rule out

A. to eliminate, to reject
B. to stifle, to hold back
C. confused
D. to appear threateningly
E. crippled with arrears
F. to cause, to spark

2 Say whether the following statements are true (T) or false (F).

1. The Channel tunnel operator announced a record net loss of £1.33bn.
2. Eurotunnel made proposals to the British and French governments about how to restructure the cross-Channel rail industry.
3. The building of the Channel tunnel and its infrastructure cost about £25 billion.
4. Eurotunnel has been a profitable investment for shareholders.
5. The shares dropped 4p in London to 34.75p.
6. Rail customers' payments to Eurotunnel amounted to almost one third of its rail revenues last year.
7. Eurotunnel is ready to cut charges for use of the tunnel in return for help with reducing debt.
8. Eurotunnel's refinancing scheme may benefit from taxpayers' money on both sides of the Channel.
9. The British government has appointed Citigroup as its adviser.

3 Find as many economic expressions as possible referring to the assessment of Eurotunnel's finances. What have these expressions in common?

4 In view of this, choose the statement which best describes Eurotunnel's financial situation.

1. Eurotunnel is

A. an economical company.

B. a loss-making company.
C. a cheap company.

2. Eurotunnel shares are
A. buoyant.
B. steady.
C. down.

3. By 2006 Eurotunnel hopes to be in a position to
A. break even.
B. be in the black.
C. repay its debt.

5 Here are some of the main share indexes of world stock markets. Say to which national stock market (city and country) each share index refers.
FTSE 100, Dow Jones, Nasdaq, Cac 40, Dax, Hang Seng, Nikkei.

6 Fill in each blank in the article with the appropriate word from the following list. Use each word only once. Verbs are given in the infinitive.

global	deal	cost-cutting	shares
comment	launch	rival	fevered
government	value	fight	company
hired	investors	hostile bid	merger
board	drugs giant		

French drugs rival moves for Aventis

By Philip Aldrick

The ...(1)... of France's second largest pharmaceutical ...(2)... Sanofi-Synthelabo, was meeting last night to approve a ...(3)... for larger ...(4)... Aventis that could come today.
An offer is likely to ...(5)... Aventis at more than $60 billion (£33 billion) and forge a French ...(6)... that would vie with Glaxo Smithkline for second place in the ...(7)... industry, behind US giant Pfizer.
The decision to ...(8)... the bid follows weeks of ...(9)... speculation that has driven the ...(10)... higher in both companies as ...(11)... welcomed the prospect of ...(12)... , combined sales forces and pooled drug pipelines.
Neither party was available for ...(13)... yesterday, though Aventis is expected to ...(14)... the approach. The company is reported to have ...(15)... Goldman Sachs, Morgan Stanley and Rothschild to work on a defence.
However, the French ...(16)... has shown tacit support for a ...(17)... . Speaking at the World Economic Forum in Davos, finance minister Francis Mer said on Saturday that a ...(18)... would be "rather positive".

The Daily Telegraph, 26/01/2004

Comcast proposes to buy Walt Disney

The cable television systems giant Comcast Corp. today proposed to buy the theme park and entertainment giant Walt Disney Co. for stock valued at about $54 billion.

Comcast, the biggest cable systems operator in the US said it would also take on $11.9 billion in Disney debt to push the total value of the deal to $66 billion. "This is a unique opportunity for all shareholders of Comcast and Disney to create a new leader of the entertainment and communications industry," Comcast President and Chief Executive Officer Brian L. Roberts said in a statement.

Comcast also released a letter sent to Disney chief executive Michael Eisner indicating that Eisner had personally rejected Roberts' offer earlier in the week. The letter from Roberts called it "unfortunate" that Eisner was not willing to enter into discussions about the proposed deal. "Given this, the only way for us to proceed is to make a public proposal directly to you and your board," the letter stated. Under the merger, Comcast said it would issue 0.78 of a share of its stock for each Disney share, and Disney shareholders would retain 42 percent of the combined company. The deal would give Disney shareholders a premium of more than $5 billion, based on Tuesday's closing stock prices. Comcast has more than 21 million cable subscribers.

AP, 11 February 2004

4

THE THIRD WORLD

LE TIERS MONDE

Vocabulaire à haute fréquence

Development and population	Le développement et la population
developing, emerging	en voie de développement
a native	un indigène, un autochtone
developed, industrialised	industrialisé
to settle	s'installer
a settlement	un peuplement, une colonie
a refugee [refju:'dʒi:]	un réfugié
a (squatter) camp	un camp (de squatters)
literacy	l'alphabétisation
illiteracy	l'analphabétisation
literate	alphabétisé
illiterate	analphabète

Production	La production
to feed on, to live on	se nourrir de, vivre de
to supply/provide sb. with sth.	fournir qch. à qn.
a supply	un approvisionnement
rainfall	les précipitations
a pump	une pompe
a well	un puits
to drill, to bore	forer
tap water	l'eau du robinet
the tap	le robinet
to tap	exploiter

untapped	inexploité
sewage	les eaux usées
to irrigate	irriguer
irrigation	l'irrigation
to grow, to cultivate	faire pousser, cultiver
to produce [prə'dju:s]	produire
farm produce ['prɒdju:s]	les produits agricoles
farming	l'agriculture
to farm	cultiver
to plough	labourer
to sow	semer
seeds	les semences
a crop	une récolte
a harvest	une moisson
livestock	le cheptel
to breed, to rear, to raise	élever
a flock of sheep	un troupeau de moutons
a herd of cattle	un troupeau de bétail
to graze	paître
grazing land, pasture land	les pâturages
self-sufficient	auto-suffisant
self-sufficiency	l'auto-suffisance
raw materials	les matières premières
a commodity	une marchandise primaire

Famine — La famine

a desert	un désert
drought [draʊt]	la sécheresse
a shortfall	une insuffisance
a shortage	une pénurie
a lack	un manque
scarce	rare, peu abondant
scarcity	la rareté, la disette
hunger	la faim
hungry	affamé
underfed	sous-alimenté
malnutrition	la malnutrition
malnourished	malnutri
to starve	manquer de nourriture
starvation	le manque de nourriture
the plight	la situation difficile/critique

Aid — L'aide

funds	les fonds
to collect, to raise	recueillir, collecter
to avert (a disaster/a catastrophe)	prévenir, éviter

	(un désastre/une catastrophe)
relief	les secours
relief workers	les équipes de secours
a charity	une organisation caritative
a Non-Governmental Organisation (NGO)	une Organisation Non Gouvernementale (ONG)
a voluntary agency	une agence bénévole
a voluntary organisation	une organisation humanitaire
a volunteer	un bénévole
a relief organisation	une organisation d'aide
relief aid, humanitarian aid	l'aide humanitaire
to donate	faire don
a donation	un don
a donor	un donateur
a consignment, a shipment	un envoi
to deliver	livrer
a delivery	une livraison
a tool	un outil
equipment	l'équipement
a project, a scheme [ski:m]	un projet
to advise	conseiller

Expressions

to wear out the soil	épuiser le sol
the standard of living	le niveau de vie
fair-trade	le commerce équitable
ethical shopping	achat éthique/équitable
help with no strings attached	l'aide sans contrepartie

Vocabulaire complémentaire

Population	La population
a census	un recensement
the population growth	la croissance démographique
the birth rate	le taux de natalité
the infant mortality rate	le taux de mortalité infantile
a mushroom city/town	une ville champignon
a nomad	un nomade
nomadic	nomade (adj.)
a hut	une hutte
a cabin	une case
a shack	une cabane
a makeshift shelter	un abri provisoire/de fortune
a shanty town	un bidonville

a slum	un taudis, un bidonville
slumdwellers	les habitants des bidonvilles
squalor	conditions sordides
filthy	sale, dégoûtant
forced resettlement	l'exode forcé
an influx	un afflux
an exodus	un exode

Production / La production

famished	affamé
a protein ['prəuti:n]	une protéine
a deficiency	une carence
topsoil	la terre végétale
to erode	éroder
erosion	l'érosion
staple food	la nourriture de base
basic commodities	les produits de première nécessité
food crops	les cultures vivrières
cash crops	les cultures de rente
a swarm of locusts	un essaim de criquets
to plague	tourmenter, affliger
fallow land	la terre en jachère
to exploit	exploiter
exploitation	l'exploitation
deforestation	le déboisement
to fell, to chop down, to log	abattre
logging	l'abattage
reforestation	le reboisement
barren	stérile, aride
parched	desséché
to desertify	désertifier
desertification	la désertification
a resource [rɪ'zɔ:s, rɪ'sɔ:s, 'ri:sɔ:s]	une ressource
to plunder	piller
plunder	le pillage

Outside aid / L'aide extérieure

to appeal to	faire appel à
an appeal	un appel
a campaign	une campagne
a convoy	un convoi
a humanitarian corridor	un couloir humanitaire
a hand-out	une aumône
to grant	accorder
a grant	une aide financière
tied aid	l'aide liée

untied aid	l'aide non liée
a string	une contrepartie
to pay back, to repay	rembourser
repayment	le remboursement
to reschedule	rééchelonner
to write off, to cancel	annuler
debt relief	l'allégement de la dette
to cooperate	coopérer
cooperation	la coopération
self-help	l'auto-assistance

Specific diseases — Les maladies spécifiques

sanitation	les installations sanitaires
water-borne diseases	les maladies contractées par l'eau
rampant	très répandu
sexually transmitted diseases/infections (STD)	les maladies sexuellement transmissibles (MST)
Aids	le Sida
the HIV virus	le virus VIH
polio	la polio
cholera	le choléra
malaria [məˈlɛərɪə]	la malaria, le paludisme
typhus [ˈtaɪfəs]	le typhus
leprosy	la lèpre
a leper [ˈlepə]	un lépreux

Trickling away ...
a life and death commodity

UN warns that underground supplies of water, crucial to billions, are remorselessly decreasing

Tim Radford, science editor

Groundwater, the unseen source of life for two billion people, is diminishing almost everywhere in the world, according to a study published today by the UN Environment Programme (Unep).

So much water has been pumped from beneath Mexico City that buildings have in some places sunk two metres. The water table under the high plains in the American Midwest has fallen on average by three metres a decade and up to 30 metres in some places. So much has been extracted from southern Florida that the aquifers are at risk of flooding by sea water.

Paradoxically, some cities in the Arabian Gulf have become waterlogged because of leaking pipes from coastal desalination plants.

Twelve cities of more than 10 million people – including Bangkok, Shanghai, London and Calcutta – rely on underground water reserves.

"Some two billion people and as much as 40% of agriculture is at least partly reliant on these hidden stores," said Klaus Toepfer, executive director of Unep. "Groundwater also supplements river flows, springs and wetlands vital for rural and urban communities and wildlife. Most of the world's liquid freshwaters are found not in rivers and lakes, but below ground." The world population has more than doubled in the past 60 years; water is used heavily by both industry and agriculture.

The report, published to mark World Environment Day today, warns that in rural India, 50% of irrigation water and 80% of drinking water comes from underground, through three million hand-pumped wells. Around 96% of Saudi Arabia's water and 69% of Bangladesh's comes from below ground. There are 1,300 boreholes tapping water below Dhaka, the Bangladeshi capital, and in some areas the water table has fallen by 40 metres. Some 450m people in 29 countries live with chronic water shortages. One person in six cannot rely on safe drinking water.

More than 2bn people have no adequate sanitation. Water-borne diseases kill a child every eight seconds, and are behind 80% of all illness and death in the developing world.

Most of all, water means food. It takes 1,000 tonnes of water to grow a tonne of wheat; 2000 tonnes to produce a tonne of rice. The worry is that the people most at risk – small farmers in poor rural districts – will be the first to suffer as wells dry and water tables sink.

"We need to learn how to value water," said Kofi Annan, UN secretary general. "While in some instances, that may mean making users pay a realistic price, it must never mean depriving already marginalised people of this resource. It is one of the crueller ironies of today's world water situation that those with the lowest income generally pay the most for their water." [...]

The Guardian, 5 June 2003

1 Choose the right explanation for each of the following words underlined in the article.

1. water table

A. the level below the surface of the ground where water can be found

B. the level above the surface of the ground where buildings are built

C. the level above the surface of the ground where water can be found

2. aquifer

A. a conduit used to convey water over a long distance

B. a deposit of rock containing water that can be used to supply wells

C. a tank, bowl, or pool in which aquatic animals and plants are kept

3. waterlogged

A. so dry that it has become very hard

B. soluble in water

C. so wet that it cannot absorb any more water

4. water-borne diseases

A. diseases which started in water

B. diseases which are carried by water

C. diseases which were born in water

2 Find words in the article which mean the same as the following.

1. entering or escaping as through a hole or crack or fissure
2. to depend on
3. a lack of something
4. the process of keeping places clean and hygienic

3 Find words in the article which mean the contrary to the following.

1. surface	2. demands
3. to increase	4. solid
5. lightly	6. dangerous

4 Say whether the following statements are true (T) or false (F).

1. The decrease in underground supplies of water is confined to a few places in the world.
2. Florida's source of freshwater could be inundated by salt water.
3. Some countries in the Arabian Gulf use sea water to produce freshwater.
4. In big cities in India, 50% of irrigation water and 80% of drinking water come from underground.
5. More than one third of the 6-billion world population has no access to proper sanitation.
6. Diseases carried by water kill about seven children every minute.
7. It takes 2,000 tonnes of water to produce either a tonne of rice or two tonnes of wheat.
8. Sadly, it's usually in developing countries that people pay the most for their water.

5 There are several ways of saying by how much an amount has increased. For example we can combine the suffix "-fold" with numbers: to increase fourfold means it is four times greater than it was originally. In the article we read: "The world population has more than doubled in the past 60 years."

Make two sentences which mean the same, using "to increase twofold" and "to multiply by two" instead of "to double".

6 Several percentages are used in the text. Fractions (e.g. one third, three-fifths) can also be used to show relative value. Transform the following percentages into fractions and vice-versa and write them down.

1. 10%	2. 25%
3. 40%	4. 80%
5. one third	6. three-fifths
7. two-thirds	8. one-twentieth

News in brief

Daily Aids toll

South Africans spend more time at funerals than on any other activities outside work, according to a survey into the effect that HIV/Aids has had on daily life. About 600 people die of Aids each day in South Africa.

The Daily Telegraph, 21 March 2004

Vaccination for 20m

About 20 million Bangladeshi children will get a polio vaccine under a campaign to free the country from the disease by 2005, said officials in the capital, Dhaka.

The Daily Telegraph, 30 March 2003

EMPLOYMENT

5

L'EMPLOI

Vocabulaire à haute fréquence

Industries and workplaces	Les industries et les lieux de travail
to employ	employer
a firm, a business	une entreprise
the service sector	le secteur des services
manufacturing industries	les industries de transformation
a plant, a factory	une usine
a steelworks	une aciérie
shipbuilding	la construction navale
a shipyard	un chantier naval
management	la direction, la gestion
to manage, to run	diriger, gérer

Employment and employees	L'emploi et les employés
to train	former
vocational training	la formation professionnelle
skilled	qualifié
unskilled	non qualifié
labour	la main-d'œuvre
to qualify for	(se) rendre apte à
qualifications	les qualifications
a workman, a worker	un ouvrier
the labour force, the workforce, the staff	le personnel
a blue-collar worker	un ouvrier

a white-collar worker	un employé
a technician	un technicien
an engineer [endʒɪ'nɪə]	un ingénieur
an executive	un cadre
a job	un emploi
a part-time/full-time job	un emploi à temps partiel/à plein temps
wages	les salaires hebdomadaires
a salary	un salaire mensuel
pay	la paie, le salaire
a pay packet, a paycheck *(US)*	une fiche de paie, une paie
a bonus	une prime
working conditions	les conditions de travail
the working population	la population active
a job centre	une agence pour l'emploi
a situation, a post	une situation, un poste
a vacancy	une offre d'emploi
job-seeking, job-hunting	la recherche d'un emploi
to apply for	être candidat à
an application	une demande
a CV, a resumé *(US)*	un CV
to interview	recevoir
an interview	un entretien
a self-employed worker	un travailleur indépendant
self-employment	le travail indépendant
to retire [rɪ'taɪə]	prendre sa retraite
retirement	la retraite
early retirement	la retraite anticipée
a pension	une pension, une retraite
a pensioner	un retraité
a pension fund	un fonds de pension

Ups and downs / Les variations

advanced technology, high technology	la technologie avancée
an order	une commande
an order book	un carnet de commandes
a robot ['rəubɒt]	un robot
productive	productif
productivity	la productivité
to compete with sb.	concurrencer qn.
competition	la concurrence
competitive	compétitif, concurrentiel
competitiveness	la compétitivité
overtime	les heures supplémentaires
short-time working	le chômage partiel
part-time working	le travail à temps partiel
temporary employment	le travail intérimaire

Consequences	Les conséquences
a job loss	une perte d'emploi
staff reductions	les compressions de personnel
to axe/shed/cut (jobs)	supprimer (des emplois)
redundant	licencié
to make redundant, to lay off	licencier
a redundancy, a lay-off	un licenciement
a redundancy payment/package	une indemnité de licenciement
a closure, a shut-down	une fermeture
to create	créer
a creation	une création

Unemployment	Le chômage
joblessness	le chômage
unemployed, on the dole	au chômage
out of work, jobless	sans emploi
to register	s'inscrire
to be eligible for, to be entitled to	avoir droit à
to claim sth.	percevoir qch.
a claimant	un bénéficiaire
unemployment benefit	l'allocation de chômage
income support	l'allocation complémentaire
a job seeker's allowance	une allocation de recherche d'emploi
a school-leaver	un jeune sorti de l'école
to gauge	mesurer
the jobless rate/level	le taux de chômage
to issue figures	publier des chiffres
to adjust	corriger
an adjustment	une correction
seasonal distortion	les variations saisonnières
to retrain	(se) reconvertir
retraining	la reconversion
a scheme [ski:m]	un plan

Expressions

a low-paid job	un emploi mal rétribué
a dead-end job	un emploi sans avenir
to work overtime	faire des heures supplémentaires
performance-related pay	le salaire au mérite
to go out of business	cesser son activité, fermer
to be on the register	être inscrit au chômage
driven out of business	contraint à la fermeture
to give notice to sb.	donner son préavis à qn.
to give a new job to sb.	reclasser qn.
a temporary employment agency	une agence de travail intérimaire

a seasonally-adjusted figure	un chiffre corrigé des variations saisonnières
to massage figures	triturer les chiffres
to attend a crash course	suivre un stage intensif
on-the-job training	la formation permanente

Vocabulaire complémentaire

Employment and employees	**L'emploi et les employés**
an apprentice	un apprenti
apprenticeship	l'apprentissage
a craftsman	un artisan
a workshop	un atelier
an industrial estate	une zone industrielle
a factory hand	un ouvrier
a casual worker	un ouvrier intérimaire
the labour market	le marché de l'emploi
a graduate	un diplômé universitaire
a skill	une compétence technique
a shift	une équipe de travail
to engage, to take on, to hire	engager, embaucher
labour demand	le besoin de main d'œuvre
a headhunter	un chasseur de têtes
to vet	enquêter sur un candidat
a prospect	une perspective
a career [kə'rɪə]	une carrière
secure	stable, sûr
job security	la sécurité de l'emploi
fringe benefits	les avantages divers
perks	les à-côtés
a share option, a stock option *(US)*	une option de souscription d'actions, une stock option
profit-sharing	la participation aux bénéfices
flexible	flexible
flexibility	la flexibilité
a workaholic	un bourreau de travail
moonlighting	le travail au noir

Ups and downs	**Les variations**
work-sharing	le partage du travail
turnover	la rotation
natural wastage	les départs en retraite et les départs volontaires
voluntary redundancies	les départs volontaires
compulsory redundancies	les licenciements secs
to refurbish, to revamp, to upgrade	rénover, remettre en état

a refurbishment, a revamp, an upgrade	une rénovation, une remise en état
to automate	automatiser
automation	l'automatisation
robotisation	la robotisation
to relocate	délocaliser
relocation	la délocalisation

Consequences — Les conséquences

to redeploy	redéployer
redeployment	le redéploiement
to restructure	restructurer
restructuring	la restructuration
outsourcing	externalisation, sous-traitance
manning levels	les effectifs
overmanning	le sureffectif
to run down	réduire l'activité
a run-down	une réduction d'activité
to streamline, to slim down	dégraisser
a development area	une zone de conversion

HSBC in pact with union on Asia jobs

by Andrew Cave, Associate City Editor

HSBC yesterday became the second major British bank to reach agreement with a trade union over outsourcing jobs to Asia.

The bank, which plans to relocate 4,000 of its 50,000 British jobs to India, Malaysia and China over the next 2.5 years, said the agreement with the banking union Unifi reaffirms its commitment to try to avoid compulsory redundancies.

Michael Geoghegan, chief executive of HSBC's British bank, said: "There are compelling reasons for global resourcing but this is about people too and our staff have my personal commitment that we will manage this process carefully. For those staff whose jobs are affected in the UK, this is a significant change and it is hard for them to see the long-term benefits of global resourcing, including the contribution this makes to narrowing the poverty gap in developing countries."

Under the agreement, which follows a deal between Unifi and Barclays last month, HSBC will give Unifi two years' notice of its "global resourcing" plans and seek to find other positions for British staff whose jobs are moved.

Employees affected by "offshoring" will get at least two weeks' notice of British vacancies before they are advertised.
Redeployment managers will help identify local job opportunities and a new HSBC redeployment forum will invite applications for voluntary redundancy or early retirement from staff in areas where more than 10 compulsory redundancies are likely.
HSBC is also providing a £4m fund for careers advice and support. Rob O'Neill, of Unifi, said: "We are confident that our objective of keeping compulsory redundancies to an absolute minimum can be achieved."

The Daily Telegraph, 17 February 2000

1 Choose the right explanation for each of the following words underlined in the text.

1. commitment
A. restructuring
B. pledge
C. belief

2. compelling
A. complicated, intricate
B. convincing, undeniable
C. contradictory, unnecessary

3. offshoring
A. flexibility
B. short-time working
C. outsourcing abroad

2 Say whether the following statements are true (T) or false (F).

1. It's the first time an agreement on outsourcing has been reached between a British bank and a trade union.
2. No mention is made of the other bank with which the same kind of agreement was reached.
3. More than one in ten British jobs will be relocated to India, Malaysia and China.
4. Outsourcing can help to bridge the poverty gap between developed and developing countries.
5. Unifi will be informed of HSBC's relocation plans two years before implementation.
6. British staff who volunteer for redundancy or early retirement can send applications to redeployment managers.
7. Rob O'Neil is in no doubt that the number of compulsory redundancies will be the smallest possible.

3 Complete the words in the following sentences. Each dash represents one letter.

1. The company said it had agreed a r _ _ _ _ _ _ _ _ _ package with the t _ _ _ _ u _ _ _ _ _.
2. The firm said it hoped the job l _ _ _ _ _ could be achieved through v _ _ _ _ _ _ _ _ _ redundancies.
3. The factory is a _ _ _ _ 180 jobs from its 1,400-strong w _ _ _ _ _ _ _.
4. The number of people o _ _ o _ w _ _ _ and claiming b _ _ _ _ _ _ is down by more than 3,000 this month.
5. In the US, up to 25 per cent of traditional IT jobs will be r _ _ _ _ _ _ _ _ from developed to d _ _ _ _ _ _ _ _ _ countries by 2010.
6. The u _ _ _ _ _ _ _ _ _ _ _ rate has fallen to its lowest level since 1984.

Bombardier to axe 1,362 jobs in UK

by Christopher Hope, Business Correspondent

Bombardier, the engineering giant, confirmed yesterday that it is cutting one in four of its total UK workforce.
The Canadian business is axing a total of 6,600 jobs across Europe – or 18.5pc of its workforce. About 37pc of these are white-collar jobs.
In all, Bombardier said that it is closing seven production sites in five European countries.
Paul Tellier, chief executive, said that some of them were operating at only half capacity. In Britain, the company is closing a small factory in Derby, as well as plants in Doncaster and Wakefield. A total of 1,362 jobs in the UK are being lost.
However, Bombardier's main train building operation in Derby – the last such plant in the UK – will stay open, despite a gap in orders from the end of the year to 2008.
Mr Tellier said: "We will maintain our manufacturing capability in the UK with the Derby Litchurch Lane facility." The factories in Doncaster, which employs 132 workers on maintenance, and Derby's Pride Park site, where rail bogies are built, will close this year. Almost 400 will be lost at the Wakefield plant, which refurbishes trains, after its closure next year.
Factories will also close in Portugal, Germany, Switzerland and Sweden over the next 24 months. Mr Tellier said excess capacity in rail transportation had to be addressed.
None of the doomed plants had any work after 2005, he said.
He said: "Plant efficiency is not adequate, with certain facilities operating at barely 50pc capacity. The urgency to move now at Bombardier Transportation has been underscored by disappointing financial results." He added: "Our goal is to improve margins."
A new team of managers in the transportation arm would help put it on better footing. Mr Tellier added: "During this year, we put in a rigorous bid review process and we are now focusing on project management."
The restructuring will cost the company C$777m (£586m). Most of that –$457m – was taken in the three months to the end of January.
The rest will be spread over two years. Costs would be cut by $600m annually, the company said.
Mr Tellier added: "Although the cost of these efforts is high, these steps are essential to maintain our competitive position in the market."
Bombardier yesterday posted a fourth-quarter, pre-tax loss of C$526m, down from a loss of C$1.5 billion in the same period last time.
For the 12 months to the end of January, there was a pre-tax profit of C$10m, against a C$930m loss last time, on revenues of C$21.3 billion.

The Daily Telegraph, 18 March 2004

1 **Choose the appropriate endings for the following sentences.**

1. Bombardier is axing
A. staff in one of its four UK factories.
B. 25% of its UK labour force.
C. 25% of its workforce across Europe.

2. Some production lines are closed because
A. they operate at 50% capacity.
B. they are small factories.
C. jobs are being lost.

3. In the UK, Bombardier is closing
A. only a small factory in Derby.
B. an unspecified number of plants.
C. three plants.

4. The main train building operation in Derby will stay open
A. although there is no order between late 2004 and 2008.
B. because there is a gap in orders after 2008.
C. despite a gap in orders until the end of the year.

5. The factories which are to close
A. operate at full capacity.
B. have no orders after 2005.
C. have no work until 2005.

6. Bombardier has to be rescaled
A. because it is in a difficult financial situation.
B. because it is on a better footing.
C. because margins have been improved.

7. Bombardier's restructuring is essential
A. because its costs are very high.
B. so as to remain competitive.
C. in order to post a fourth-quarter, pre-tax loss.

2 **Which of the words in each list does not have the same meaning as the first word?**

1. workforce, wages, labour force, staff
2. to cut, to axe, to retrain, to shed
3. to refurbish, to revamp, to vet, to upgrade
4. business, company, firm, plant
5. to close, to gauge, to shut down, to liquidate

3 **Fill in the ten lines across the grid with translations of the corresponding French words. This will give you the answer to number 11 in Column D.**

1. partage du travail
2. chômage
3. bénéficiaire
4. impasse, blocage
5. supprimer
6. licencié
7. un retraité
8. s'inscrire
9. concurrentiel
10. se reconvertir
11. chasseur de têtes

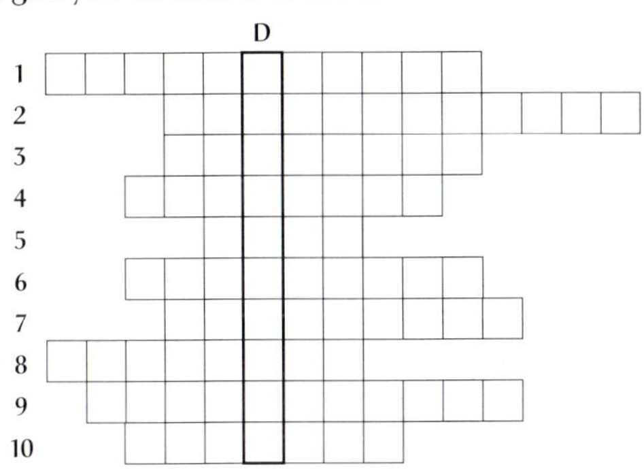

4 **The words in italics in the article have been scrambled. Put the letters back into the right order.**

Kodak cuts 15,000 jobs as film fades

By Simon English

Eastman Kodak, the company that popularised photography, *is lgsihasn* up to 15,000 jobs over the next three years as it fights to save the *sisubsen*.

The job cuts will see its *fwrokecro* cut by a fifth across the world, reflecting the falling demand for film cameras as digital photography becomes the norm.

Kodak admits it needs to dramatically overhaul its products. It expects that the job *stcu* will save as much as $1billion by 2007, *nyoem* it can invest in commercial printing and digital health imaging. The Kodak Camera was invented in 1888, after which the company dominated the industry for decades.

Chief executive Daniel Carp said: "Obviously when you have to *yla fof* as many people as we have, that's gut wrenching, but we know we are doing it for the better good of the whole *nmopcya*."

The *hsrase* rose $3.19 to $30.65 in early trading in New York, the highest since last summer.

The Daily Telegraph, 23 January 2004

DISPUTES AND TENSION

6

LES TENSIONS

Vocabulaire à haute fréquence

The world of labour	Le monde du travail
a wage earner	un salarié
a trade union, a labor union *(US)*	un syndicat ouvrier
a member	un adhérent
a trade unionist	un syndicaliste
a (trade) union leader/official/ representative	un leader/responsable/représentant syndical
the general secretary	le secrétaire général
a local branch	une section locale
a shop steward	un délégué syndical
the management	la direction
a pay claim	une revendication salariale
a mass meeting	une assemblée générale
a rally	un rassemblement
to ballot	consulter par vote
a ballot	une consultation

International tension	La tension internationale
tense, strained	tendu
a relationship, a relation, a tie	une relation
a chill	un refroidissement
a strain	une tension
to deteriorate	se dégrader
a deterioration	une dégradation
the axis of evil	l'axe du mal

rogue states	les États voyous
a thaw	un dégel
to ease	se détendre
a summit	un sommet
a conference	une conférence
a pact	un pacte
to violate	violer
a violation	une violation
to impose	imposer
a sanction	une sanction
a boycott	un boycott
an embargo [em'bɑːgəʊ]	un embargo
to lift an embargo	lever un embargo
a blockade	un blocus
a ban	une interdiction

Negotiations — Les négociations

a delegate	un délégué
an official	un responsable
to talk	s'entretenir, discuter
a talk	un entretien, une discussion
bilateral talks	des discussions bilatérales
a pay round	une négociation salariale
to claim	revendiquer, affirmer
a claim	une revendication, une affirmation
to demand	exiger
a demand	une exigence
to organise, to stage	organiser
to consider	examiner, étudier
a consideration	un examen, une étude
to bargain, to negotiate	négocier
the bargaining/negotiating table	la table des négociations
an agenda	un ordre du jour
an issue	une question, un problème
to propose	proposer
a proposal	une proposition
to offer	offrir
an offer	une offre
a step	une mesure, une disposition
a move	une décision, une initiative
a gesture	un geste
a formula ['fɔːmjʊlə]	une formule

Disagreement — Le désaccord

to reject, to turn down	rejeter, décliner
a rejection	un rejet

to refuse	refuser
a refusal	un refus
a stalemate, a deadlock, a gridlock	une impasse, un blocage
an obstacle, a hurdle	un obstacle
to disagree	être en désaccord
to warn	avertir, mettre en garde
a warning	un avertissement
to threaten ['θretn]	menacer
a threat	une menace
to break off	rompre
to break down	(se) rompre, échouer
to walk out	quitter la salle
a walk-out	une sortie, un départ
to fail to	ne pas réussir à
a failure	un échec
a crisis ['kraɪsɪs]	une crise

Industrial disputes — Les conflits sociaux

to walk out	débrayer
a walk-out	un débrayage
to stop work	cesser le travail
a work stoppage	un arrêt du travail
to back	soutenir, supporter
to strike, to go on strike	se mettre en grève
a strike	une grève
a non-striker	un non-gréviste
to disrupt	perturber
a disruption	une perturbation
to picket	installer un piquet
a picket (line)	un piquet (de grève)
a picketer	un piquet de grève (la personne)
to suspend	mettre à pied, suspendre
a suspension	une mise à pied
to dismiss, to sack	renvoyer, limoger
a dismissal, a sacking	un renvoi

A settlement — Un règlement

to resume	reprendre
a resumption	une reprise
to compromise	transiger
a compromise	un compromis
to give in, to yield, to cave in	céder
to back down	renoncer, abandonner sa position
to repeal	abroger, annuler
a repeal	une abrogation, une annulation
to betray	trahir

a backlash	un contrecoup, un retour de bâton
to grant	accorder
to draw up, to work out	établir, élaborer
a breakthrough, a step forward	une avancée
a term	une condition
to accept	accepter
an acceptance	une acceptation
to agree	être d'accord
an agreement, a deal	un accord
to manage to, to succeed in	réussir à
to solve, to resolve	résoudre, solutionner
to overcome	surmonter
a difference	une divergence, un différend
to settle	régler
a spokesperson	un(e) porte-parole
a statement	une déclaration

Ending a strike — La fin d'une grève

a peace formula	une formule d'apaisement
a peace process	un processus de paix
a pay settlement, a pay deal, a wages agreement	un accord salarial
a pay rise/raise	une augmentation de salaire
to call off a strike	terminer/annuler une grève

Expressions

Trades Union Congress	la Fédération des syndicats
to press a claim, to lodge a claim	déposer une revendication
to come to a halt	s'arrêter (production)
to come to a standstill	être paralysé
to refer to arbitration	soumettre à l'arbitrage
to take industrial action	entamer une action revendicative
to cross the picket line	franchir le piquet de grève
to call out/for a strike	appeler à la grève
to fight to the bitter end	lutter jusqu'au bout
to enter into negotiations	entamer des négociations
a round of talks	une série d'entretiens
to come to a deadlock	aboutir à une impasse
to break the deadlock/stalemate	débloquer la situation, sortir de l'impasse
to get negotiations back in gear	reprendre les négociations
to pave the way	préparer la voie
to prepare the ground	préparer le terrain
to strike a deal	conclure un accord
to come to/reach (an) agreement	parvenir à un accord

an across-the-board increase	une augmentation générale uniforme
to put to a vote	soumettre au vote
to be back to normal	être de retour à la normale
to break off diplomatic links	rompre les liens diplomatiques
to sever diplomatic ties	rompre les relations diplomatiques
to mend diplomatic ties	rétablir les relations diplomatiques
a show of strength	une démonstration de force
a trial/test of strength	une épreuve de force
to make representations	élever une protestation
to issue a statement	publier une déclaration
to get the sack	se faire virer

Vocabulaire complémentaire

The world of labour — Le monde du travail

collective bargaining	la négociation collective
the shopfloor	les ouvriers, la base
rank and file	la base
closed shop	le monopole de l'embauche
organised labour	les ouvriers syndiqués
a pay packet	une enveloppe de paie
a pay check *(US)*	une paie, un salaire
working conditions	les conditions de travail
working hours, the working week	la durée du travail
work patterns	les tableaux de service
safety standards	les normes de sécurité

International tension — La tension internationale

to go sour	se gâter
to escalate	monter, faire monter
escalation	l'escalade
a breach	une rupture
the UN security council	le conseil de sécurité de l'ONU
a resolution	une résolution
a diplomat ['dɪpləmæt]	un diplomate
diplomacy	la diplomatie
diplomatic [dɪplə'mætɪk]	diplomatique
an embassy	une ambassade
an ambassador [æm'bæsədə]	un ambassadeur
at large, roving	itinérant
a hot line	un numéro spécial
to extradite	extrader
extradition	l'extradition
to normalise	normaliser
normalisation	la normalisation
reconciliation	la réconciliation

a peace bid	une offre de paix
an envoy	un envoyé, un émissaire
an emissary	un émissaire
a counterpart, an opposite number	un homologue
the West Bank	La Cisjordanie
the Gaza Strip	la bande de Gaza
the Near East	le Proche-Orient
the Middle East	le Moyen-Orient

Negotiations	**Les négociations**
a stand, a stance	une attitude, une position
to keep under pressure	maintenir sous pression
to founder	achopper
a sticking point, a stumbling block	un point de désaccord, une pierre d'achoppement
to be bogged down, to be mired down	s'enliser
a log jam	un blocage, une impasse
a stand-off	un face-à-face
a counterproposal	une contre-proposition
a row [raʊ]	une querelle
a pre-condition	un préalable
to hammer out	élaborer/obtenir par discussion
a draft	un projet
a draft agreement	un protocole d'accord
a framework	un cadre
a showdown	un bras de fer
confrontation	l'affrontement
a deadline	une limite de temps, une date butoir
behind the scenes, backstage	dans les coulisses
to attempt to	tenter de
an attempt	une tentative
to mediate	servir d'intermédiaire
a mediator	un médiateur
mediation	la médiation
to defuse	désamorcer
to placate, to appease	apaiser
an appeasement	un apaisement
to conciliate	concilier
conciliation	la conciliation
conciliatory [kən'sɪlɪətrɪ]	conciliant
to trade off for	échanger contre
a trade-off	un échange, une contre-partie
a bargaining chip	une monnaie d'échange
an accord	un accord

Industrial disputes	Les conflits sociaux
a grievance ['griːvəns]	une doléance
pace	les cadences
working practices	l'organisation du travail
to consult	consulter
a consultation	une consultation
strike pay	l'allocation de grève
a scab	un jaune
a strike breaker	un briseur de grève
national strike action	un mouvement de grève national
a pay strike/row/dispute	une grève/un conflit sur les salaires
a lightning strike	une grève éclair
a selective strike	une grève limitée, ponctuelle
an all-out strike	une grève totale
a token strike	une grève d'avertissement
a go-slow, a work-to-rule	une grève du zèle
a sympathy strike	une grève de solidarité
a sit-down strike	une grève avec occupation
an official strike	une grève préparée, légale
an unofficial strike	une grève spontanée
a wildcat strike	une grève sauvage
a rolling strike	une grève tournante
an indefinite strike	une grève illimitée
a hunger strike	une grève de la faim

Consequences	Les conséquences
to cripple, to paralyse	paralyser
to lay off	mettre en chômage technique
lay-off	le chômage technique
a court ruling	une décision de justice
to discipline	punir, sanctionner
to fire	virer
an industrial tribunal	un Conseil de prud'hommes
unfair dismissal	le licenciement abusif
to reinstate	réintégrer
reinstatement	la réintégration

Deadlock in Korea nuclear crisis

by Richard Spencer in Beijing

Hopes of an early end to the North Korean nuclear crisis vanished yesterday, with delegations from Pyongyang and Washington blaming each other for failing to come up with a solution.

The only deal at the talks in Beijing was a vague agreement to keep trying. But both the United States and North Korea also toned down their rhetoric and American officials said progress had been made.

The comments seemed to shut the door firmly on any chance of Washington threatening sanctions before the next round of talks, which may be as late as July.

President George W. Bush is unlikely to gamble by provoking the North Koreans so soon before the presidential election in November. Analysts say the North Koreans may well wait to see if a more emollient adversary emerges.

Washington is demanding a commitment to "complete, verifiable, and irreversible dismantling" of Pyongyang's weapons programme. North Korea says it sees the freezing and then dismantling of its nuclear weapons programme as a goal, but says that to promise to do so before a deal would be to give in to Washington's "hardline stance".

According to some analysts, the North Korean leader Kim Jong-Il believes he can "slice the onion thinly" and win four separate stages of economic compensation: first for a freeze; then for dismantling his plutonium recycling plant; then for admitting and destroying stocks of enriched uranium; and finally for ruling out dual-use nuclear power stations.

The Daily Telegraph, 1 March 2004

1 **Choose the right explanation for each of the following words underlined in the article.**

1. to tone down
A. to stop
B. to moderate
C. to exaggerate

2. emollient
A. soft
B. hard
C. happy

3. to give in
A. to refuse
B. to yield
C. to offer

2 **Say whether the following statements are true (T) or false (F).**

1. There is still hope of an early settlement between the White House and Pyongyang.
2. The US and North Korea have both softened their rhetoric.
3. There will probably be no retaliation from the US government against North Korea.
4. According to analysts, North Koreans hope that a new, more lenient president will be elected in the US in November.
5. North Korea is ready to commit itself to dismantling its weapons programme immediately.
6. Pyongyang wants to buy time for its dismantling of its nuclear weapons programme so as to bargain for financial help.

3 **The first word in each list comes from the article. Which of the other three should not be associated with it?**

1. chance, gamble, risk, proposal
2. deadlock, stalemate, mediation, gridlock
3. an agreement, a deal, a bargain, a claim
4. adversary, partner, opponent, foe

4 **Complete the missing words in the following sentences. Each dash represents a letter.**

1. A recent t _ _ _ in ties has raised hopes for talks on a range of issues.
2. The EU r _ _ _ _ _ _ _ _ _ has been submitted to the UN nuclear w _ _ _ _ _ _ _ which meets on Thursday to discuss Iran.
3. Thousands of workers will w _ _ _ o _ _ threatening travel chaos in the capital.
4. The White House has urged both sides to h _ _ _ _ _ _ _ t a deal.
5. The t _ _ _ _ u _ _ _ _ _ have not implemented an _ _ l - _ _ _ strike to demonstrate their willingness to talk to resolve the issue.

University lecturers to strike over pay

By Liz Lightfoot

University lecturers have voted to strike over pay later this month. The final decision on the form their action will take and its timing will be made by the executive committee of the Association of University Teachers today but it is likely to endorse a mixture of walk-outs and disruption during the week beginning Feb 23.

Their action would coincide with the campaign of disruption planned by the National Union of Students in protest at the introduction of top-up fees. The NUS has backed the lecturers' action.

Sally Hunt, general secretary of the association, said lecturers' pay had declined by 40 per cent in comparison with the rest of the workforce.

The union has rejected a pay package which vice-chancellors say will modernise salaries and give rises worth 6.44 per cent for both 2003-04 and 2004-05.

It claims that many lecturers, researchers and senior support staff would lose out in future because of the changes to the way their salaries are calculated.

There was a 54.4 per cent turn-out for the ballot, which showed two thirds in favour of a strike and 81 per cent backing industrial action in which they would refuse to mark students' work.

Vice-chancellors told the Government earlier this week that they needed a further £8.8 billion to protect the standard of higher education.

The Daily Telegraph, 14 February 2004

1 Choose the right explanation for each of the following words underlined in the article.

1. to endorse

A. to refuse

B. to approve

C. to reject

2. lecturers

A. academics

B. readers

C. writers

2 Say whether the following statements are true (T) or false (F).

1. University lecturers have already voted to walk out and disrupt classes.
2. The NUS's campaign of disruption and the AUT's strike will be simultaneous.
3. Students will have to pay less for higher education.
4. Lecturers have lost out compared to the rest of the labour force as regards pay.

5. The pay round between vice-chancellors and the union led to an agreement.
6. There will be no marking of students' work as a result of the ballot.
7. Vice-chancellors have turned down the government's £8.8 billion offer to protect the standard of higher education.

3 Fill in the eight lines across the grid with translations of the corresponding French word. This will give you the answer to number 9 in column D.

1. négocier
2. tendu
3. échec
4. extrader
5. contrecoup
6. blocus
7. un responsable, un cadre
8. avancée
9. impasse, blocage

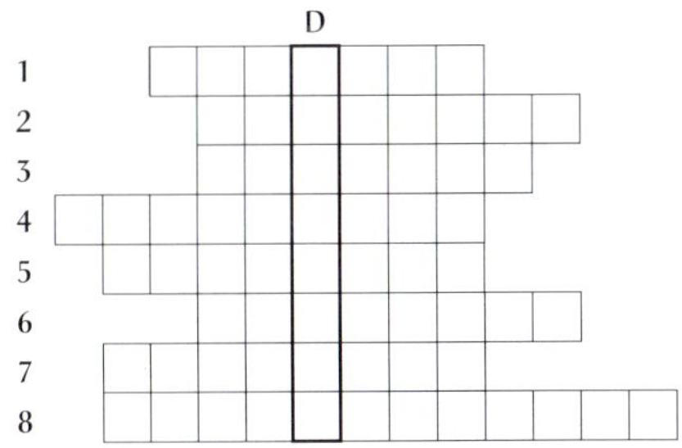

Civil servants go on strike

Sarah Hall, political correspondent

Almost 100,000 civil servants in three government departments will go on strike today in what is expected to be the biggest civil service industrial action for more than a decade. Some 90,000 staff in Jobcentres and benefit offices in England, Wales and Scotland will walk out for 48 hours in an increasingly acrimonious dispute over pay. They will be joined by 4,500 workers from the prison service in England and Wales in a separate wage dispute which could disrupt the transfer of prisoners, and by 1,500 workers from the Office of National Statistics who will stage a 24-hour strike – the first in the office's history.

The industrial action comes less than two months after 90,000 staff from the Department for Work and Pensions went on strike, leading to the closure of some Jobcentres and benefit offices.

The DWP workers are opposed to the imposition of a new pay performance structure. They argue it is does little to address the growing problem of low wages for many civil servants.

Starting salaries for all three departments range from £10,300 to £10,575, and the Public and Commercial Services Union, which is organising the strike, says more than 20,000 staff in the DWP have to claim the same low pay benefits they administer. The union has warned it will take the DWP to the high court unless it withdraws the scheme, arguing its "unilateral imposition" was a breach of contract.

Managers in the department have said they have offered workers a substantial pay deal worth an average 5% aimed at junior and the worst-paid staff, but the union insists it is worth 2.9%.

Mark Serwotka, the union's general secretary, said yesterday: "Rather than try to find compromise with its workforce, senior management prefer the bully-boy tactics of imposing divisive bonus schemes and real term pay cuts."

The Guardian, 13 April 2004

Land Rover strikes

Workers at Land Rover's West Midlands plants in Solihull and Gaydon are likely to announce further strike dates next week.

Some 1,100 workers are set to stage a 24-hour stoppage starting tomorrow after rejecting a 6.5 per cent two-year pay offer from Land Rover's owner, Ford. Last month, members of Amicus and the Transport Union voted for strike action and an overtime ban.

The Observer, 25 January 2004

7

MEDICINE

LA MÉDECINE

Vocabulaire à haute fréquence

Health and disease	La santé et la maladie
ill, sick	malade
an illness, a sickness, a disease	une maladie, un mal
to suffer from	souffrir de
pain	la douleur
painful	douloureux
back pain	le mal de dos
sore	endolori
a sore throat	un mal de gorge
a headache	une migraine
dizziness	le vertige
nausea	la nausée
to hurt	faire mal
temperature, fever	la fièvre
a fit	un accès, une attaque
a fit of coughing	une quinte de toux
a cough	la toux
critical	critique
a condition	un état
healthy	bien portant
a virus ['vaɪrəs]	un virus
a bacterium (*pl.* -ia) [bæk'tɪərɪəm]	une bactérie
contagious, infectious, catching	contagieux
to pass on, to transmit	transmettre
to develop, to contract	attraper contracter
an outbreak	un début d'épidémie

an epidemic	une épidémie
a case	un cas
a cold	un rhume
measles [mi:zlz]	la rougeole
chicken pox	la varicelle
flu, influenza [ɪnflu:'enzə]	la grippe
to spread	se répandre, s'étendre
to infect	infecter
an infection	une infection
to contaminate	contaminer
contamination	la contamination
to incubate	incuber
incubation	l'incubation
a carrier	un porteur
benign [bɪ'naɪn]	bénin
a malignant tumour	une tumeur maligne
cancer	le cancer
leukaemia [lu:'ki:mɪə]	la leucémie
Aids	le sida
an Aids sufferer	un malade du sida
HIV positive	séropositif
the immune system	le système immunitaire
an antibody	un anticorps
to faint, to pass out	s'évanouir
to come to	reprendre connaissance
disabled, impaired	handicapé
a heart attack	une crise cardiaque
a heart failure	une défaillance cardiaque
a nervous breakdown	une dépression nerveuse
a victim	une victime
mentally handicapped	handicapé mental
life expectancy	l'espérance de vie
euthanasia [ju:θə'neɪzɪə]	l'euthanasie

Organs and tissues / Les organes et les tissus

blood	le sang
a cell	une cellule
a blood cell	un globule
a blood sample	une prise de sang
blood pressure	la tension artérielle
a kidney	un rein
the liver	le foie
a breast	un sein
a lung	un poumon
the brain	le cerveau
a neuron	un neurone
the womb [wu:m]	l'utérus
a nerve	un nerf

Health service and treatment — Les services de santé et le traitement

the World Health Organisation (WHO)	l'Organisation Mondiale de la Santé (OMS)
the Food and Drug Administration (FDA) *(US)*	l'office de contrôle pharmaceutique et alimentaire
the National Health Service (NHS) *(GB)*	la sécurité sociale
a general practitioner (GP)	un médecin généraliste
a surgeon	un chirurgien
surgery hours	les heures de consultation
a surgery	un cabinet médical
a chemist, a pharmacist	un pharmacien
a hospital	un hôpital
a nurse	une infirmière
an outpatient	un malade de jour
a ward	une salle, un service
an emergency	une urgence
to examine	examiner
an examination	un examen
to check	vérifier
a check-up	un contrôle
to diagnose ['daɪəgnəuz]	diagnostiquer
a diagnosis	un diagnostic
a test	une analyse
a probe	une sonde
to detect	déceler, dépister
detection	le dépistage
to screen	examiner pour dépister
screening	examen de dépistage
mass screening	le dépistage massif
to prescribe	prescrire
a prescription	une ordonnance
a drug/pharmaceutical company	une société pharmaceutique
a medicine, a drug	un médicament
a generic drug	un médicament générique
a tailored drug	un médicament sur mesure/personnalisé
a dose	une dose
a pill	une pilule
a tablet	un comprimé, un cachet
a tranquilliser	un tranquillisant
to treat	traiter, soigner
to respond	réagir
efficient, effective	efficace
efficacy, efficiency	l'efficacité
a side effect	un effet secondaire
to relieve	soulager
a relief	un soulagement

to cure	guérir
a cure	une guérison, un remède
a remedy	un remède
incurable	incurable
to save	sauver
to recover	se rétablir
a recovery	un rétablissement
a diet	un régime
a slimming diet	un régime amincissant

Operations / Les opérations

surgery	une intervention
to perform	effectuer
to undergo	subir
an operating theatre	une salle d'opération
intensive care	les soins intensifs
to resuscitate	réanimer
resuscitation	la réanimation
a transfusion	une transfusion
blood donation	le don du sang
to remove	enlever
a removal	une ablation
to transplant [træns'plɑ:nt]	transplanter
a transplant ['trænsplɑ:nt]	une transplantation
to donate	faire un don
a donor	un donneur
a recipient	un receveur
to reject	rejeter
a rejection	un rejet

Research / La recherche

a survey	une étude, une enquête
a trial	un test, un essai
to research	faire de la recherche
a scientist	un scientifique
a laboratory	un laboratoire
to carry out	effectuer
an experiment	une expérience
to discover	découvrir
a discovery	une découverte
findings	les résultats (recherche)
to develop	mettre au point
development	la mise au point
a breakthrough	une percée, une avancée

Childbearing	La maternité
sterile, infertile	stérile
childless	sans enfant
to fertilise	féconder
in vitro fertilisation	la fécondation in vitro
a test tube	une éprouvette
sperm	le sperme
to inseminate	inséminer
insemination	l'insémination
an embryo ['embrɪəʊ]	un embryon
pregnant	enceinte
a pregnancy	une grossesse
a fœtus ['fiːtəs]	un fœtus
labour	le travail
a maternity hospital	une maternité
to deliver	accoucher
a delivery	un accouchement

Cloning and genetics	Le clonage et la génétique
the human genome	le génome humain
the genetic make-up	le patrimoine génétique
DNA	l'ADN
a chromosome	un chromosome
a gene [dʒiːn]	un gène
a mutated gene	un gène muté
to inherit	hériter
a gene test	un test génétique
genetic engineering	le génie génétique
a geneticist	un généticien
gene therapy	la thérapie génique
to clone	cloner
a clone	un clone
cloning	le clonage
a biotech company	une société de biotechnologie
pharmacogenetics	la pharmacogénétique
embryonic stem cells	les cellules souches embryonnaires
to harvest	récolter
therapeutic/reproductive cloning	le clonage thérapeutique/reproductif
cystic fibrosis	la mucoviscidose
muscular dystrophy	la myopathie

Expressions

to be on a diet	suivre un régime
to take a sample	faire un prélèvement
a sexually transmitted disease (STD)	une maladie sexuellement transmissible (MST)
to have an X-ray	passer une radio
to be operated on	subir une opération
to be on a life support machine	être sous assitance respiratoire
he is making good progress	son état s'améliore
to be doing well	être en bonne voie
to nurse a cold	soigner un rhume
to have a heart condition	avoir une affection cardiaque
to take to hospital	transporter à l'hôpital
to spark an epidemic	déclencher une épidémie
to be available on prescription	être délivré sur ordonnance
to be available over-the-counter	être délivré sans ordonnance

Vocabulaire complémentaire

Health and disease	La santé et la maladie
sound	sain
a deficiency	une carence
stamina	le tonus
a complaint	une affection
acute	aigu
chronic	chronique
to quarantine	mettre en quarantaine
a quarantine	une quarantaine
a germ	un germe
a microbe ['maɪkrəub]	un microbe
a bug	un microbe, un virus
a prion	un prion
a strain	une souche
an enzyme	une enzyme
allergies	les allergies
bronchitis	la bronchite
pneumonia	la pneumonie
flu-like pneumonia	pneumonie atypique
severe acute respiratory syndrome (SARS)	syndrome respiratoire aigu sévère (SRAS)
hepatitis [hepə'taɪtɪs]	l'hépatite
diabetes [daɪə'bi:ti:z, daɪə'bi:tɪz]	le diabète
asthma ['æsmə]	l'asthme
arthritis [ɑ:θ'raɪtɪs]	l'arthrite
rheumatism ['ru:mətɪzm]	le rhumatisme

multiple sclerosis	la sclérose en plaques
meningitis [menɪn'dʒaɪtɪs]	la méningite
rabies ['reɪbi:z]	la rage
angina [æn'dʒaɪnə]	l'angine de poitrine
a stroke	une attaque cérébrale
epilepsy	l'épilepsie
Legionnaire's disease	la maladie du légionnaire
Parkinson's disease	la maladie de Parkinson
Creutzfeld Jakob Disease (CJD)	la madie de Creutzfeld Jakob
cholesterol	le cholestérol
a symptom	un symptôme
a sick note	un certificat de maladie
sick/sickness leave	un congé de maladie
a growth, a lump	une grosseur, une tumeur
cancerous	cancéreux
carcinogenic	cancérigène
passive smoking	le tabagisme passif
a stage	un stade
mercy killing	l'euthanasie
a hæmophiliac [hi:mə'fɪlɪæk]	un hémophile
food poisoning	l'intoxication alimentaire
salmonella	la salmonellose
listeria	la listeriose

Organs and tissues — Les organes et les tissus

a vessel	un vaisseau
a vein	une veine
an artery	une artère
coronary	coronaire, coronarien
a blood clot	un caillot de sang
the belly, the tummy	le ventre
the bladder	la vessie
bone marrow	la moëlle des os
the uterus	l'utérus
an intestine	un intestin
the bowels	les entrailles
the cervix	le col de l'utérus
cervical	du col de l'utérus
a gland	une glande
a mole	un grain de beauté
a boil	un furoncle

Health service and treatment — Les services de santé et le traitement

a physician, a doctor	un médecin
a consultant, a specialist	un spécialiste

a heart specialist, a cardiologist	un cardiologue
a junior doctor	un interne
a sister	une infirmière chef
a unit	un service
to hospitalise	hospitaliser
a clinic	une clinique, un service de consultation
a nursing home	une maison de santé
a mental hospital	un hôpital psychiatrique
terminal care, palliative care	les soins palliatifs
antibiotics [æntɪbaɪ'ɒtɪks]	les antibiotiques
a painkiller	un analgésique
to vaccinate	vacciner
a vaccine	un vaccin
to immunise	immuniser
immunisation	l'immunisation
to eradicate	éradiquer
eradication	l'éradication
a swab [swɒb]	un prélèvement
a smear [smiːə]	un frottis (vaginal)
a biopsy [baɪ'ɒpsɪ]	une biopsie
chemotherapy	la chimiothérapie
radiation therapy	radiothérapie
metastasis	les métastases
a serum	un sérum
a report, a bulletin	un bulletin
to pull through	s'en sortir

Operations / Les opérations

surgical	chirurgical
cosmetic/plastic surgery	la chirurgie esthétique
keyhole surgery	la chirurgie mini invasive, la vidéo chirurgie
under anæsthetic	sous anesthésie
a bypass	un pontage
to implant	implanter
an implant	un implant
a pioneer [paɪə'nɪə]	un pionnier
to graft	greffer
cross-species	inter-espèces
a graft	une greffe
a pacemaker	un stimulateur
a respirator	un respirateur
a dialysis machine	un rein artificiel

Childbearing	La maternité
to conceive	concevoir
conception	la conception
an ovary ['əʊvərɪ]	un ovaire
ovulation	l'ovulation
Fallopian tubes	les trompes
periods	les règles
semen ['siːmən]	la semence
a miscarriage	une fausse couche
stillborn	mort-né
stillbirth	mort à la naissance
newborn	nouveau-né
a surrogate mother	une mère porteuse
surrogacy ['sʌrəgəsɪ]	la substitution
Caesarian section	une césarienne
an offspring	un descendant
to breastfeed	nourrir au sein
to bring up	élever
premature	prématuré
cot death	la mort subite du nourrisson
twins	des jumeaux
abnormal	anormal
malformed	malformé
malformation	la malformation
a disability	un handicap
a wheelchair	un fauteuil roulant

UN postpones global human cloning ban

by Celeste Biever

The United Nations' General Assembly in New York narrowly voted to postpone any ban on human cloning until 2005 on Thursday, leading many scientists around the world to breathe a sigh of relief. The main alternative to the two-year moratorium was a Costa Rican-led blanket ban on both human reproductive and therapeutic cloning, backed by the US government and 43 other countries.

Reproductive cloning – creating babies – is regarded by virtually everyone as dangerous and unethical. But opinion is split on therapeutic cloning – the use of cloned embryos to harvest stem cells for medical use. Supporters say the approach offers unrivalled promise for the treatment of many diseases, such as Parkinson's and diabetes. Opponents, many of whom also oppose abortion, say that the resultant death of the embryo is absolutely unacceptable.

Scientists see the Iranian-led compromise as the least worst option. "No decision is better than the wrong decision," says Bob Ward, spokesperson for the UK's premier scientific association, the Royal Society. Ian Wilmut, who led the cloning of the first adult mammal, Dolly the sheep, agrees: "I think it is a lesser evil to have this solution than to have a complete ban."

Nuclear transfer

Both reproductive and therapeutic cloning begin with the same procedure. The genetic material in the nucleus of a human cell is transferred to an egg from which the nucleus has been removed. This egg can then be prompted to grow into an early embryo. Implanting the early embryo into a woman's womb could produce a baby. But the cells could also be collected, killing the embryo, for therapeutic use.

Cloned animals have suffered serious health problems, and for this and ethical reasons, reproductive cloning is already banned in over 30 countries. But until it is banned worldwide, "safe havens for unscrupulous scientists" will remain, says Bernard Siegel, director of the Human Cloning Policy Institute in Florida.

However, many scientists believe therapeutic cloning shows remarkable medical promise. The stem cells harvested from cloned embryos can develop into any type of tissue and would not be rejected after implantation into the original donor. "I am convinced that therapeutic cloning offers health opportunities that you could not attain in any other way," says Wilmut, at the Roslin Institute in Edinburgh, Scotland.

Third way

This is why the governments of the UK, Japan, China, Germany, France and other countries, as well as most of the world's scientific institutions, backed a third UN proposal. This would have banned reproductive cloning globally, while leaving the decision on therapeutic cloning up to individual countries. But with 14 countries, this proposal had less backing than the proposed ban on both types of cloning.

Thursday's UN vote means the both proposals will have to wait two years before being re-evaluated, prompting an angry response from some scientists. "Rather than ban the thing that we all agree on, we end up with no ban, because the extremists refuse to compromise," says Larry Goldstein, a stem cell researcher at the University of California, San Diego.

But Jose Cibelli of the University of Michigan is confident that the two-year interlude will give researchers just enough time to come up with the compelling results to persuade the public of the huge medical value of therapeutic cloning.

New Scientist, 7 November 2003

1 Say whether the following statements are true (T) or false (F).

1. If a moratorium on cloning had not been voted, human cloning would have been banned overall.
2. Almost no scientists are against reproductive cloning.
3. Therapeutic cloning is attacked by opponents mainly on abortion grounds.
4. Iran was in favour of the two-year moratorium.
5. Bernard Siegel is in favour of a worldwide ban on reproductive cloning.
6. No rejection is observed after the implantation of stem cells.
7. Therapeutic cloning shows unrivalled promise to treat health problems, according to Ian Wilmut.
8. Larry Goldstein is angry because some countries refuse a compromise that would allow therapeutic cloning while banning reproductive cloning.

2 Reorder the following statements to fit the order of the text.

A. Technically speaking, the early stages of reproductive and therapeutic cloning are very similar.
B. A complete ban on any human cloning has been avoided by the UN General Assembly.
C. So far, cloning experiments on animals have led to serious medical concerns.
D. Some scientists hope that in two-years' time people will be more open about therapeutic cloning when seeing the promising results of this medical practice.
E. The disagreement that divides scientists concerns therapeutic cloning.
F. A minority group of countries had put forward a plan banning only reproductive cloning.

3 Which of the words in each list does not have the same meaning as the first word?

1. to ban, to bar, to forgive, to forbid
2. to postpone, to cancel, to put off, to delay
3. dangerous, hazardous, unsafe, unfit
4. to back, to support, to oppose, to defend

4 Two different sentences have been cut into parts and the parts

scrambled. Put them back into the right order. (The capital letters have been removed at the beginning of the sentences).

1. growing embryos / that can grow / to supply stem cells / consists in / into any tissue / therapeutic cloning / in a test tube
2. on 5 July 1996, / cloned mammal / aged 6 / , who became / Dolly the sheep / was euthanised / the first / when she was born

5 In English we add "–ly" to an adjective to form an adverb:

beautiful (adj.) → beautifully (adv.)
biological (adj.) → biologically (adv.)
extreme (adj.) → extremely (adv.)

Find the adjectives or adverbs corresponding to the following words taken from the article.

1. narrowly (adv.)
2. virtually (adv.)
3. absolutely (adv.)
4. scientific (adj.)
5. complete (adj.)
6. reproductive (adj.)
7. therapeutic (adj.)
8. genetic (adj.)
9. ethical (adj.)
10. remarkable (adj.)
11. medical (adj.)
12. original (adj.)
13. globally (adv.)
14. individual (adj.)
15. angry (adj.)
16. confident (adj.

Obesity close to smoking as cause of death in US

David Teather in New York

Obesity is closing in on smoking as the number one cause of death in the US as Americans continue to pack on the pounds. A report from the Centres for Disease Control and Prevention said that tobacco remained the number one killer, accounting for 435,000 deaths in the US during 2000, around 18.1% of all those who died that year.

But illnesses related to weight problems are catching up fast. A poor diet and physical inactivity accounted for 400,000 deaths in 2000, some 16.6% of the total. That figure was one-third higher than in 1990. Tobacco-related illnesses grew by just 9% over the same ten-year period. An estimated 59m Americans are classified obese, generally held to be 30 pounds overweight for women and 35 to 40 pounds for men. Obesity sharply increases chances of serious health problems like heart disease, cancer and diabetes.

The results appeared in yesterday's Journal of the American Medical Association. «Our worst fears were confirmed,» said Dr Julie Gerberding, the CDC's director and an author of the study. The research is the latest to highlight the issue. A separate report by the Rand think tank found that an increase in obesity threatens to wipe out many of the recent advances in health among middle-aged and older Americans. The House of Representatives yesterday voted in favour of a bill to ban fast food restaurants' liability for consumers' health problems.

The Guardian, 11 March 2004

8

SPACE
L'ESPACE

Vocabulaire à haute fréquence

Getting ready	Les préparatifs
a space agency	une agence spatiale
a rocket	une fusée
a spacecraft, a spaceship	un vaisseau spacial
a shuttle	une navette
onboard, aboard	embarqué, à bord
a cabin	une cabine
training	l'entraînement, la préparation
a spaceman	un spationaute
an astronaut	un astronaute
a cosmonaut	un cosmonaute
a taikonaut	un taïkonaute
a spacesuit	un scaphandre
a crew	un équipage
a human/manned (space) flight	un vol habité
to check	vérifier
safety	la sécurité
the countdown	le compte à rebours
a schedule ['ʃedju:l, 'skedju:l]	un horaire
on schedule	comme prévu
to delay	retarder
a delay	un retard
to put off, to postpone	reporter, ajourner
a postponement	un ajournement
to cancel	annuler
a cancellation	une annulation

a setback	un échec
a fault, a defect, a flaw	un défaut, une anomalie
defective, faulty	défectueux
to fix	réparer
to work	marcher, fonctionner

Lift-off — Le décollage

to ignite	allumer, mettre à feu
ignition	l'allumage, la mise à feu
to launch	lancer
a launch	un lancement, un tir
a launching-pad	un pas de tir
to blast off, to lift off, to take off	décoller
a blast-off, a lift-off, a take-off	un décollage, un envol
a propulsion system	un système de propulsion
fuel	le carburant
a tank	un réservoir
a booster	un propulseur d'appoint
to soar	s'élever, s'élancer
a stage	un étage
to separate	se séparer
to fall off	se détacher
to circle/orbit (a planet)	tourner en orbite (autour d'une planète)
an orbit	une orbite
orbit insertion	la mise en orbite
an orbiter	un orbiteur
to monitor, to track	suivre la trace de

In Space — Dans l'espace

a stage, a leg	une étape
the away leg	l'aller
a flightpath	une trajectoire de vol
to glide	planer
on route to	en route vers
to dock (with)	accoster, (s')arrimer (à)
to link up	(se) relier, (se) rattacher
a docking, a link-up	un amarrage, un arrimage
to latch on to	(s')accrocher, (s')attacher à
a space station	une station spatiale
a weather satellite	un satellite météo
a spy satellite	un satellite espion
weightlessness	l'apesanteur
a pull	une attraction
a laboratory	un laboratoire
to carry out	effectuer
an experiment	une expérience

a cargo	une cargaison
a payload	une charge utile
a pay-off, a spin-off	une récompense, une retombée
a drug	un médicament
the cargo bay, the hold	la soute
to deploy	déployer
a (solar) panel	un panneau (solaire)
a device	un dispositif
a robotic arm	un bras motorisé
to eject	éjecter
ejection	l'éjection
a rover	un rover
a lander	un robot, un atterrisseur
a landing site	un site d'atterrissage
to touch down	atterrir
a touchdown	un atterrissage
to retrieve, to recover	récupérer, reprendre
retrieval, recovery	la récupération
a spacewalk	une sortie dans l'espace
a spacewalker	un piéton de l'espace
a lifeline	un filin, une ligne de vie
a backpack	un fauteuil de l'espace
to steer [stɪə]	diriger, gouverner
to manœuvre [mə'nu:və]	manœuvrer
a manœuvre	une manœuvre

Crashes — Les accidents

to desintegrate	se désintégrer
to crash	s'écraser
to blow up, to break up	exploser
to scuttle	saborder
to lose contact	perdre le contact
a technical failure	une défaillance technique
a collision	une collision
debris	les débris
an investigation	une enquête
a blunder, an error	une erreur, une bourde

Return — Le retour

to complete	terminer
to re-enter	rentrer
re-entry	la rentrée
the atmosphere	l'atmosphère
to land	atterrir
landing	l'atterrissage
a base	une base

Expressions

to be behind schedule	être en retard
to be out of order	être en panne
there was something wrong with...	il y avait quelque chose qui n'allait pas dans ..
to put/to place into orbit	mettre en orbite
to go into/to enter orbit	se mettre en orbite
the International Space Station (ISS)	la station spatiale internationale
to put something right	remédier à quelque chose

Vocabulaire complémentaire

Flight	**Le vol**
space sickness	le mal de l'espace
space tourism	le tourisme spatial
a space tourist	un touriste spatial
a commercial space launch	un lancement spatial commercial
lunar	lunaire
a module	un module
a capsule	une capsule
a retro-rocket	une rétrofusée
a rendez-vous, an encounter	un rendez-vous
to team up	s'assembler
a back-up system	un système de secours
a repair kit	un kit de réparation
remote control	le contrôle à distance
a tracking station	une station de repérage
supersonic speeds	des vitesses supersoniques
a meteorite [ˈmiːtɪəraɪt]	un météorite

Missions	**Les missions**
geostationary	géostationnaire
to relay	relayer
to beam back	renvoyer, réfléchir
a telescope	un télescope
an astronomer	un astronome
to probe	sonder
a probe	une sonde
an antenna [ænˈtenə]	une antenne
outer space, the cosmos	le cosmos
a planet	une planète
interplanetary	interplanétaire
a galaxy	une galaxie
the solar system	le système solaire
gravitation	la gravitation
gravity	la pesanteur
vacuum	le vide

Opportunity knocks in latest Mars landing

Scientists jubilant at success after "six minutes of terror" as another US rover heads off in search of more signs of water

Tim Radford, science editor

A second US robot rover crashed through the atmosphere of Mars early yesterday at 12,000mph and bounced to a standstill in a region called the Meridiani Planum. The arrival makes Mars a relatively crowded place. There are already three satellites in orbit around the red planet and the six-wheeled rover Opportunity was the third landing on Mars since Christmas Day.

The first, the British Beagle 2, has been silent since its Yuletide arrival at a plain called Isidis. The second, Spirit, a twin of Opportunity, made a successful landing on January 4 at a place called the Gusev crater, but ran into serious communication problems on Wednesday. On Friday, it began to transmit again, giving engineers enough evidence to identify a software flaw which they hope to correct. But this could take weeks.

So the successful landing of Opportunity was greeted with more than the usual jubilation. In the last four decades more than half of all missions to Mars have come to grief.

To make a safe landing, Opportunity had to hit the Martian atmosphere at just the right angle, survive a sudden burst of intense heat as it ploughed through the thin air of the planet, open a parachute, then fire a set of retro rockets, and finally inflate a set of airbags to cushion its impact with the arid rocks of Mars. One engineer called such a descent "six minutes of terror". Then the rover had to settle the right way up, flip away its inflated cocoon, unfold its solar panels, and prepare to send a postcard home to mission control 100m miles away in Pasadena, California. "I came here prepared for a funeral," said Ed Weiler, second in command at Nasa. "Talk about a rollercoaster ride: I saw the resurrection of one rover and the birth of another."

Like Spirit before it, Opportunity will stay on its landing platform, gathering up solar energy and checking its faculties before trundling off with its stereoscopic, eye-level camera and geological tools to investigate its new home and look for evidence of water on the parched planet.

The Americans chose the Gusev touchdown because it looked like an old lake bed. They selected Meridiani because it seemed to be rich in the mineral haematite, normally linked with water. But the two rovers are, in effect, only geologists. Water is a prerequisite for life, but neither Spirit nor Opportunity is designed to look for signs of life.

Beagle 2, put together by a British consortium led by the Open University's Colin Pillinger, would have been the first working biologist on Mars. It was the first robot specifically engineered to probe beneath the Martian surface to "sniff" for telltale organic chemicals usually linked with life.

Mission scientists have not yet entirely given up hope, but its silence has been a cruel blow.

The pain was softened a little on Friday, however, by the first data from Beagle's mothership, Mars Express, which has begun to send back stunning images of the planet. It has also begun a search for water by radar and other sensing instruments.

The Guardian, 26 January 2004

1 Choose the right explanation for each of the following words underlined in the article.

1. a standstill
A. a silence
B. a halt
C. a breakdown

2. to inflate
A. to blow up
B. to explode
C. to shrink

3. to cushion
A. to worsen
B. to increase
C. to soften

4. a rollercoaster ride
A. a ride as in a capsule rolling through space
B. a ride as in a railway in an amusement park
C. a ride along the coast

5. trundling off
A. orbiting
B. studying
C. rolling away

6. beneath
A. on
B. over
C. below

2 Which of the three or four words in each list should not be associated with the others.

1. landing, touchdown, grinding
2. flaw, delay, fault, defect
3. jubilation, glee, grief, joy
4. to probe, to examine, to investigate, to identify
5. stunning, ordinary, fabulous, marvellous
6. engineered, sent, programmed, designed
7. telltale, trivial, meaningful, significant

3 Say whether the following statements are true (T) or false (F).

1. The rover Opportunity exploded when going through the Mars atmosphere.
2. There are three satellites in orbit around Mars and six rovers on the planet.
3. Spirit and Opportunity are similar rovers.
4. The British Beagle 2, silent since its arrival on Mars, began to transmit again on Friday.
5. Less than 50% of all missions to Mars have been successful.
6. Opportunity made a smooth landing.

7. Ed Weiler was not optimistic when he arrived in Passadena.
8. Spirit's and Opportunity's landing sites were chosen because they are thought to have been rich in water.
9. Scientists are pessimistic about the future of Beagle 2.
10. Mars Express is circling the Red Planet.

5 The nine planets in our solar system. Order them from the nearest to the farthest from the sun.

Venus, Mercury, Jupiter, Mars, Uranus, Saturn, Pluto, Earth, Neptune

4 Fill in the fourteen lines across the grid with translations of the corresponding French words. This will give you the answer to number 15 in column D.

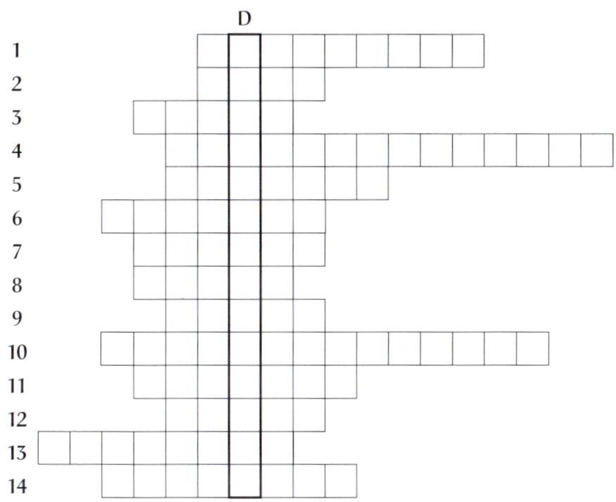

1. atterrissage 2. équipage 3. sonde 4. l'apesanteur 5. échec, revers 6. la pesanteur 7. lancer 8. s'écraser 9. diriger 10. interplanétaire 11. saborder 12. planer 13. la mise à feu 14. entraînement, préparation 15. mise en orbite

Rosetta blasts off at last

Europe's comet-chasing spacecraft, Rosetta, is finally on its way after lifting off into the tropical skies of Kourou, French Guiana, on Tuesday.

The successful launch of the billion-euro mission will come as a relief to both the European Space Agency (ESA) and to Arianspace, manufacturer of the Ariane-5 launch rocket.

ESA is hoping to trump NASA with the ambitious mission, which will go into orbit around comet 67P/Churyumov-Gerasimenko in 2014, then send a lander down onto its icy surface. Meanwhile Arianspace, which already cost the mission a year's delay after one of its rockets self-destructed, needs to prove its reliability in an increasingly competitive launch market.

So the past week at Kourou has been a tense one. Mission managers and technicians worked round the clock through heavy rainstorms as the launch was postponed two days in a row. On 26 February the countdown was stopped 20 minutes short of lift-off because high-altitude winds could have rained debris down on Kourou if the rocket had blown up in flight.

The next day, the launch was cancelled again after a chunk of insulating foam fell off the rocket's cryogenically cooled main stage, and it had to be rolled back into the assembly building for the foam to be reattached to the spacecraft.

Success came four days later. Rosetta will swing past the Earth three times and Mars once on its 10-year journey to comet Chury.

New Scientist, 6 March 2004

European plan for man on Mars

French, German or Italian astronauts could be walking on Mars within three decades – but Britain remains opposed to manned space flight.

The European Space Agency said yesterday it planned to put a man on the Moon by 2020 and on Mars by 2030, as it set out its "road map" for space exploration.

Britain is supporting the earliest stages, which involve robotic exploration of the Moon and Mars – but is unlikely to take in the more ambitious later stages unless there is a clear change of heart by Government.

In 2011 or 2014, the European space agency will attempt to bring back one pound of rock and soil from Mars to Earth for analysis.

The Daily Telegraph, 4 February 2004

POLITICS I

9

LA POLITIQUE I

Vocabulaire à haute fréquence

Political parties	Les partis politiques
to join sth.	adhérer à qch.
to quit	démissionner, claquer la porte
a member	un adhérent, un membre
membership	les adhérents, l'adhésion
a policy	une politique
a politician	un homme politique
radical	radical, maximaliste
extreme [ɪks'triːm]	extrême
an extremist	un extrémiste
a nationalist	un nationaliste
moderate	modéré
left-wing, leftist	de gauche
right-wing, rightist	de droite
Tory, Conservative	conservateur
Labour	travailliste
Republican	républicain
Democrat *(n.)*, Democratic *(adj.)*	démocrate
a green party	un parti vert/écologiste
a programme	un programme
a view, an opinion	une opinion
a coalition	une coalition

Before the election	Avant l'élection
an opinion poll	un sondage d'opinion
to publish	publier
to survey	interroger (échantillon)
a survey	une enquête, une étude
a figure	un chiffre
a rating	une cote, un score
a lead [li:d]	une avance
to trail	avoir du retard
a margin	une marge
popular	populaire
popularity	la popularité
dissatisfaction	le mécontentement
a referendum	un référendum
local	locale, municipale
general, legislative	législative
presidential	présidentielle
an election	une élection
a by-election	une élection partielle
to fight	disputer
to stand for, to run for	se présenter à, être candidat à
a candidate	un candidat
the front-runner	le mieux placé
a constituency	une circonscription
a deposit	une caution
a campaign	une campagne
a campaign official	un responsable de campagne
to promise	promettre
a promise	une promesse
to pledge	promettre, s'engager
a pledge	une promesse, un engagement
funding	le financement
to donate	faire un don
a donation	un don

Elections	Les élections
a ballot	un scrutin
a ballot paper	un bulletin de vote
polling day	le jour des élections
a polling station	un bureau de vote
a ballot box	une urne
to vote	voter
a vote	une voix, un suffrage
a voter	un électeur
the voters, the electorate	l'électorat
a round	un tour (de scrutin)
turnout, polling	la participation

to count	dépouiller
counting	le dépouillement
a seat	un siège
to elect	élire
to win, to carry	remporter, enlever
a win, a victory	une victoire
overwhelming	écrasant
close	serré
to retain	conserver
a defeat	une défaite
an overall majority	une majorité absolue
to swing	faire pencher, basculer
a swing	un basculement, un transfert
to shift	changer, se déplacer
a shift	un changement, un déplacement
results	les résultats
the outcome	le résultat, la conclusion

The United States — Les États-Unis

a primary	une primaire
a caucus	un comité de primaire
a convention	une convention
a delegate	un délégué
nomination	la désignation
Congress	le Congrès
a congressman	un membre du Congrès
the Senate	le Sénat
a senator	un sénateur
the House of Representatives	la Chambre des représentants
a representative	un représentant
to inaugurate	investir
inauguration	l'investiture

Expressions

to launch a party	créer un parti
to be in the lead	être en tête
they are 2 points ahead	ils ont 2 points d'avance
the run-up to an election	la période pré-électorale
to call an election	provoquer une élection
to hold an election	procéder à une élection
to go to the country	en appeler aux électeurs
to field a candidate	présenter un candidat
to run for office/election	se présenter aux élections
to jump on the bandwagon	prendre le train en marche
to hit the campaign trail,	se lancer dans la campagne

to launch a campaign	lancer une campagne
to go barnstorming *(US)*	électorale
to be a vote winner	attirer les suffrages
to take votes from	prendre des voix à
to go to the polls	aller aux urnes
to cast a vote	déposer un bulletin
to top the poll	remporter les élections
to win by default	gagner par défaut
first-past-the-post system	système majoritaire à un tour
a two-thirds majority	une majorité aux deux tiers
the five per cent threshold	le seuil des 5 pour cent
to gain/win/secure/take seats	gagner des sièges
to concede defeat	admettre la victoire
to hold the balance of power	détenir la minorité de blocage
to be sworn in	prêter serment

Vocabulaire complémentaire

Political parties	**Les partis politiques**
the leadership	la direction, les dirigeants
an apparatus	un appareil
the political spectrum	l'éventail politique
the rank and file, the grass roots	la base
an activist, a campaigner	un militant
influential	influent
seasoned, veteran	expérimenté
reactionary	réactionnaire
progressive	progressiste
reformist	réformiste
a hardliner, a diehard	un dur
a conference	un congrès
a quota system	un système de quota
an umbrella organisation	un collectif, une fédération
to chair	présider
a rival	un rival
rivalry	la rivalité
a split	une division, un désaccord
a rift	un fossé, une faille
in-fighting	les luttes internes
a tendency	une tendance
to fall apart	éclater, se séparer
to break away	se détacher
maverick	indépendant, dissident
a breakaway group	un groupe dissident
dissent	en dissidence
an independent bid	une candidature indépendante

a fringe party	un groupuscule
the far right	l'extrême droite

Before the election — Avant l'élection

a pollster, a poll taker	un sondeur
the don't knows	les indécis
the floating vote	l'électorat instable, mouvant
to conduct	organiser
a straw poll	une consultation improvisée
a standing	une position, un classement
a showing	une performance, une prestation
to lag	être à la traîne
neck and neck	au coude à coude
a constituent	un électeur (circonscription)
proportional representation	la représentation proportionnelle
an election manifesto	un manifeste électoral
a platform	une plate-forme
a feel-good factor	un sentiment de confiance, une impression d'optimisme
bread and butter issues	les questions matérielles
on the hustings, on the stumps *(US)*	en campagne
an electioneering promise	une promesse électorale
to canvass	faire du porte à porte
a whistle stop (tour)	une visite électorale éclair
a rostrum	une tribune
to heckle	harceler
a soundbite	une petite phrase, une formule
to smear [smɪə]	diffamer
to taunt	railler, ironiser
a smear campaign	une campagne de diffamation
character assassination	atteinte à la réputation
mudslinging	les coups bas
dirty tricks	les coups tordus
gerrymandering [dʒerɪ'mænderɪŋ]	les tripatouillages
to hit back	riposter
to stand against sb.	se présenter contre qn.
to contend, to contest	disputer
a contest	une compétition, une lutte
a contender, a contestant, a challenger	un concurrent
to pull out	se retirer
a safe seat	un siège sûr
a marginal seat	un siège menacé
a stronghold, a heartland	un bastion, un fief
to commit	engager
a commitment, an undertaking	un engagement
to vow to [vaʊ]	s'engager à

propaganda [prɒpə'gændə]	la propagande
a ward	une circonscription (élections locales)
an image	une image

Elections	**Les élections**
a snap election, an early election	une élection anticipée
a run-off election	un deuxième tour avec deux candidats
mid-term	mi-mandat
to register	s'inscrire
to poll	recueillir
the poll	les suffrages, les élections
a polling-booth	un isoloir
an exit poll	un sondage à la sortie
returns	les résultats partiels
a tally	un décompte
to recount	recompter
a recount	un nouveau décompte
to declare	proclamer (résultats)
a declaration	une proclamation
the runner-up	le vaincu, le second
an absolute majority	une majorité absolue
a commanding majority	une majorité confortable
a landslide victory, an outright/ sweeping victory	une victoire écrasante
a rout, a drubbing	une déroute, une raclée
to trounce, to thrash	écraser
a groundswell	une lame de fond
a share of the vote	un pourcentage de voix
a protest vote	un vote sanction
a hung Parliament	un Parlement sans majorité
a mandate	un mandat (contrat)
a term	un mandat (durée)
the wilderness, limbo	le désert (politique)
fraud	la fraude
to rig	truquer
ballot rigging	le trucage électoral

The United States	**Les États-Unis**
the presidency	la présidence
the incumbent president	le président en exercice
the outgoing president	le président sortant
the president elect	le président élu
a ticket	un ticket électoral, une liste électorale
an elector	un grand électeur

Kerry starts campaign with attack on Bush

from Roland Watson in Washington

John Kerry fired the opening shots of an eight-month presidential campaign today, branding President Bush "the great divider" and vowing to remake America into a beacon for the rest of the world. Moving swiftly to capitalise on his sweeping victory for the Democratic crown, Mr Kerry headed straight to Florida, scene of the climactic 2000 presidential showdown, as he pledged to "give America back its future and its hope". Mr Bush will respond tomorrow, unleashing the first of his campaign advertisements as he begins to spend his \$100 million (£56 million) war chest in earnest. The ads will air in 17 swing states for five days at a cost of \$4.5 million. Mr Bush's strategists, anxious not to let Mr Kerry settle, sent an e-mail to six million voters nationwide portraying the Massachusetts Senator as too liberal and out of touch for middle America.

Hours before Mr Kerry's overwhelming triumph in the Super Tuesday primaries, the Bush campaign fielded Dick Cheney, the Vice-President, to overshadow the Democratic victory parade. Mr Cheney used Mr Kerry's Senate voting record to accuse him of being soft on defence and inconsistent on the use of American force.

The exchanges mean that a sharply divided America faces one of the longest ever presidential campaigns, even by US standards. The accelerated primary process has produced a Democrat nominee earlier in the year than usual, and Mr Bush has a record war chest. Mr Bush and Mr Kerry shared a cordial phone conversation last night in which the President congratulated his rival.

The Kerry campaign barely paused for breath as it switched gears from the primaries to the presidential showdown. "Boy, wait till you see the fire in my belly," Mr Kerry said. He pitched straight into the heart of the campaign, aiming to make national security one of his signature themes. Democrats feared that an election fought against the backdrop of the War on Terror would favour Mr Bush.

Much of Mr Kerry's primary victory owed itself to his claim that as a decorated Vietnam veteran he could credibly battle Mr Bush on national security. "The Bush Administration has run the most inept, reckless, arrogant and ideological foreign policy in the modern history of our country. And we will reverse that course," he said.

Mr Kerry starts with a huge financial disadvantage. Mr Bush has raised nearly \$150 million, a third of which he has spent on setting up the most sophisticated grassroots network the Republicans have ever had. Mr Bush aims to raise another $50 million in the next few months. It must all be spent before the Republican convention in September, when both candidates receive $70 million of federal funds. [...]

Mr Kerry made clear in his victory speech that he will paint Mr Bush as a President who has led the US astray. He invoked Lincoln, saying he would once again ensure the country was, "the last, best hope of Earth". He said voters had lost faith in Mr Bush's presidency and were wondering, as they did in the 1970s, whether they could trust their leaders. "Our campaign is about restoring that faith."

The Times, 3 March 2004

1 Match the words (1-5), underlined in the article, with their corresponding definitions (A-I)

1. to brand	A. overwhelming
2. to vow	B. to eclipse
3. sweeping	C. to launch
4. a showdown	D. rank-and-file members
5. to unleash	E. to label
6. a war chest	F. to make a solemn promise
7. to overshadow	G. a fund to finance an investment
8. reckless	H. a confrontation
9. grassroots	I. rash, irresponsible

2 Say whether the following statements are true (T) or false (F).

1. Pro-Republican TV ads will be broadcast in states in which voters are still undecided about who they will vote for.
2. E-mails have been sent to voters across the US by Bush's tacticians.
3. The 2004 primary process has been faster than usual.
4. Kerry stopped to make a pause between the race for the Democratic nomination and the presidential election.
5. Mr Kerry wants to be seen as tough on national security.
6. Voting for Mr Kerry was somewhat tactical.
7. Mr Kerry's war record makes him a convincing opponent for Mr Bush on security issues.
8. Mr Bush has spent around $50 million on establishing an intricate network of Republican rank-and-file members.
9. Mr Kerry will receive $35 million of federal funds.

3 Complete the words in the following sentences. Each dash represents one letter.

1. John Kerry emerged today as the man who will c _ _ _ _ _ _ _ _ President Bush for the White House in November

2. Opinion p _ _ _ _ asking people how they would vote if the e _ _ _ _ _ _ _ _ was today show Mr Kerry with a healthy lead over George W. Bush. But will it last?
3. The nomination process, which began in January, sees each state return a certain number of d _ _ _ _ _ _ _ _ to the Democratic Party convention, held in the summer.
4. By winning 9 of the 10 states in the Super Tuesday primaries, Senator Kerry secured the Democratic n _ _ _ _ _ _ _ _ _.
5. Mr Edwards is a strong contender to stand as v _ _ _ _ _ _ _ _ _ _ _ _ on a Kerry-Edwards ticket to challenge President George W. Bush and Dick Cheney in November.

4 **Fill in the twelve lines across the grid with translations of the corresponding French words. This will give you the answer to number 13 in Column D.**

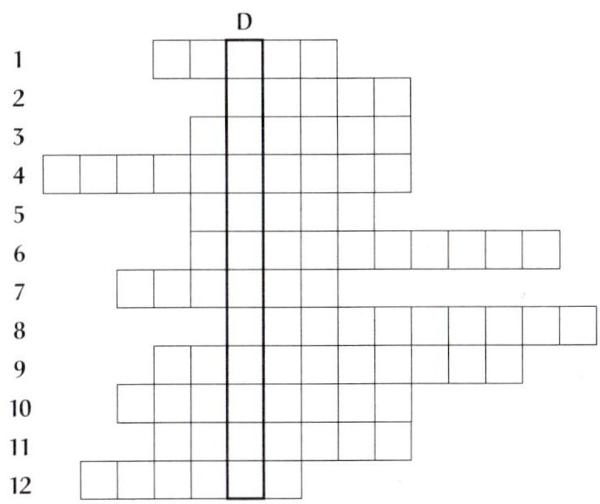

1. serré 2. électeur 3. adjoint 4. la base 5. basculer, faire pencher 6. concurrent 7. défaite 8. direction, dirigeants 9. désignation 10. militant 11. financement 12. promesse 13. écrasant

Russia votes to return Putin with landslide

by Andrew Jack and Arkady Ostrovsky in Moscow and Guy Dinmore in Washington

Vladimir Putin on Sunday won his predicted landslide re-election as Russian president, putting him under the spotlight to deliver on promises to boost economic growth, reduce poverty and reform the military over the next four years. With 99 per cent of the vote counted on Monday morning Mr Putin scored 71.2 per cent of the vote, with his nearest rival, the hardline Communist Nikolai Kharitonov, winning a higher-than-expected 13.7 per cent.

The result contrasted with a lacklustre campaign, with Mr Putin refusing to take part in debates with his five rivals, who complained about bias in media reporting and periodic harassment by local officials while on the hustings.

Mr Kharitonov's score followed a surge in coverage of his campaign on state television in the final days, and strong negative coverage for Sergei Glaziev, the leftwing populist. His Motherland party scored unexpectedly well in the parliamentary election and he represented a potential political challenge to Mr Putin.

The election was assessed to have fallen short of a "genuine democratic contest" by the Organisation for Security and Co-operation in Europe, who on Monday released their preliminary statement. But, the organisation praised the administration of the polls, calling them "well managed."

In the wake of publicity to encourage people to vote and steps to reach even the most isolated among the country's 109m electorate, turnout at more than 62 per cent was well above the 50 per cent minimum needed for the election to be valid. However, that was well short of the 68 per cent in Russia's previous presidential poll in 2000, suggesting disinterest among voters.

Reflecting the chillier tone in US-Russia relations, Colin Powell, US secretary of state, said on Sunday on Fox News that the Bush administration was "concerned" over the conduct of the elections. Given that Mr Putin was going to win so easily, he questioned other candidates' lack of access to the media.

Mr Putin has called for Mikhail Fradkov, the prime minister, to push ahead with streamlining government and introducing further tax and other economic reforms.

The Financial Times, 14 March 2004

10

POLITICS II

LA POLITIQUE II

Vocabulaire à haute fréquence

Power	Le pouvoir
to set up, to establish	établir, installer
a regime	un régime
a dictator	un dictateur
a dictatorship	une dictature
to liberalise	libéraliser
liberalisation	la libéralisation
a say	une voix au chapitre
a status	un statut
a constitution	une constitution
constitutional	constitutionnel
democracy [dɪ'mɒkrəsɪ]	la démocratie
democratic [demə'krætɪk]	démocratique
a republic	une république
office	les fonctions
powerful	puissant
to rule	diriger, gouverner
the ruling party	le parti au pouvoir
rule	l'autorité, l'administration
majority rule	le gouvernement de la majorité
self-rule	l'autonomie
a state	un État
a statesman	un homme d'État
to corrupt	corrompre
corrupt	corrompu
corruption	la corruption

to bribe	soudoyer
a bribe	un pot de vin
bribery	la corruption
sleaze	les pratiques douteuses, la corruption
immunity (from prosecution)	l'immunité parlementaire

Parliament — Le parlement

a Member of Parliament (MP)	un député
the House of Commons	la Chambre des députés
the House of Lords	la Chambre des lords
a select committee	une commission (parlementaire)
to sit	siéger
a sitting	une séance
to put forward	proposer, soumettre
to table	déposer
a motion	une motion
a bill	un projet de loi
a private member's bill	une proposition de loi
to amend	amender
an amendment	un amendement
to reject	rejeter
a rejection	un rejet
to rule out	exclure la possibilité de
to abolish	abolir
abolition	l'abolition
to carry	faire passer
to defeat	repousser, mettre en minorité
to adopt	adopter
an adoption	une adoption
a law	une loi

Debate — Les débats

to debate	débattre
an issue	une question, un problème
to propose	proposer
a proposal	une proposition
to discuss	discuter
a discussion	une discussion
to approve of sth.	approuver qch.
approval	l'approbation
to praise sth.	faire l'éloge de qch.
to criticise	critiquer
criticism	la critique
to argue	argumenter, faire valoir
to state	déclarer
a statement	une déclaration

to advocate	prôner
an advocate	un défenseur, un partisan
to support, to back	soutenir
support, backing	le soutien
to favour	être partisan de
confidence	la confiance
to agree to sth.	consentir à qch.
to agree with sb.	être d'accord avec qn.
an agreement	un accord
to disagree with sb.	être en désaccord avec qn.
a disagreement	un désaccord
a difference	une divergence
to explain	expliquer
an explanation	une explication
to contradict	contredire
a contradiction	une contradiction
to deny	nier
a denial	un démenti
to claim	affirmer
a claim	une affirmation
to maintain	continuer d'affirmer
to complain	se plaindre
a complaint	une plainte, une réclamation
to advise	conseiller
advice	les conseils
to press sb. to	pousser qn. à
pressure	la pression
to urge	exhorter
to blame sb. for sth.	reprocher qch. à qn.
to blame sth. on sb.	rendre qn. responsable de qch.
blame	la responsabilité
to protest [prə'test]	protester
a protest ['prəutest]	une protestation
a controversy	une polémique
controversial	controversé, polémique
to contest	contester
to oppose sth.	s'opposer à qch.
an opponent	un opposant
opposition	l'opposition
to challenge	défier
a challenge	un défi
to denounce	dénoncer
denunciation	la dénonciation
to accuse	accuser
an accusation	une accusation
to condemn	condamner
a condemnation	une condamnation

to outrage	provoquer l'indignation de
an outrage	un scandale
a row [raʊ]	une querelle, une dispute
a crisis ['kraɪsɪs]	une crise
a division	un vote au Parlement
to abstain	s'abstenir
abstention	l'abstention

Government — Le gouvernement

to govern	gouverner
to appoint	nommer
an appointment	une nomination
a (senior) minister	un ministre
a minister of state	un sous-secrétaire d'État
a junior minister	un secrétaire d'État, un ministre délégué
the Prime Minister, the premier	le Premier ministre
a cabinet	un cabinet
to deal with sth.	s'occuper de qch.
to tackle sth.	s'attaquer à qch.
to handle sth.	traiter, gérer qch.
to implement	mettre en œuvre
an implementation	une mise en œuvre
a move	une démarche, une initiative
a step	une disposition, une mesure
a road map	une feuille de route
a stand, a stance	une position
an objective	un objectif
an aim	un but
to back down	faire marche arrière
to climb down	faire des concessions
a climb-down	une reculade
to yield, to give in	céder
to reform	réformer
a reform	une réforme
to reshuffle	remanier
a reshuffle	un remaniement
a setback	un revers, une déconvenue
to bring down	faire chuter
to overthrow, to topple	renverser
an overthrow	un renversement
the downfall	la chute
to resign [rɪ'zaɪn]	démissionner
the resignation	la démission
to hand in	remettre
the former Prime Minister	l'ancien Premier ministre

Expressions

to take office	entrer en fonction
to remove from office	démettre de ses fonctions
the ousted president	le président déchu
to go to the vote	être soumis au vote
to put to the vote	soumettre au vote
a vote of no confidence	un vote de censure
to put through a legislation	faire voter une loi
to come to power	accéder au pouvoir
to hold on to power	se maintenir au pouvoir
to bring into force	mettre en application
to come under pressure	subir des pressions
to bow to pressure	céder aux pressions
to address an issue	aborder un problème
to make political capital out of	faire de la récupération politique
to take issue with sb.	engager une controverse avec qn.
to be critical of	trouver à redire à
to take sb. to task	prendre qn. à partie
to level a charge at sb.	lancer une accusation contre qn.
to be at loggerheads	être en conflit
to come under fire	être vivement critiqué
to resign the whip	démissionner d'un groupe parlementaire
to carry a lot of clout	avoir beaucoup d'influence

Vocabulaire complémentaire

Power	Le pouvoir
emergency powers	les pouvoirs d'urgence
dictatorial	dictatorial
a military regime	un régime militaire
tyranny	la tyrannie
a tyrant	un tyran
a despot	un despote
despotism	le despotisme
totalitarian	totalitaire
to purge	purger
a purge	une épuration, une purge
a monarchy	une monarchie
a monarch ['mɒnək]	un monarque
autocracy	l'autocratie
misuse	abus
influence peddling	le trafic d'influence
a kickback, a backhander	un pot de vin, un backchich
cronyism	le copinage

Parliament	Le parlement
a parliamentarian	un parlementaire

parliamentary	parlementaire
a session	une session
the Speaker	le Président de la Chambre
a rotating presidency	une présidence tournante
a whip	un chef de file
disciplinary action	mesure disciplinaire
a front-bencher	un député porte-parole
a back-bencher	un député de la base
question time	la séance des questions
to sponsor	présenter (une proposition)
the sponsor	l'auteur (d'une proposition)
to endorse	appuyer, approuver, donner son aval
an endorsement	un soutien, une approbation
to legislate	légiférer
legislation	la législation
a framework	un cadre (de discussion)
a draft	une ébauche, un avant-projet
a loophole	une faille, une lacune
to outlaw	mettre hors la loi
a leak	une fuite
an Act	une loi
to lobby	chercher à influencer
a lobby	un groupe d'intérêts
a surgery	une permanence (de député)
a deputy	un député (à l'étranger)
deputy	vice, adjoint
a life peer	un pair à vie

Debate / Les débats

to stress sth., to insist upon sth.	insister sur qch.
to emphasise	bien préciser
to underline	souligner
to highlight	mettre en valeur
to prop up	étayer, soutenir
to vindicate	justifier, donner raison à
vindication	confirmation du bien-fondé
to placate	apaiser
to tone down	modérer, mettre en sourdine
to dismiss	écarter, rejeter
unanimous	unanime
unanimity	l'unanimité
consensus	le consensus
to alter	modifier
an alteration	une modification
to repeal	abroger
a repeal	une abrogation
to antagonise sb.	provoquer l'hostilité de

to incense	mettre en fureur
an outcry	un tollé
an uproar	un tapage
turmoil	les remous, la tourmente
to barrack	chahuter
to castigate	critiquer, fustiger
to deride	railler, se moquer (de)
to lambast	éreinter, fustiger
a scathing attack	une attaque cinglante
a stooge	un fantoche
a puppet	un pantin
a pawn	un pion
to filibuster	faire de l'obstruction
a guillotine	une limitation des débats
to rescind	révoquer, résilier
a turning-point, a watershed	un tournant, un virage
a milestone, a landmark	un moment décisif, un jalon
to turn around/about	faire volte-face
a turn-around, an about-turn, a U-turn	une volte-face
to stifle	étouffer
to cover up	camoufler, étouffer
a cover-up	un étouffement (scandale)
the Dispatch Box	la tribune du gouvernement
a White Paper	un avant-projet de loi
to censure	censurer
censure	la censure parlementaire
a no-confidence motion	une motion de censure
a split vote	un vote sans majorité
a casting vote	une voix prépondérante
to assemble	se réunir
to adjourn	suspendre, reporter
an adjournment	une suspension, un report
to convene [kən'viːn]	convoquer (parlement)
recess ['riːses, rɪ'ses]	les vacances parlementaires
to re-assemble	rentrer (parlementaires)
to dissolve [dɪ'zɒlv], to disband	dissoudre
dissolution	la dissolution

The United States — Les États-Unis

an aide	un collaborateur
bipartisan	bipartite
to veto sth. ['viːtəʊ]	opposer son veto à qch.
a veto	un veto
to override sth.	passer outre à qch.
to overrule sth.	annuler, casser qch.
to impeach	mettre en accusation
an impeachment	une procédure de destitution

the State Department	le ministère des Affaires étrangères
the Secretary of State	le ministre des Affaires étrangères
the Attorney General	le ministre de la Justice
the Supreme Court	la Cour suprême

Government / Le gouvernement

the Queen's speech	le discours du Trône
provisional	provisoire
interim	intérimaire
caretaker	chargé des affaires courantes
to cohabit	cohabiter
cohabitation	la cohabitation
a portfolio	un portefeuille
to shake up	réaménager, remodeler
a shake-up	un réaménagement
a decree	un décret, une ordonnance
a by(e)law	un arrêté municipal
a package of measures	un ensemble de mesures
to review	réexaminer
a review	un réexamen
a body	un organisme
a watchdog	un comité de surveillance, un " gendarme "
an ombudsman	un médiateur
a quango	un organisme paragouvernemental
a record	un bilan
to achieve	accomplir
an achievement	une réalisation
accountability	l'obligation de rendre compte
to mishandle sth.	se montrer maladroit
a spin doctor	un conseiller en communication
to scrap	mettre au rebut
to phase in	introduire progressivement
to phase out	abandonner progressivement
to undermine	saper, affaiblir
to step down	se désister
to stand down	se démettre
devolution	l'autonomie régionale
a Cabinet meeting	un conseil de cabinet
the Shadow Cabinet	le contre-gouvernement
the Lord Chancellor	le ministre de la Justice
the Home Secretary	le ministre de l'Intérieur
the Education Secretary	le ministre de l'Éducation
the Foreign Secretary	le ministre des Affaires étrangères
the Foreign Office	le ministère des Affaires étrangères
the Treasury	le ministère du Budget
the Statute Book	le Registre des lois

Chirac swaps top ministers after debacle

Jon Henley in Paris

France's hugely popular interior minister, Nicolas Sarkozy, was handed the job yesterday of pushing through an immensely unpopular programme of reforms as Jacques Chirac made sweeping changes to his cabinet after the centre-right's humiliating defeat in regional elections.

Mr Sarkozy was appointed finance minister in a reshuffle that also saw President Chirac's close ally, the smooth and aristocratic foreign minister, Dominique de Villepin, take over at the interior ministry, and a European commissioner, Michel Barnier, step into Mr de Villepin's shoes at the Quai d'Orsay.

Mr Chirac has come under mounting pressure to show that he had heard the electorate's message of widespread discontent with government spending cuts in Sunday's second-round vote, which saw the Socialist opposition win a landslide victory with 21 of mainland France's 22 regional councils and a 50% share of the national vote, compared with 37% for the ruling conservatives.

The president's decision on Tuesday to give his embattled prime minister, Jean-Pierre Raffarin, a 10-week stay of execution until at least the European elections in June was met with incredulity in the Socialist camp yesterday.

The affable Mr Raffarin is seen as unpopular, burned out and so severely weakened by the regional election pounding that he will be unable to push through the government's cost-cutting reforms without provoking potentially crippling strikes and demonstrations.

"On the one hand we have a society which has shown its anger in dramatic fashion. On the other, we have political leaders who are displaying a certain deafness," said Jerome Sainte-Marie of the polling organisation BVA. "It is quite an explosive cocktail."

Mr Sarkozy, on the other hand, who constantly tops opinion polls as France's most popular politician, may have the charisma, stature and gift of the gab for the job. The appointment has the added benefit for Mr Chirac that if he fails to convince France's fickle voters of the need for reform, Mr Sarkozy will see his bid to become president in 2007 badly undermined. He faces a huge task overcoming anger over high unemployment, pension reform and budget cuts.

The new job will in effect make or break Mr Sarkozy's ambitions. The minister has cracked down on street crime, illegal immigrants and prostitution, but is by no means certain to make such a success of his new role.

The same could, however, be said of Mr Villepin, the part-time poet and arch Chirac loyalist who won over the French public by eloquently voicing France's opposition to the US-led war on Iraq. "To be honest, I just can't see De Villepin visiting some rundown housing estate to talk about rising levels of street crime with youth gang leaders," said one government official who asked not to be named. But other observers discerned a longer-term strategy in Mr Chirac's choice. "This is an interim appointment," said one commentator, Marie Eve Malouine. "It's setting up De Villepin to take over from Raffarin as prime minister, probably after the June elections, and establishing his credentials as Chirac's preferred successor. This is all about keeping out Sarkozy."

The Guardian, 1 April 2004

1 Choose the right explanation for each of the following words underlined in the article.

1. to swap
A. to sack
B. to change
C. to congratulate

2. crippling
A. rewarding
B. stimulating
C. damaging

3. the gift of the gab
A. the ability to speak easily, confidently and persuasively
B. the ability to offer gifts out of generosity
C. the ability to make jokes

4. fickle
A. constant
B. changeable
C. faithful

2 Say whether the following statements are true (T) or false (F).

1. Michel Barnier is the new foreign minister.
2. People showed their discontent by voting massively for the opposition party.
3. According to Mr Sainte-Marie, French political leaders have well understood the voters' message.
4. Mr de Villepin is in the same situation as Mr Sarkozy: his political future depends on his success or failure as interior minister.
5. According to Ms Malouine, Mr Chirac's strategic reshuffle aims at eliminating Mr Sarkozy from the 2007 presidential race.

3 Choose the appropriate endings for the following sentences.

1. President Chirac made
A. just a few changes to his cabinet.
B. no changes to his cabinet.
C. extensive changes to his cabinet.

2. The president's decision to maintain Mr Raffarin in his role
A. left the Socialist camp indifferent.
B. was backed by the Socialist camp.
C. amazed the Socialist camp.

3. If Mr Sarkozy is successful in his new role

A. he will see his bid to become president in 2007 badly undermined.

B. he will be seen as Chirac's natural successor.

C. he will fail to convince French voters of the need for reform.

4 The first word in each of the following lists is taken from the article. Which of the other three words should not be associated with it?

1. discontent, anger, passion, disenchantment
2. landslide, qualified, sweeping, overwhelming
3. bid, attempt, try, loss
4. to crack down on, to clamp down on, to control, to promote

5 The suffix "-en", added to a noun or an adjective, is used to form verbs: "Mr Raffarin [...] so severely <u>weakened</u>". Use the definitions to find the 10 verbs ending in "–en".

1. to make or become longer	l _ _ _ _ _ en
2. to make or become wide or wider	w _ _ en/b _ _ _ _ en
3. to make or become deep or deeper	d _ _ _ en
4. to make shorter	s _ _ _ _en
5. to make or grow strong or stronger	s _ _ _ _ _ _ _ en
6. to make or become tight, more constricted	t _ _ _ _ en
7. to make less tight, to unfasten	l _ _ _ en
8. to rise, to elevate, to intensify	h _ _ _ _ _ en
9. to suppress, to mute	d _ _ _ en

Immigration minister resigns

Beverley Hughes, the immigration minister, has resigned because she misled Parliament over the row about her handling of eastern European migrants, Downing Street has said.

Miss Hughes has been embroiled in a embarrassing row after leaks showed that the Home Office failed to act on warnings 18 months ago of an eastern European immigration racket and routinely allowed bogus visa applicants to enter Britain.

David Blunkett, the Home Secretary, suspended all immigration applications from Romania and Bulgaria on Tuesday and promised an inquiry into the allegations.

But the issue erupted into a full-blown political storm at Prime Minister's Questions in the Commons yesterday, when Conservative leader Michael Howard accused the Government of cutting asylum figures by ordering officials to wave through other applications based on forged papers.

Miss Hughes said that her conscience was clear over the affair. "I am neither incompetent nor dishonest and I intend to carry on doing my job as long as the Prime Minister and the Home Secretary want me to," she said.

But the Prime Minister's official spokesman said today that Miss Hughes had decided to quit after it became clear she had given a "misleading impression – albeit unwittingly" to Parliament.

The civil servant whose revelations first sparked the row is today appearing before a Home Office disciplinary hearing. Steve Moxon will be asked about his disclosure to a newspaper that key checks were being waived for visa applicants from countries due to join the EU on May 1. Mr Moxon was suspended from his post at the Sheffield office of the Immigration and Nationality Directorate after he exposed details of the scheme, codenamed Operation Brace, to a newspaper.

The Daily Telegraph, 1 April 2004

1 **Choose the right explanation for each of the following words underlined in the article.**

1. to mislead
A. to mistake
B. to misinform
C. to testify

2. embroiled
A. involved
B. hired
C. expelled

3. bogus
A. authentic
B. genuine
C. fake

4. forged
A. false
B. sincere
C. real

5. unwittingly
A. involuntarily
B. carefully
C. knowingly

6. to spark off
A. to deactivate
B. to trigger
C. to worsen

11

RELIGION

LA RELIGION

Vocabulaire à haute fréquence

Religions	Les religions
religious [rɪ'lɪdʒəs]	religieux
a Jew	un juif
Jewish	juif
a Christian	un chrétien
a Roman Catholic	un catholique
a Protestant	un protestant
Islam ['ɪzlɑːm]	l'islam
a Moslem, a Muslim	un musulman
a god	un dieu
a goddess	une déesse
faith	la foi
faithful	fidèle
to obey sb.	obéir à qn.
obedience	l'obéissance
to venerate, to worship	adorer, vénérer
a worshipper	un fidèle
to follow	suivre
a follower	un adepte
to believe	croire
a belief	une croyance
a creed	un credo, les principes
a dogma	un dogme
a verse	un verset
a doctrine	une doctrine
to endoctrinate	endoctriner

endoctrination	l'endoctrinement
a denomination	une confession religieuse
denominational	confessionnel
a non-believer	un incroyant
an atheist	un athée
an agnostic	un agnostique
a pagan, a heathen ['hi:ðən]	un païen
an idol ['aɪdl]	une idole
a deity	une divinité
supernatural	surnaturel
to save	sauver
salvation	le salut
tolerance	la tolérance
tolerant	tolérant
intolerance	l'intolérance
intolerant	intolérant
conspicuous/overt religious symbols	les signes religieux ostensibles
an Islamic headscarf (*pl.* -ves)	un voile islamique
a Jewish skullcap	une kippa
a cross	une croix
to persecute	persécuter
persecution	la persécution
a fundamentalist, an extremist	un intégriste
fundamentalism, extremism	l'intégrisme

Worship / La pratique religieuse

a cathedral [kə'θi:drəl]	une cathédrale
a churchgoer	un pratiquant
an abbey	une abbaye
a mosque [mɒsk]	une mosquée
a temple	un temple
a chapel	une chapelle, un temple
a sanctuary	un sanctuaire
to pray	prier
a prayer	une prière
to celebrate	célébrer
a celebration	une célébration
mass	la messe
a service	un office
to bless	bénir
a blessing	une bénédiction
the congregation	l'assemblée des fidèles
church attendance	l'assistance aux offices, la fréquentation
the choir [kwaɪə]	le chœur
a hymn	un cantique
a hymnbook	un recueil de cantiques
to preach	prêcher

a preacher	un prédicateur, un pasteur (*US*)
an evangelical	un évangélique, un protestant
a sermon	un sermon
a homily	une homélie
the pulpit	la chaire
a saint	un saint
sainthood	la sainteté
holy	saint
evil ['iːvəl]	le mal
to sin	pécher
a sin	un péché
blasphemy	le blasphème
a soul	une âme
to convert	convertir
a conversion	une conversion
a convert	un converti
a disciple	un disciple
secular	laïque
secularity	la laïcité

Christianity — Le christianisme

Christ [kraɪst]	le Christ
the Lord	le Seigneur
the Holy Spirit	le Saint-Esprit
the Blessed Virgin	la Sainte Vierge
the Bible	la Bible
the Gospel	l'Évangile
Good Friday	le Vendredi saint
Easter	Pâques
Whitsun	la Pentecôte
Anglican	anglican
an angel	un ange
to damn	damner
a devil	un diable
Satan ['seɪtən]	Satan
heaven	le ciel
hell	l'enfer
to cross oneself	se signer

The servants — Les serviteurs

an ayatollah [aɪə'tɒlə]	un ayatollah
a rabbi ['ræbaɪ]	un rabbin
clergy	le clergé
a clergyman, a cleric	un ecclésiastique
a priest	un prêtre
a vicar	un curé

a parish	une paroisse
a parishioner	un paroissien
a parson, a minister, a pastor	un pasteur
the ministry	le ministère religieux, le sacerdoce
a deacon	un diacre
a bishop	un évêque
an archbishop	un archevêque
a cardinal	un cardinal
the Pope	le pape
the papacy	la papauté
to ordain	ordonner
an ordination	une ordination

Cults	**Les sectes**
to join sth.	adhérer à qch.
a cult	une secte, un culte
a sect	une secte
a member	un membre, un adhérent
membership	les adhérents
a Freemason	un franc-maçon
Freemasonry	la franc-maçonnerie
a Jehovah's Witness	un Témoin de Jéhovah
to recruit [rɪ'kru:t]	recruter
a recruit	une recrue
recruitment	le recrutement

Expressions

a born-again Christian	un chrétien régénéré
a place of worship	un lieu de culte
the Established Church	l'Église officielle
to take vows	prononcer des vœux
the Garden of Eden	le paradis terrestre

Vocabulaire complémentaire

Religions and cults	**Les religions et les sectes**
a state religion	une religion d'état
the Koran	le Coran
Muhammad, Mohammed	Mahomet
a Shiite, a Shiah, a Shia	un chiite
a Sunni	un sunnite
Mecca	la Mecque
Buddha	Bouddha
Buddhism	le bouddhisme

a Buddhist	un bouddhiste
Hinduism	l'hindouisme
a Hindu	un hindouiste
to revere	révérer
a guru ['guru:], a cult leader	un gourou
a prophet	un prophète
a prophecy	une prophétie
prophetic	prophétique
a martyr	un martyr
martyrdom	le martyre
a saviour	un sauveur
a miracle	un mirade
miraculous	miraculeux
a godsend	un don du ciel
the divine	le divin
devout [dɪ'vaʊt]	dévot
a persuasion	une confession, religion
a devotee	un fervent, un adepte
to lapse	ne plus pratiquer
to curse	maudir
a curse	une malédiction
mass suicide	le suicide collectif
to immolate oneself	s'immoler

Worship — La pratique religieuse

to practise	pratiquer
practice, chruchgoing	la pratique
spiritual life	la vie spirituelle
a synagogue ['sɪnəgɒg]	une synagogue
circumcision	la circoncision
a shrine	un lieu saint
a rite	un rite
a sacrament	un sacrement
sacramental	sacramentel
a pilgrim	un pèlerin
a pilgrimage	un pèlerinage
an altar	un autel
an address	une allocution
to fast	jeûner
Ramadan ['ræmədæn]	le ramadan
to swear	jurer
a swear-word, an oath	un juron
to tempt	tenter
temptation	la tentation
sacrilege	un sacrilège
a zealot ['zelət]	un fervent, un ultra
to consecrate	consacrer

a consecration, a dedication	une consécration
a beatification	une béatification
to desecrate	profaner
desecration	la profanation
a crusade	une croisade
sectarian	sectaire, confessionnel
bigotery, sectarianism	fanatisme, sectarisme

Christianity — Le christianisme

the Messiah [mɪ'saɪə]	le Messie
the Almighty	le Tout-Puissant
the Scriptures	les Écritures
a lesson	une lecture des Écritures
a Testament	un Testament
the Apostles	les apôtres
Christendom	la chrétienté
celibacy	le célibat
a diocese ['daɪəsɪs]	un diocèse
the Holy See	le Saint-Siège
ecumenical	œcuménique
a flock	un troupeau
the fold	le bercail
Lent	le Carême
to baptise, to christen	baptiser
a christening	un baptême
Communion	la communion
the Eucharist	l'Eucharistie
to redeem	racheter
redemption	le rachat, la rédemption
atonement	l'expiation
absolution	l'absolution
penance	la pénitence
doomsday	le jour du jugement dernier
the last rites	les derniers sacrements
your neighbour	votre prochain

The servants — Les serviteurs

a lay member	un membre laïque
a layman	un laïc
secular	séculier
the Pontiff	le souverain pontife
a primate	un primat
a curate	un vicaire
a dog collar	un col ecclésiastique
the vicarage, the rectory	le presbytère
a churchwarden	un conseiller paroissial

a missionary	un missionnaire
a chaplain	un aumônier
a monk	un moine
a monastery	un monastère
a nun	une religieuse
a religious order	un ordre religieux
theology	la théologie
a theologian	un théologien
a theocracy	une théocratie

Children to study atheism at school

Gaby Hinsliff, chief political correspondent

Children will be taught about atheism during religious education classes under official plans being drawn up to reflect the decline in churchgoing in Britain. Non-religious beliefs such as humanism, agnosticism and atheism would be covered alongside major faiths such as Christianity or Islam under draft guidelines being prepared by the Qualifications and Curriculum Authority, which regulates what is taught in schools in England.

Although some schools already cover non-religious beliefs, there is currently no national guidance for what is taught, even though all schools must provide religious education.

The draft plans being drawn up by the QCA will not be compulsory, allowing religious schools the freedom to keep devout parents happy. But they will be regarded as best practice for heads, and are likely to be followed across the country.

A spokesman for the QCA said its guidance would be released for consultation in the summer term, but added: "It is very much the intention that young people in the context of religious education should be studying non-religious beliefs. There are many children in England who have no religious affiliation and their beliefs and ideas, whatever they are, should be taken very seriously."

The plans risk sparking a conflict between evangelists, who want to strengthen faith teaching, and secularists, who argue it is becoming irrelevant to modern life.

The first shot in the debate will be fired with a controversial report to be published tomorrow calling for RE to be renamed religious, philosophical and moral education and children encouraged to debate such ethical issues as whether it is permissible to express racist views.

"The whole thing is terribly biased in favour of religion right now - it's all about encouraging an identification with religion," said Ben Rogers, author of the report for the Institute for Public Policy Research thinktank. "There are huge numbers of people who are atheists or whose families are atheists and who are coming into a class where their family's view is not acknowledged. You should be able to have a conversation about ethics that doesn't collapse into a conversation about religion."

While 19 per cent of Britons attended a weekly religious service in 1980, by 1999 that had fallen to 7 per cent – prompting some to argue that RE should be scrapped as a compulsory subject. Secularists say there is little point trying to drum religion into sceptical children at school. [...]

The Observer, 15 February 2004

1 **Choose the right explanation for each of the following words underlined in the article.**

1. draft plans
A. definite plans
B. provisional plans
C. irrelevant plans

2. biased
A. prejudiced
B. objective
C. wrong

3. thinktank
A. a committee that does research and analyses complex problems with a view to practical applications
B. a committee that designs and builds tanks
C. a committee that believes in strength as a source for action

2 **Choose the appropriate endings for the following sentences.**

1. Non-religious beliefs could be introduced as part of religious education
A. to acknowledge the diversity of views among young people.
B. to replace major faiths.
C. to boost churchgoing in Britain.

2. The plans risk sparking off a conflict because
A. religious education could disappear.
B. faith teaching could be strengthened.
C. secularists have a different approach to RE.

3. Some argue that RE should be scrapped as a compulsory subject because
A. only 19 per cent of Britons attend a weekly religious service.
B. there has been a decline in churchgoing.
C. religion is a difficult subject to teach to children.

3 **Say whether the following statements are true (T) or false (F).**
1. RE is compulsory in all schools across England.
2. Schools will have the choice to implement the draft plans prepared by the QCA or not.
3. With the changes brought to religious education, non-believers will have their beliefs and ideas taken into account.
4. Ben Rogers believes that religious education should encourage an identification with religion.

4 **Find words in the article which mean the same as the following.**
1. practice
2. pious
3. a denomination
4. churchgoers
5. religious belief
6. non-believers

5 **A few religions and non-religious beliefs are mentioned in the article. Match the following beliefs (1-6) with their corresponding definitions (A-F).**
1. atheism
2. agnosticism
3. humanism
4. Christianity
5. Islam
6. Judaism

A. the belief that people can achieve happiness and fulfilment without the need for religion
B. a religion that is based on the teachings of Jesus Christ and the belief that he was the son of God
C. a religion based on the Old Testament of the Bible and the Talmud
D. the belief that there is no god
E. a religion that teaches that there is only one God and that Mohammed is His prophet
F. the belief that it is not possible to say definitely whether or not there is a god

Church may end up as sect, warns bishop

Matthew Taylor

A leading Anglican bishop has warned that the Church of England could become a minority sect within "a generation".

The Bishop of Manchester, the Right Rev Nigel McCulloch, said that the established Church is in danger of completely disappearing.

Bishop McCulloch said the clergy were being diverted from their true mission of evangelism by the debate over sexuality, 25 years of Church legislation and more red tape caused by secular regulations.

Figures published in The UK Christian Handbook: *Religious Trends* show that, at the current rate of decline, total Church membership will have fallen to 5,598,000 by 2005, down by more than a million people in 15 years. Over the same period, the number of church buildings will have fallen by 1,400 to 48,600 and the number of ministers by 1,000 to 35,400. Even if there is no further decline, by the turn of the next century, there will still be thousands of churches and ministers, but they will have no Christians to minister to.

The waning interest in organised Christianity contrasts with the findings of the 2001 census, which included a voluntary question about religion for the first time. In response, 72% of the population said they were Christians. The Handbook acknowledges a "yawning gap" between what people say and church attendance.

Writing the foreword to the *Handbook*, published by Christian Research, Bishop McCulloch said: "The overall picture presented by this book serves to highlight the dilemma which Christian churches in the United Kingdom currently face. It has long been said that there is a yearning for spirituality across our countries, but until now the evidence has been largely anecdotal."

Bishop McCulloch is not the first senior cleric to voice such concerns. In September 2001, the Archbishop of Westminster, Cardinal Cormac Murphy-O'Connor, caused dismay in ecclesiastical circles when he said Christianity in Britain had been all but vanquished. He blamed the rising secular interests of British society for the inevitable decline of the religious doctrine.

The Guardian, 20 March 2004

1 **Choose the appropriate endings for the following sentences.**

1. The Church of England is in danger of completely disappearing because

A. the clergy has implemented more red tape.
B. it is already a minority sect.
C. it has forgotten its evangelistic mission.

2. In 1990 Church membership was as high as

A. 5,598,000.
B. less than 6,598,000.
C. more than 6,598,000.

3. In 2005 there will be

A. 48,600 church buildings.
B. 50,000 church buildings.
C. 47,200 church buildings.

4. There is a "yawning gap" between what people say and church attendance because

A. a lot of people go to church but few say they are Christians.
B. a lot of people say they are Christians but few go to church.
C. a lot of people say they are Christians but even more go to church.

5. In the foreword of the Handbook, Bishop McCulloch says that

A. spirituality in England is anecdotal.
B. a longing for spirituality has not yet materialised.
C. the evidence of spirituality is obvious.

6. When they heard Cardinal Cormac Murphy-O'Connor's comments, ecclesiastical circles were

A. pleased.
B. surprised.
C. shocked.

2 **Read the article again and find the following.**

1. a noun synonymous with "a cult"
2. a noun which means "the teaching of Christianity"
3. a phrase synonymous with "bureaucracy"
4. four nouns which refer to clergymen

3 **Three sentences have been cut up into parts and the parts scrambled. Put them back into the right order. (Punctuation and the capital letter at the beginning of the sentences have been removed.)**

1. to tackle religious / a leading academic / extremism and hatred / education is the only way / has warned that
2. 10 people in Scotland / on a Sunday according / go to church / to the latest figures / only one in
3. is going to be / to have somewhere / built for the town's / a mosque / quiet to worship / Muslim communi

Teacher in head scarf charge

A 42-year-old woman teacher is to appear before magistrates today on a charge of religiously aggravated assault after allegedly forcing a pupil to remove her head scarf at Bretton Woods community school in Peterborough. Nearly 40% of its 900 pupils are from ethnic minorities.

The Guardian, 19 September 2003

ENTERTAINMENT AND THE MASS MEDIA 12

LES SPECTACLES ET LES MASS MEDIA

Vocabulaire à haute fréquence

The world of entertainment	Le monde des spectacles
to entertain	divertir, amuser
to act	jouer
an actor	un acteur
an actress	une actrice
to interpret [ɪn'tɜːprɪt]	interpréter
an interpretation	une interprétation
to play (a part, a role)	jouer (un rôle)
a part, a role	un rôle
the leading part, the lead	le rôle principal
a supporting role	un rôle secondaire
a character	un personnage
a character part	un rôle de composition
an artist	un artiste
a plot	une intrigue
to direct	mettre en scène, réaliser
a director	un metteur en scène, un réalisateur
to cast	choisir comme interprète
a cast	une distribution
to produce	produire
a production	une production
a performance	une représentation
the setting, the scenery	le décor
a designer	un décorateur
to design [dɪ'zaɪn]	dessiner, concevoir
to release	sortir, publier

a release	une sortie, une parution
a blockbuster	un film (un livre, etc.) à succès
a comedian	un comédien, un comique
a conjuror	un prestidigitateur
a trick	un tour
an act	un numéro
a circus	un cirque
a show	une revue, un spectacle
ballet	le ballet
ballet dancing	la danse classique
a ballerina	une ballerine
a pantomime	un spectacle musical de Noël

Success and failure — Le succès et l'échec

fame	la célébrité
the box office	le guichet, la caisse
a (smash) hit	un succès, un tube
a flop	un four
a fanatic, a fan, an admirer	un admirateur
an idol ['aɪdl]	une idole
a craze, a fashion, a fad	une mode, un engouement
a masterpiece	un chef-d'œuvre
a review	une critique
a reviewer, a critic	un critique
a film contest	une compétition cinématographique
an award	une récompense
a prize	un prix
a shortlist	une liste des candidats sélectionnés
to nominate	nommer
a nominee	un nommé
an award contender	un candidat à un prix
a juror	un juré
an Oscar winner	un lauréat des Oscars
the runner-up	le second

The theatre — Le théâtre

a play	une pièce de théâtre
a playwright	un auteur dramatique
a tragedy	une tragédie
a comedy	une comédie
a drama	un drame
to stage	monter (une pièce)
the stage	la scène
to rehearse [rɪ'hɜːs]	répéter
a rehearsal	une répétition
an act	un acte

act two	le deuxième acte
the interval	l'entracte
a curtain call	un rappel

Cinema and television — Le cinéma et la télévision

the movie/film industry	l'industrie cinématographique
independent movie making	le cinéma indépendant
a screen	un écran
to screen	projeter
a film, a movie, a motion picture *(US)*	un film
a cult film	un film culte
a première	une avant-première
the opening	les chiffres des premiers jours
a record opening	un record d'entrées au premier jour, des entrées record le jour de sortie
a silent movie	un film muet
the feature film	le film principal
an animated cartoon	un dessin animé
a filmmaker	un cinéaste
to shoot, to film	tourner
shooting	le tournage
a shot	un plan
a cameraman	un opérateur
to edit	monter
an editor	un monteur
editing	le montage
a sequence	une séquence
the soundtrack	la bande sonore
a scenario |sɪ'nɑːrɪəʊ|	un scénario
a script, a screenplay	un scénario détaillé
a screenwriter, a scenarist	un scénariste
to star	avoir pour vedette
a star	une vedette
a studio	un studio
pornography |pɔː'nɒgrəfɪ|	la pornographie
pornographic |pɔːnə'græfɪk|	pornographique
a documentary	un documentaire
a detective film	un film policier
a thriller	un film à suspense
a horror movie	un film d'horreur
an art film	un film d'art et d'essai
to dub	doubler
an undubbed film	un film en version originale
subtitles	les sous-titres

Music	La musique
a concert	un concert
a gig [gɪg]	un concert unique, un show case
an encore	un rappel
an orchestra ['ɔːkɪstrə]	un orchestre
to conduct	diriger (un orchestre)
a conductor	un chef d'orchestre
a concerto [kən'ʃɜːtəʊ]	un concerto
a symphony	une symphonie
a sonata [sə'nɑːtə]	une sonate
a piece	un morceau
a score	une partition
classical	classique
a bar	une mesure
a tune	un air
an instrument	un instrument
a band	une formation, un groupe
to split up	se séparer
lyrics	les paroles
a musical (comedy)	une comédie musicale
to record [rɪ'kɔːd]	enregistrer
a tape/cassette recorder	un magnétophone
a record ['rekɔːd]	un disque
a single	un single, un CD un titre
an album	un album
a double album	un double album
a compact disc	un disque compact
a CD	un CD
a DVD	un DVD
a CD/DVD player	un lecteur de CD/DVD
a track	une chanson, une piste
online music	la musique sur Internet
a record shop	un magasin de disques
a record company	une maison de disques
a record label	un label de disque
a cassette	une cassette
the charts	le hit-parade
a partygoer	un teuffeur

Journalism	Le journalisme
a journalist, a newspaperman	un journaliste
a news agency	une agence de presse
to report	signaler, faire savoir
a report	un reportage
an account	un compte-rendu
reporting	le reportage
an article	un artide

the Times editor	le directeur du Times
the sports editor	le rédacteur sportif
a correspondent	un correspondant
a freelance	un journaliste indépendant
a column	une chronique
a columnist	un chroniqueur
the leading article, the leader	l'éditorial principal
an editorial	un éditorial
to publish	éditer
a publisher	un éditeur
to investigate	enquêter
an investigation	une enquête
to interview	interviewer
an interviewer	un interviewer
an interviewee	une personne interviewée
to reveal	révéler
a revelation	une révélation
the popular press	la presse à sensation
a tabloid	un journal de petit format
the quality papers	les journaux sérieux
a copy	un exemplaire
an issue	un numéro (publication)
a headline	un titre
a banner headline	une manchette
the front page	la une
front page splashes	les gros titres
advertisements	les publicités
classified advertisements	les petites annonces
circulation	le tirage

Radio and television / La radio et la télévision

a radio set, a TV set	un poste de radio, de télé
a transmission	un programme, une retransmission
to broadcast, to air	émettre
a broadcast, a programme	une émission
a broadcaster	une personnalité du PAF
to listen in to	écouter (la radio)
a listener	un auditeur
a frequency	une fréquence
a wavelength	une longueur d'ondes
a waveband	une gamme d'ondes
to watch TV, to view	regarder la télé
satellite TV	la télévision par satellite
to digitalise	numériser
digital (terrestrial) TV	la télévision numérique (terrestre)
a viewer	un téléspectateur
a video	un enregistrement vidéo

a video recorder	un magnétoscope
a station	une station
a channel	une chaîne, un canal
a network	un réseau, une chaîne
the news	les informations
a news bulletin, a newscast	un bulletin d'information
a newsreader, a newscaster	un présentateur de journal
to announce	annoncer, présenter
an announcer	un présentateur
to comment	commenter
a commentator	un commentateur
to present	présenter
a presenter	un présentateur
a TV crew	une équipe de télé
peak time, prime time	les heures de grande écoute
the ratings	l'indice d'écoute
audience	l'audience
a schedule	une grille
a slot	une tranche horaire
a commercial	une annonce publicitaire
a spot	une coupure publicitaire
a series	une série
a serial	un feuilleton
a soap opera	un feuilleton mélo
a sitcom	un feuilleton, une série comique
reality TV	la télé réalité

Events — Les événements

to cover	couvrir
coverage	la couverture
blanket coverage	une large couverture
live	en direct
an exclusive deal	une exclusivité
a summary	un résumé
to highlight	mettre en valeur
the highlights	les moments forts
a source	une source
a leak	une fuite
a topic	un sujet, un thème
current affairs	l'actualité
sensational	sensationnel
sensationalism	recherche du sensationnel
off the record	hors antenne, en privé
to distort	déformer
distortion	la déformation
bias ['baɪəs]	le préjugé, le parti pris
biased, one-sided	partial, partisan

unbiased, objective	impartial, objectif
a news conference	une conférence de presse
a statement	une déclaration
a communiqué [kə'mju:nɪkeɪ]	un communiqué
to pirate	pirater
pirated film/music	film/musique piraté(e)
piracy	la piraterie
to download	télécharger

Expressions

to be a sell-out	se jouer à guichets fermés
to be shortlisted	être selectionné
an award-winning film	un film primé
to be presented with an award	recevoir une distinction
to be acclaimed by critics	être plébiscité par la critique
to be in the limelight	être sous les projecteurs
to be cast against type	jouer à contre-emploi
to bring to the screen	porter à l'écran
a box-office attraction	un spectacle à grand succès
to break box-office records	battre tous les records d'entrées
What's on tonight?	Que peut-on voir ce soir ?
the top of the ratings	la tête du classement
to hit the headlines	faire les gros titres
to be given front-page treatment	faire la une des journaux
to give prominence to	mettre en vedette
to fuel rumours	alimenter la rumeur
to be contracted to	être sous contrat avec
to carry an exclusive tag	porter la mention " en exclusivité "
to appear on television	paraître à la télévision
to go on television	se montrer à la télévision
to be glued to the TV set	être rivé devant la télé
to be on the air	être à l'antenne
to go off the air	quitter, rendre l'antenne
to name sources	révéler ses sources
letters to the editor	le courrier des lecteurs

Vocabulaire complémentaire

The world of entertainment	**Le monde des spectacles**
characterisation	la peinture des caractères
costumes	les costumes
make-up	le maquillage
to impersonate [ɪm'pɜ:səneɪt]	imiter
an impersonator	un imitateur

a stand-up comedian	un comique (en solo)
to audition	auditionner
an audition	une séance d'essai
a spoof	une parodie
a theatre buff	un mordu, un cinglé de théâtre
a slapstick comedy	une comédie bouffonne
a role model	un modèle exemplaire
an icon ['aɪkɒn]	une figure emblématique
glamour	l'éclat, la séduction
a festival	un festival
a tour	une tournée
a rerun	une reprise
a preview	une avant-première
farewell	les adieux
mainstream	institutionnalisé, dominant
underground	avant-gardiste, underground

The theatre — Le théâtre

a cue	une réplique
a dress rehearsal	une répétition générale
the first night	la première
stagecraft	l'art de la scène
stage fright	le trac
a stage manager	un régisseur
a repertory company	une troupe du répertoire
an understudy	une doublure

Radio and television — La radio et la télévision

a press review	une revue de presse
a rerun, a repeat	une rediffusion
to rebroadcast	rediffuser
a plug	une publicité clandestine
the tube, the box *(fam.)*	la téloche
a newsflash	un flash d'information
a news update	un dernier point
a news round-up	un tour d'horizon
an anchorman	un présentateur
a host	un animateur
a signature tune	un indicatif sonore
on the line	en ligne (téléphone)
airtime	le temps d'antenne
a phone-in	un programme à ligne ouverte
a quiz	un jeu avec questions
a quizmaster	un meneur de jeu
a radio car	une voiture émettrice
an aerial ['ɛərɪəl]	une antenne

a dish (aerial)	une parabole
pay per view	paiement à la séance
a digital box/decoder	un décodeur numérique
a remote control	une télécommande
cable	le câble
to tune in to	se brancher sur
to zap	zapper

Cinema and television — Le cinéma et la télévision

an animated feature	un dessin animé de long métrage
a full-length film	un long métrage
a short film	un court métrage
a filmgoer, a cinemagoer	un cinéphile
a television film, a made-for-TV movie	un téléfilm
to commission	commander
to adapt	adapter
an adaptation	une adaptation
a take	une prise de vue
a close-up	un gros plan
location	les extérieurs
an extra	un figurant
a cameo part	un mini rôle (pour vedette)
a set	un plateau
a stunt	une cascade
a stuntman	un cascadeur
the props	les accessoires
a propman	un accessoiriste
an X-rated film	un film classé X
a U-rated film	un film pour tous
the flicks	le cinoche
footage	une bande filmée
in slow motion	au ralenti
to replay	faire revoir
(action) replay	un retour sur l'action
a reel	une bobine
a trailer	une bande annonce
the credits	le générique
an episode, an instalment	un épisode
a sequel	une suite
an impresario [ɪmprə'sɑːrɪəʊ]	un imprésario
gore	l'hémoglobine
a video nasty	une cassette porno et/ou très violente
a camcorder	un caméscope
to videotape	enregistrer sur cassette
a DV-cam	un caméscope numérique

Journalism	Le journalisme
a tycoon	un magnat
a newshound	un reporter
to feature	figurer, faire figurer
a feature	un artide de fond
a dispatch	une dépêche
a note	un billet
obituaries	la rubrique nécrologique
the agony column	le courrier du cœur
the agony aunt	le journaliste du courrier du cœur
the gossip column	les commérages
a gossip columnist	un chroniqueur mondain
a chief editor	un rédacteur en chef
readership	le lectorat
to contribute to	collaborer à
a contributor	un collaborateur
a broadsheet	un journal grand format
a rag	une feuille de chou
the gutter press	la presse à scandales
a hack	un pisse-copie
a box	un encadré
a cartoon	un dessin humoristique
a cartoonist	un dessinateur humoristique
a caption	une légende
a comic strip	une bande dessinée
the lay-out	la mise en page
a press cutting	une coupure de joumal
an excerpt	un extrait
a pull-out supplement	un supplément détachable
news in brief	les nouvelles brèves
miscellaneous news	les faits divers
newsprint	le papier journal

Events	Les événements
a development	une évolution de situation
to hype	matraquer
media hype	le matraquage des médias
to fabricate	inventer, fabriquer
a news blackout	un refus d'informer
to gag	bâillonner
a gag	un bâillon
to censor	censurer
censorship	la censure
propaganda [prɒpə'gændə]	la propagande
disinformation	la désinformation
an authoritative source	une source autorisée
a reliable source	une source sûre

a press release	un avis à la presse
to brief	mettre au courant
a press briefing	un point de presse
lurid reporting	reportage à sensation
muckraking	la recherche du sordide
to pander to sb.	flatter bassement les goûts de qn.
slanted	tendancieux, partial
slant	le parti pris
libel [ˈlaɪbəl]	la diffamation écrite
defamatory	diffamatoire
to slander	calomnier
slander	la calomnie
to sue [sjuː, suː]	poursuivre en justice
a breach of, an intrusion of privacy	une atteinte à l'intimité, la vie privée
damages	des dommages-intérêts

Zellweger and Pink to star in rival films on Janis Joplin

By Terry Kirby, Chief Reporter

One is a pop diva with an extravagant haircut and an outrageous new stage show. The other is an Oscar-winning movie star best known for her portrayal of a fictional British heroine. Now both want to be Janis Joplin.

Pink, the singer, was named yesterday as the director's choice to play the legendary rock star, who died from heroin at 27, in a forthcoming biopic, *The Gospel According to Janis*.

But Renée Zellweger, of Bridget Jones fame, is already to star in another film biography of Joplin, entitled *Piece of My Heart*, after one of her most famous songs.

Actress and singer now face difficulties with their roles, which critics will relish. Pink, real name Alecia Moore, although critically applauded as a singer, has no track record as an actress. And while few would doubt Zellweger's on-screen ability after her Oscar for *Cold Mountain*, she has yet to prove she can sing as well as her idol.

Then there is the problem of two films being made on the same subject at the same time; precedent suggests only one will enjoy box-office success. Both have tentative 2005 release dates, but have not yet begun shooting.

The trade paper *Variety* says Pink's screen test, in which she sang two Joplin standards, as well as acting in two scenes, convinced Penelope Spheeris, the director, that she was the right choice. Pink is now featuring Joplin songs in her stage

show, which is earning strong reviews for its music and choreography.
Spheeris told Variety: "After trying to make a picture on Janis's life for 15 years, I'd call Alecia's screen test the most gratifying moment in my film career." Spheeris directed *Wayne's World*, the 1992 film that helped make a star of Mike Myers.
The producers are trying to raise finance. They have the rights to several Joplin songs, and the endorsement of her family. A soundtrack deal is in the pipeline with Arista, the label headed by Clive Davis, who signed Joplin to CBS more than 30 years ago.The film appears further advanced than *Piece of My Heart*, a <u>pet project</u> for Zellweger, who has said she grew up worshipping her fellow Texan. The film, being developed for Paramount, has a recognised writer, Anne Meredith, but no director.
Joplin's story is great film material. Born into a middle-class home, she dropped out to the West Coast scene of the late 1960s, <u>belting out</u> blues and R'n'B with her powerful, earthy voice. Fast-living Joplin died from a heroin overdose in 1970. The 1979 Bette Midler film, *The Rose*, was loosely based on her life.
Several films have been made at the same time on similar subjects. The most notorious example was Stephen Frear's *Dangerous Liaisons* and Milos Foreman's *Valmont*, both based on the stage play *Les Liaisons Dangereuses*. Both were made at the same time but *Valmont* was held back for a year to avoid a box-office clash. It stood no chance, despite the opinion of many that it was the better film.

The Independent, 3 April 2004

1 Choose the right explanation for each of the following words underlined in the article.

1. forthcoming
A. present
B. future
C. past

2. to relish
A. to enjoy
B. to dislike
C. to run down

3. tentative
A. tempting
B. stimulating
C. provisional

4. a pet project
A. a favourite plan
B. an unpopular plan
C. a difficult plan

5. to belt out
A. to sing softly
B. to sing loudly
C. to sing tastelessly

2 Say whether the following statements are true (T) or false (F).

1. Zellweger and Pink are rivals to star in the same film.
2. No further mention is made of "a British fictional heroine".

3. *Piece of my Heart* is both the title of the film and the title of one of Joplin's songs.
4. Alecia Moore has already played in several films.
5. While Zellweger has proved herself as an actress, she has no track record as a singer.
6. There have already been examples of two films on the same subject at the same time enjoying box-office success.
7. Pink's interpretation of Joplin's songs as part of her stage show has been acclaimed by critics.
8. Penelope Spheeris is optimistic about Moore's ability as an actress.
9. Joplin's family is backing Zellweger's film biography project.
10. An agreement on the music of Spheeris' motion picture is in the making with Arista.
11. Zellweger has always been a big fan of Joplin's music.
12. There has already been a film faithfully portraying Joplin's life.
13. Stephen Frear's film was released before *Valmont*.
14. Milos Foreman's film was better than Stephen Frear's and enjoyed box-office success.

3 Which of the four words in each list should not be associated with the others.

1. fame, familiarity, celebrity, renown
2. a success, a hit, a gig, a triumph
3. to film, to take, to edit, to shoot
4. reviews, awards, appraisals, critiques
5. a score, a flop, a washout, a failure

4 Complete the words in the following sentences. Each dash represents one letter.

1. *The Lord of The Rings*, the final part of the Tolkien trilogy, became the first f _ _ _ _ _ _ film to win best picture – and equalled the record trophy tally at the Hollywood ceremony.
2. Donald Trump's r _ _ _ _ _ _ _ television show in the US, *The Apprentice*, has attracted audiences of 20 million every week.
3. Singapore is changing its cinema ratings system in a move to relax c _ _ _ _ _ _ _ _ _.
4. Canadian singer-songwriter Alanis Morissette's first a _ _ _ _ for four years has entered the United States c _ _ _ _ _ at number one.
5. *The Independent* became the first n _ _ _ _ _ _ _ _ in recent times to reduce the page size of its d _ _ _ _ edition, in September 2003. *The Times* quickly followed suit. *The Guardian* has told its staff that the title will remain a b _ _ _ _ _ _ _ _ _.

5 Fill in each blank in the following article with a word from the list below. Use each word only once.

websites	legal
worldwide	play
downloaded	albums
success	Internet
CDs	music
singles	

Soaring sales of music downloaded from Net threaten future of CDs

by Severin Carrell

Sales of "personal jukeboxes" that play music ...(1)... from the Internet are set to triple over the next few years – wrecking sales of CD ...(2)... and ...(3)... .

Music industry analysts predict that Britons will buy 12.5 million devices like the Apple iPod over the next four years to ...(4)... songs downloaded from ...(5)... or copied on to their personal computers.

In a report last week, experts at the ...(6)... industry consultancy Understanding & Solutions revealed that the British download more music from the ...(7)... and use computers for playing music more often than the Americans, Japanese and French.

Earlier this year, ...(8)... downloads of songs out-stripped the sales of ...(9)... , cassettes and vinyl records for the first time in Britain when more than 150,000 songs were sold over the internet in January.

The latest predictions follow the runaway ...(10)... of the iPod, the palm-sized "personal jukebox" made by Apple, since its launch in the UK last year. It sold out over Christmas, and at least 2.5 million iPods have now been sold ...(11)..... [...]

The Independent, 21 March 2004

Beckham may tackle role in Pink Panther

by Mark Sage

David Beckham has been approached to appear in the forthcoming Pink Panther movie. The England midfielder would play a cameo role as a footballer in the film, which follows a detective trying to solve the murder of a famous soccer coach and the theft of the Pink Panther diamond. The Hollywood Reporter newspaper said Beckham had to resolve a scheduling clash before committing to the film.

The MGM production would be the first feature film in which the Real Madrid player would appear. He would be alongside Steve Martin and Beyoncé Knowles. Archive footage of Beckham on the field was used in the British production *Bend It Like Beckham*.

The new film, which is due to go into production in May and is scheduled for a July 2005 release, is being directed by Shawn Levy. Also in the movie are Kevin Kline and Jean Reno.

A spokeswoman for Beckham said: "They have approached him to be in the film but he hasn't made a decision."

The Independent, 27 March 2004

INTRODUCTION TO CHAPTERS 13-20

INTRODUCTION AUX CHAPITRES 13-20

Crime	La criminalité
Drugs	La drogue
Demonstrations	Les manifestations
Revolutions	Les révolutions
War	La guerre
Miscellaneous Topics	Centres d'intérêt divers
Accidents	Les accidents
Natural Disasters	Les catastrophes naturelles

Vocabulaire à haute fréquence

Physical damage	Les dégâts matériels
to blast	faire sauter, détruire
to explode	exploser, faire exploser
a blast, an explosion	une explosion
an explosive	un explosif
to set off	déclencher
to go off	se déclencher, exploser
to damage	endommager, abîmer
damage	les dégâts
to wreck	saccager, détruire
a wreck	une carcasse, une épave
wreckage	les débris, les décombres
to destroy	détruire
destruction	la destruction
to happen	se produire
to occur	survenir

to scatter	disperser
to devastate	ravager, dévaster
devastation	la dévastation, les ravages
devastating	dévastateur, catastrophique
to collapse	s'effondrer
rubble	les décombres, les gravats
debris	les débris
ruins	les ruines
to demolish	démolir
demolition	la démolition
to assess	évaluer
an assessment	une évaluation
scope, extent	l'étendue
a scale	une échelle de grandeur
the scene	les lieux
a disaster	un désastre
a catastrophe [kə'tæstrəfɪ]	une catastrophe
the aftermath	les conséquences, la suite

Casualties — Les victimes

to injure, to hurt	blesser
to wound	blesser (attaque)
slight, minor ['maɪnə]	léger
serious, major	grave
to sustain injuries	être blessé
an injury	une blessure
minor injuries	des blessures sans gravité
serious/life-threatening injuries	des blessures mettant la vie en danger
a stable condition	un état de santé stable
a wound	une blessure (attaque)
to bury	ensevelir
to trap	coincer, bloquer
a shock	une commotion
unhurt	indemne
to escape	s'en sortir
alive	vivant
to shelter	abriter
a shelter	un abri, un refuge
a death toll	un bilan des morts

Rescue work — Intervention des secours

alarm	l'alarme, l'alerte
to survive	survivre
a survivor	un rescapé
to attempt	tenter
an attempt, a bid	une tentative

to rescue	secourir
a rescue operation	une opération de secours
relief	l'aide, le secours
relief/rescue/aid workers	les secouristes
a paramedic	un aide-soignant, un auxiliaire médical
first aid	les premiers soins
artificial respiration	respiration artificielle
chest massage	massage cardiaque
to save	sauver
an emergency	une urgence
a refugee	un réfugié
to clear	déblayer
to pull clear	dégager
a heap	un tas
a pile	un amas
to recover	retrouver, récupérer
recovery	la récupération
to name	communiquer les noms
a helpline	un numéro spécial
a stretcher	une civière
to take to	transporter à
an ambulance	une ambulance
to identify	identifier
to name	nommer
to evacuate	évacuer
evacuation	l'évacuation
supplies	l'approvisionnement

Weapons — Les armes

the weapon culture	la culture des armes
a knife, a blade	un couteau, une lame
to shoot	tirer
a shot	un coup de feu
to fire	tirer (un coup de feu)
a firearm	une arme à feu
to arm	armer
a pistol	un pistolet
a handgun	une arme de poing
a gun, a rifle	un fusil
gunfire	une fusillade
a shotgun	un fusil de chasse
a gunman	un homme armé
a bullet	une balle
a grenade	une grenade
automatic	automatique
a bomb	une bombe
to bomb	bombarder (avion)

a bombing	un bombardement
to machine gun	mitrailler
a machine gun	une mitrailleuse
a gun	un canon
a mortar	un mortier
a mortar shell	un obus de mortier
a rocket	une roquette
to shell	bombarder (obus)
a shell	un obus
artillery	l'artillerie
ammunition	les munitions
to mine	miner
a mine	une mine
an armoured car	un véhicule blindé
a tank	un char d'assaut
a missile	un missile

Violent actions / Les actions violentes

to threaten ['θretn]	menacer
a threat [θret]	une menace
to blackmail	faire du chantage
blackmail	le chantage
to kidnap, to abduct	kidnapper, enlever
an abduction, kidnapping	un enlèvement, un rapt
to loot	piller
looting	le pillage
to attack	attaquer
an attack, an onslaught	une attaque
to clash with	se heurter à, affronter
a clash	un affrontement
to raid	attaquer
a bank raid	une attaque de banque
to burst into	faire irruption dans
to demand	exiger
a demand	une exigence
a ransom	une rançon
to take over	s'emparer de
to mask	masquer
a mask	un masque
to blow up	faire sauter
a target	une cible
to assassinate	assassiner
an assassination	un assassinat
to gun down, to shoot dead	abattre
a network, a ring	un réseau
to fight	lutter, combattre
a fight	un combat, une lutte

a battle	une bataille
a gunfight	un échange de coups de feu
a siege [si:dʒ]	un siège
to besiege	assiéger

Security — La sécurité

to tighten/to step up security	renforcer la sécurité
to crack down on sth.	réprimer qch.
a crackdown on, a blitz on	une répression de
to clamp down on sth.	donner un coup d'arrêt à, durcir la lutte contre
a clampdown on sth.	un durcissement de la lutte contre qch., un tour de vis
to combat sth.	mener une lutte contre qch.
a measure	une mesure
to look for, to search for	rechercher
a search	une recherche, une fouille
to seal off	boucler, interdire l'accès
to enquire	enquêter, se renseigner
an enquiry	une enquête
to investigate	examiner, enquêter
an investigation, a probe	une enquête, une investigation
a detective constable	un inspecteur de police
a detective inspector	un inspecteur principal
a detective superintendent	un commissaire de police
a detective chief superintendent	un commissaire divisionnaire
the security forces	les forces de sécurité
a security guard	un vigile, un convoyeur de fonds
a bodyguard	un garde du corps
to patrol	patrouiller
a patrol	une patrouille
to block	bloquer
a road block	un barrage routier
to flee	fuir, s'enfuir
to surround	cerner, entourer
to overpower	maîtriser
to arrest	arrêter
an arrest	une arrestation
to hold	interpeller
to detain	garder à vue
to outlaw	mettre hors la loi
to ban	interdire
a ban	une interdiction
a raid	une descente
to curb	juguler
to quell	étouffer, réprimer
to storm	donner l'assaut

to dismantle	démanteler
to impose	imposer
a curfew	un couvre-feu
a truce	une trêve
a ceasefire	un cessez-le-feu
a peacekeeping force	une force d'interposition
to give oneself in/up, to turn oneself in	se rendre, se livrer
to surrender	se rendre, capituler
a surrender	une reddition
to prevent	empêcher, prévenir
prevention	la prévention
to free, to set free, to release	relâcher, libérer
a release	une libération

Expressions

to set fire to sth., to set sth. on fire	mettre le feu à qch.
to set sth. alight, ablaze	embraser qch.
to raise the alarm	donner l'alarme
to lift a ban	lever une interdiction
to make a getaway	prendre la fuite
to be in hiding	se cacher
to be on the loose, to be on the run,	ne pas avoir été arrêté,
to be at large	être dans la nature, être en cavale
to take refuge	prendre refuge
to keep an open mind	ne rejeter aucune piste
to pose a threat	constituer une menace
tit for tat	la loi du talion
to be under arrest	être en état d'arrestation
to raise a ransom	réunir une rançon
at point-blank range	à bout portant
to level a gun at sb., to take aim at sb.	pointer une arme sur qn.,
	diriger une arme contre qn.
to be caught in crossfire	être pris entre deux feux
to hold sb. at gunpoint	braquer une arme sur qn.
to take up arms	prendre les armes
to be up in arms against	s'insurger contre
to lay down (one's) arms	déposer les armes
riddled with bullets	criblé de balles
to lay siege to	faire le siège de
a surface to air missile	un missile sol-air
to take one's toll	prélever son tribut
to claim 20 lives,	faire 20 morts
to leave 20 people dead	
to lose one's life	trouver la mort
to die instantly	mourir tout de suite

to be killed outright	être tué sur le coup
to be in a coma	être dans le coma
to lose consciousness	perdre connaissance
the kiss of life, mouth to mouth resuscitation	le bouche à bouche
to recover consciousness	reprendre connaissance
to be unaccounted for	ne pas avoir été retrouvé
to go/to be missing	être porté disparu
flags at half mast	les drapeaux en berne
to offer condolences	présenter des condoléances

Vocabulaire complémentaire

Physical damage	**Les dégâts matériels**
to rip through	souffler
to shatter	fracasser
to gut	éventrer
a tangle	un enchevêtrement
remains	les restes, les dépouilles
to cave in, to subside	s'affaisser
catastrophic	catastrophique

Casualties and rescue work	**Les victimes et l'intervention des secours**
to dial 999, to dial 911 *(US)*	appeler police-secours
unscathed [ʌn'skeɪðd]	indemne
a cut	une coupure
to bruise [bruːz]	meurtrir, tuméfier
a bruise	une meurtrissure, un hématome
to mutilate, to maim	mutiler
belongings	les possessions
to pass out	s'évanouir
to come to	revenir à soi
to resuscitate	réanimer
resuscitation	la réanimation
survival	la survie
a theory	une hypothèse
a corpse	un cadavre
an autopsy	une autopsie
a tally of deaths	un décompte des morts
a coffin	un cercueil
a shroud	un linceul
a mortuary	une morgue, une chapelle ardente
a memorial service	une cérémonie commémorative
relatives	la famille

to shed blood	répandre le sang
bloodshed, bloodletting	l'effusion de sang
a bloodbath	un bain de sang
to mourn sb.	porter le deuil de qn.
mourning	le deuil

Violent actions and security — Les actions violentes et la sécurité

on the alert	en état d'alerte
to outlaw	mettre hors la loi
captive	captif
captivity	la captivité
to occupy	occuper
an occupation	une occupation
a skirmish	une escarmouche, un accrochage
to ambush	tendre une embuscade, tomber dans une embuscade
to erupt, to flare up	se déclencher brusquement
an eruption	un déclenchement brusque
a flare-up	une flambée
an upsurge, a surge	une recrudescence
a spate, a rash	(toute) une série
to trigger, to spark	déclencher, provoquer
to mastermind	organiser
a mastermind	un cerveau
a scheme [ski:m]	un stratagème, un projet
a ploy	un stratagème
to avenge	venger
revenge	une revanche
to respond	répliquer
a response	une réplique
retribution	le châtiment, la vengeance
to retaliate	riposter
retaliation	la riposte
reprisals	les représailles
a carbon copy	une réplique exacte
an assumed name	un nom d'emprunt
the whereabouts	l'endroit où est qn.
to vanish	disparaître
to conceal	dissimuler
a hideaway, a hide-out	une cachette, une planque
a weapons cache [kæʃ]	une cache d'armes
a haul	une prise, un butin
a hood	une cagoule
a wig	une perruque
a sniper	un tireur isolé
a ringleader	un meneur

an accomplice	un complice
complicity	la complicité
an informant, an informer	un informateur
a repentant informer	un repenti
a tip, a tip-off	un renseignement
surveillance	la surveillance
to thwart, to foil	contrecarrer, déjouer
to stalk	traquer, filer
to move in	intervenir
to trap, to entrap	piéger
a trap	un piège, une souricière
a sting operation	une opération piège
a strike	un coup de main, un raid
to rage	faire rage
to bombard	bombarder (obus, bombes)
bombardment	le bombardement
headquarters	le quartier général
a deadline	une limite de temps, une date butoir
to cordon off	boucler, interdire l'accès
to barricade oneself	se barricader
a police cordon	un cordon de police
to handcuff	passer les menottes à
handcuffs	les menottes
to regain (control)	reprendre (le contrôle)
to extradite	extrader
an extradition	une extradition
beleaguered	assiégé, investi
a shoot-out	une fusillade
a bulletproof vest, a flak jacket	un gilet pare-balles
body armour	un gilet d'armes
a marksman, a sharpshooter	un tireur d'élite
a stray bullet	une balle perdue
a state of emergency	un état d'urgence
a state of siege	un état de siège
martial law	la loi martiale
to swoop	faire une descente
a swoop	un coup de filet
to round up	effectuer une rafle
a round-up	un regroupement, une rafle
to sweep	ratisser
a sweep	un ratissage
to sift through	passer au crible
to comb	fouiller, ratisser
a manhunt	une chasse à l'homme
to massacre, to slaughter	massacrer
a massacre, a slaughter	un massacre
to exterminate	exterminer

an extermination	une extermination
to execute	exécuter
a summary execution	une exécution sommaire
to liquidate, to eliminate	liquider, éliminer
a mass grave	une fosse commune
genocide	le génocide

Weapons	Les armes
an arms dealer	un marchand d'armes
gun running	le trafic d'armes
a battery	une batterie
the butt	la crosse
a gun barrel	un canon de fusil
a silencer	un silencieux
the trigger	la détente
to pull the trigger	presser la détente
a sawn-off shotgun	un fusil à canon scié
a pump action shotgun	un fusil à pompe
a submachine gun	une mitraillette
an arms dump	un dépôt d'armes
ammunition	les munitions
a round of ammunition	une balle, une cartouche
a cartridge	une cartouche
a blank shot	un tir à blanc
a live bullet	une balle réelle
a volley	une rafale
to strafe	mitrailler, bombarder
gunshot	le plomb de chasse
a rubber/plastic bullet	une balle de caoutchouc
a limpet mine	une mine ventouse
a fire bomb	une bombe incendiaire
shrapnel	les éclats
a time bomb	une bombe à retardement
a cluster bomb	une bombe à fragmentation

13 CRIME AND PUNISHMENT

DÉLITS ET SANCTIONS

voir Introduction p. 142

Vocabulaire à haute fréquence

General background	Contexte général
an offence	un délit, une infraction
a crime	un délit, un crime
to commit	commettre
to break	transgresser, violer
to uphold the law	faire respecter, maintenir la loi
law enforcement	l'application de la loi
a criminal	un criminel
an offender	un délinquant
a law-breaker	un contrevenant
crime	la délinquance
petty crime	la petite délinquance
the crime rate	le taux de criminalité
law-abiding	respectueux de la loi
security	la sécurité
insecurity	l'insécurité

Non-violent crime	Les délits sans violence
antisocial behaviour	les incivilités
motoring offences	les délits de la route
shoplifting	le vol à l'étalage
a shoplifter	un voleur à l'étalage

to smuggle	passer en fraude
smuggling	la contrebande
to forge	contrefaire
forgery	la contrefaçon
to deceive [dɪ'siːv]	tromper
deception	la tromperie
confidence	la confiance
to con sb.	escroquer, duper qn.
a con	une supercherie, escroquerie
a conman	un escroc, un imposteur
to trust sb.	avoir confiance en qn.
libel ['laɪbəl]	la diffamation écrite
to steal sth. from sb.	dérober qch. à qn.
a thief (*pl.* -ieves)	un voleur
a theft	un vol

Violent crime — Les délits avec violence

to rob sb. of sth.	voler qch. à qn.
a robber	un voleur
a robbery	un vol qualifié
an armed robbery	un vol à main armée
car jacking	détournement de véhicule
to hold up	braquer, neutraliser
a hold-up, a raid	un braquage
to burgle	cambrioler
a burglary	un cambriolage
a burglar	un cambrioleur
to break in	entrer par effraction
a break-in	une effraction
a hooligan	un casseur
to vandalise	vandaliser
a vandal	un vandale
vandalism	le vandalisme
a thug, a yob	un loubard
to mug, to assault	agresser
a mugger	un aggresseur
a mugging, an assault	une agression
to rape	violer
a rape	un viol
a rapist	un violeur
child abuse	les sévices aux enfants
a pædophile ['piːdəufaɪl]	un pédophile
a child porn offender	un pédophile
manslaughter	homicide involontaire/par imprudence
to murder	assassiner
a murder	un meurtre
attempted murder, a murder attempt	tentative de meurtre

to stab	poignarder
to strangle	étrangler

Enquiries and arrests / Enquêtes et arrestations

a constable, an officer	un agent, un gendarme
a cop, a copper	un flic
to suspect	soupçonner
a suspect	un suspect
suspicion	les soupçons
suspicious	soupçonneux, suspect
a description	un signalement
a clue	un indice
a lead [li:d]	une piste
to give away	dénoncer
evidence	témoignage, preuve
to question	interroger
an interrogation	un interrogatoire
to accuse	accuser
an accusation	une accusation
alleged	présumé
to charge	inculper, accuser
a charge	une inculpation, une accusation

Justice / La justice

a court	un tribunal
a magistrate	un magistrat, un juge d'instance
to judge	juger
a judge	un juge
a judg(e)ment	un jugement
a trial	un procès
a case	une affaire, un procès
a loophole	un vide juridique
to prosecute	poursuivre
prosecution	des poursuites, l'accusation
a prosecutor	un procureur
to witness sth.	être témoin de qch.
a witness	un témoin
to testify	témoigner, déposer
a testimony	un témoignage
to admit, to own up	reconnaître
to confess	avouer
to deny	nier
a denial	un démenti, une dénégation
guilt	la culpabilité
guilty	coupable
not guilty	non coupable

innocent	innocent
to plead	plaider
to sentence	condamner
a sentence	une peine, une condamnation
tough, harsh, stiff	dur, rigoureux
lenient	indulgent
leniency	l'indulgence
punishment	le châtiment
to fine	donner une amende
a fine	une amende
a prison	une prison
a jail, a gaol [dʒeɪl]	une prison
to jail, to gaol	emprisonner
life imprisonment	la réclusion à vie
a life sentence	une condamnation à perpétuité
a suspended sentence	une condamnation avec sursis
a warder, a prison officer	un gardien, un surveillant
to escape, to break out, to run off	s'évader
an escape, a break-out	une évasion
the death penalty	la peine de mort
capital punishment	la peine capitale
to abolish	abolir
abolition	l'abolition
to restore	rétablir
restoration	le rétablissement

Expressions

to force one's way into	s'introduire de force dans
to be set upon	se faire attaquer
to produce a weapon	sortir une arme
grievous bodily harm	coups et blessures
to appear before magistrates, to appear in court	être présenté au juge
to help with enquiries	être entendu par la police
to be placed under investigation	être mis en examen
to act suspiciously	avoir une attitude suspecte
to arouse suspicion	éveiller les soupçons
to be caught red-handed	être pris sur le fait
to issue a photofit picture, to release an identikit picture	publier un portrait robot
the Serious Crime Squad	la Brigade de répression du banditisme
to be remanded on bail	être laissé en liberté sous caution, sous contrôle
to be remanded in custody	être placé en détention, être incarcéré
under house arrest	assigné à résidence

to bring to court/justice	poursuivre en justice
to bring to trial	assigner en justice
to bring an action against,	intenter une action
to serve a writ on	en justice contre
to be tried in one's absence	être jugé par contumace
to settle out of court	régler à l'amiable
to drop a charge	rendre un non-lieu
to dismiss a case	prononcer la relaxe
to serve a sentence	purger une peine
to uphold a judg(e)ment	confirmer un jugement
to quash a conviction	casser une condamnation
a miscarriage of justice	une erreur judiciaire
a travesty of justice	une parodie de justice
to speak under duress	parler sous la contrainte
to have jurisdiction over	relever de la juridiction de
to take the law into one's own hands	se faire justice soi-même
to tighten the law	renforcer la loi
to be jailed for three months, to be given/to get a three-month jail term	être condamné à trois mois de prison
to receive a jail sentence	être condamné à une peine d'emprisonnement
a non-custodial sentence	une peine autre que la prison
to commute a sentence	commuer une peine
to run into trouble	avoir des ennuis
to stay out of trouble	ne plus avoir d'ennuis

Vocabulaire complémentaire

General background	**Contexte général**
wrongdoing	indélicatesse, méfait
a wrongdoer	un malfaiteur
a misdemeanour [mɪsdɪ'miːnə]	un méfait, un délit
lawful	légal
unlawful	illégal
illicit	illicite
an infringement	une infraction
a first offender	un délinquant primaire
a hardened criminal	un repris de justice

Non-violent crime	**Les délits sans violence**
misconduct	l'indélicatesse
to trespass	s'introduire sans permission
a trespasser	un intrus
trespassing	l'intrusion illégale
to poach	braconner
joyriding	"emprunt" de voiture, rodéo

contraband	la contrebande
to fake	falsifier
a counterfeit note, a fake note	un faux billet
a fence	un receleur
a breach	une violation
a breach of trust	un abus de confiance
to trick sb.	tromper qn.
a trick	un tour, une supercherie
a trickster	un filou
a confidence trick	un abus de confiance
a crook	un escroc, un filou
to swindle	escroquer, estamper
a swindle	une escroquerie
to rip off	arnaquer
a rip-off	une arnaque
to defraud	spolier, gruger
fraud	la fraude
a fraudster	un fraudeur
to cover up	dissimuler, étouffer
to embezzle	détourner des fonds
embezzlement	le détournement de fonds
defamation [defə'meɪʃən]	la diffamation
defamatory [dɪ'fæmətrɪ]	diffamatoire
to slander	calomnier
slander	la diffamation orale
to solicit [sə'lɪsɪt]	racoler
a prostitute	une prostituée
a pimp	un souteneur
indecent exposure	outrage public à la pudeur
gross indecency	outrage aux bonnes mœurs

Violent crime — Les délits avec violence

a firebug	un pyromane
an affray	une rixe
a brawl	une bagarre
indecent assault	attentat à la pudeur
gang rape	le viol collectif
a serial killer	un tueur en série
a highwayman	un bandit de grand chemin
to tie (up), to bind	attacher
to blindfold	bander les yeux
to gag	bâillonner
a safe	un coffre-fort
a vault	une chambre forte
to get away	se sauver
a getaway	une fuite
the mob, the mafia	la mafia

a gang	une bande
a gangster, a mobster	un truand, un gangster
a godfather	un parrain
a hired gunman	un tueur à gages
a contract	un contrat
organised crime	le crime organisé, le grand banditisme
the underworld	le milieu
to racketeer [rækɪ'tɪə]	racketter
conspiracy	association de malfaiteurs

Enquiries and arrests / Enquêtes et arrestations

an eye witness	un témoin oculaire
a statement	une déclaration, une déposition
a reward	une récompense
a beat	une ronde, un ilôt
a trail	une piste
a fingerprint	une empreinte digitale
an alibi ['ælɪbaɪ]	un alibi
a warrant	un mandat
to hound, to track down	traquer
to come forward	se présenter à la police
a jailbreak	une évasion
to recapture	reprendre (évadé)
to be involved in	être mêlé à
a motive	un mobile
to prove	prouver
a proof	une preuve
to substantiate	fournir des preuves à l'appui de
hard evidence	preuves réelles, matérielles
incriminating evidence	une pièce à conviction
an inquest	une enquête après mort
a post-mortem	une autopsie
forensic medicine	la médecine légale
forensic evidence	expertise médico-légale
a coroner	un chargé d'enquête après mort suspecte
the culprit, the perpetrator	l'auteur, le coupable
a put-up job, a set-up, a frame-up	une machination, un coup monté
to frame sb.	monter un coup contre qn.
a supergrass	un indicateur, un repenti
trumped up, fabricated	fabriqué
an allegation	une allégation
to lock up	mettre sous les verrous
remand	la détention préventive

Justice	La justice
a youth court	un tribunal pour mineurs
a youth offender	un délinquant juvénile
a (court) summons	une citation à comparaître
a criminal record	un casier judiciaire
previous convictions	condamnations antérieures
a persistent offender	un multirécidiviste
a crime spree	une série de délits
a jury	un jury
a juror	un juré
to sue [sjuː, suː]	intenter une action contre
to try sb.	faire passer qn. en jugement
a lawsuit	un procès
the defendant	le prévenu
the plaintiff	le plaignant
in camera	à huis-clos
a lawyer	un homme de loi
a solicitor	un notaire, un avocat-conseil
a counsel, a barrister	un avocat à la cour
a defence attorney *(US)*	un avocat
a district attorney *(US)*	un procureur
prosecution	le ministère public
the dock	le banc des accusés
the witness stand	la barre des témoins
a hearing	une audience, une audition
an account	une déclaration
an affidavit	une déposition sous serment
a confession	un aveu
plea-bargaining	le plaider coupable
to indict [ɪn'daɪt]	mettre en accusation
an indictment	un acte d'accusation
a count	un chef d'accusation
to cross-examine	interroger un témoin de la partie adverse
a cross-examination	un contre-interrogatoire
to recant	se rétracter
a recantation	une rétractation
to sum up	conclure
summing-up	les conclusions
to rule	décider, ordonner
a ruling	une décision, un jugement
a verdict	un verdict
in absentia	par défaut
to acquit	acquitter
an acquittal	un acquittement
to discharge	relaxer
a discharge	une relaxe
to caution	mettre en garde

a caution	un avertissement
contempt of court	outrage à magistrat
extenuating/mitigating circumstances	circonstances atténuantes
to exonerate, to clear	disculper, innocenter
to convict	déclarer coupable
a conviction	une condamnation
to appeal	faire appel
a court of appeal	une court d'appel
mercy	la clémence
to pardon	grâcier, amnistier
pardon	la grâce
amnesty	l'amnistie
remission	remise de peine
on parole	en liberté conditionnelle
a bar	un barreau
a cell	une cellule
an inmate, a detainee	un détenu
solitary confinement	l'isolement carcéral
a prison mutiny	une mutinerie de prisonniers
a prison governor	un directeur de prison
a remand centre, a detention centre	un centre de détention
exercise	la promenade (en prison)
community work	les travaux d'intérêt général
electronic tagging	le bracelet électronique
alternative punishment	peine de substitution
probation	mise à l'épreuve
a probation officer	un agent de tutelle
death row [rəʊ]	le couloir de la mort
a stay of execution	un sursis à exécution
an executioner	un bourreau
to deter	dissuader
deterrent	dissuasif
to prevent	prévenir, empêcher
prevention	la prévention
a neighbourhood watch scheme	un comité de vigilance de quartier

British FBI "will hunt down Mr Bigs"*

by John Steele, Home Affairs Correspondent

Major extensions of the powers of investigators and courts to tackle top-level gangsters were proposed yesterday in a White Paper on the creation of an organised crime agency. Convicted major criminals could be forced to hand over bank and credit statements for up to a decade after their release from jail to prove they had not returned to crime.
A more formal and transparent legal framework was outlined to encourage plea-bargaining and sentence reductions for supergrasses who give Queen's Evidence against fellow gangsters.
The Home Office document raised the prospect of lengthier prison terms for organised crime convictions, similar to those in America. Those involved in conspiracies to smuggle class A drugs, such as heroin and cocaine, routinely face sentences of 20 years in the United States, compared with between five and 14 years in Britain.
The paper also indicated, as reported in *The Daily Telegraph* on Saturday, that the Government wanted to follow America and most other advanced nations and allow records of telephone taps to be used in evidence against gangsters.
Other proposals for powers and procedures to help the new Serious Organised Crime Agency (Soca) is an improved national witness protection programme and a new offence of "belonging to an organised crime group".
Soca, dubbed the "British FBI", will be able to force lawyers and accountants to disclose documents which could put criminals behind bars. It will replace the National Crime Squad, the National Criminal Intelligence Service and the investigative arms of Customs and Excise and the immigration service. It will employ about 5,000 agents.
The paper says it would be "lawfully audacious" in cracking down on organised crime. Soca will require legislation and is expected to be operational by 2006.
The White Paper rejects the idea of creating a unified border agency but urges closer work between Customs, Special Branch and immigration.

The Daily Telegraph, 30 March, 2004

** Mr Bigs est une allusion aux gros bonnets de la pègre.*

1 Say whether the following statements are true (T) or false (F).

1. Suspected major criminals could be forced to provide bank and credit statements to prove that they aren't criminals.
2. Criminals giving evidence against other gangsters could benefit from sentence reductions.
3. The law is more lenient in the US than in the UK on criminals convicted of organised crime involvement.
4. So far, records of telephone taps aren't recognised as evidence against gangsters.
5. Soca will work closely with the "British FBI".

6. With this new agency, strong legal action to clamp down on organised crime will be taken.
7. For Soca to be fully operational new laws will have to be passed.
8. The White Paper encourages the extension of an organised crime agency to the whole of Europe.

2 The first word in each list is taken from the article. Which of the other three should not be associated with it.

1. convicted, sentenced, condemned, indicted
2. gangster, thug, mob, yob
3. jail, sentence, gaol, prison
4. offence, crime, felony, case
5. lawfully, innocently, legally, rightfully

3 Read the article again and find words which mean the following.

1. a defendant's pleading guilty to a lesser charge rather than being tried on a more serious one.
2. a criminal turned informer
3. to import or export illegally
4. a formal judgement, including terms of punishment

4 In the article are the words "investigators", "gangsters", "lawyers". The suffixes "-er" or "-or" can be used with a wide range of verbs to make them into nouns. Use the suffixes to give the nouns corresponding to the following verbs.

1. to photograph
2. to play
3. to offend
4. to donate
5. to write
6. to supervise
7. to poach
8. to sail
9. to work
10. to shoplift
11. to trespass
12. to prosecute
13. to murder
14. to rob
15. to smuggle
16. to act
17. to operate
18. to shop

15 arrested in crackdown on beggars

Westminster Council has said that 15 people were arrested on the first night of a controversial drive to clear beggars off the streets of London's West End.

Council staff, including roadsweepers and traffic wardens, were briefed in advance to report beggars who would then be arrested by police and have their fingerprints and DNA taken.

Kit Malthouse, <u>deputy</u> leader of the council said today: "Last night we managed to arrest 15 people who were begging in Westminster. They were being processed today. It seems to be going pretty well, hopefully the message has got out."

The operation is targeting an estimated 300 beggars operating in a few square miles around areas including Soho, Covent Garden, Piccadilly and Victoria – many of them at Tube stations and cash machines.

Beggars identified as repeat offenders and those <u>lurking</u> at cashpoints may be issued with anti-social behaviour orders after they are convicted,...

...which would prevent them returning to their begging areas.

Crisis, a charity for the homeless, attacked the operation and said it would "criminalise" the homeless.

A spokesman for Crisis said: "All this will create is a series of additional barriers for people wanting to escape homelessness for good. Many of the people who will be rounded up this weekend are among the hidden homeless, living isolated lives in hostels, squats, emergency B&Bs and friends' floors."

The Daily Telegraph, 28 February 2004

1 Choose the right explanation for each of the following words underlined in the article.

1. deputy
A. vice-
B. minister
C. spokesperson

2. lurking
A. vandalising
B. stealing
C. hiding

3. to round up
A. to arrest
B. to release
C. to report

2 Choose the appropriate endings for the following sentences.

1. The decision to clear beggars off the streets of London's West End was
A. unanimous.
B. disputed.
C. undisputed.

2. Council staff
A. were instructed to arrest beggars.
B. were given very brief instructions.
C. received instructions to report beggars to the police.

3. Convicted beggars
A. will be expelled from the streets of London's West End.
B. will lurk at cashpoints not to be seen by the police.
C. will return to their begging areas.

4. This measure will
A. help the homeless to escape homelessness.
B. make it even more difficult for the homeless to escape homelessness.
C. provide the homeless with hostels, squats, emergency B&Bs and friends' floors.

3 Suffixes are used extensively in the article: "hopefully", "homeless", "homelessness", "criminalise".

A. "-less" (to indicate that sb. or sth. does not have the thing the noun refers to) and "-ful" (to refer to the quantity of a substance that an object contains or can contain) are added to nouns to form adjectives. Sometimes both suffixes can be used with one noun. Use the suffixes to give the adjectives corresponding to the following nouns.

1. blood
2. home
3. hope
4. job
5. law
6. use
7. forget
8. harm
9. cloud
10. dread

B. "-ness" is used to make nouns from adjectives as in "homelessness". Use the suffix to give the noun corresponding to the following adjectives.

1. good
2. ready
3. forgetful
4. happy
5. sad
6. weak
7. jobless
8. serious

C. "-ise" (or "-ize") is used to make verbs from adjectives as in "to criminalise". Use the suffix to give the verb corresponding to the following adjectives.

1. penal
2. modern
3. industrial
4. legal
5. commercial
6. central

4 Fill in the blanks in the artcle with the appropriate words from the following list. Use each word only once.

abducted	hunt	searched
treatment	arrested	officers
questioning	knifepoint	missing

"Abducted" girls found safe and well

by Louise Barnett, PA News

A nationwide ...(1)... for two girls allegedly ...(2)... from their foster parents at ...(3)... ended after they were found safe and well, police said today.

Sisters Salina Hafeez, five, and Sarah, three, went ...(4)... from Middlesbrough on Wednesday. They were found at an address in the town centre shortly after midnight when ...(5)... searched a number of properties, Cleveland police said.

Four men and three women have been ...(6)... in connection with the abduction and are being held for ...(7)... at police stations in the Middlesbrough area.

A Cleveland police spokesman today said: "Several premises were ...(8)... at around midnight in the Middlesbrough area. The children were found safe and well at one of the addresses that were searched. They did not need any medical ...(9)... . They were fit and well." The find came after the girls' unnamed foster mother made an emotional appeal for their safe return.

The Independent, 2 April 2004

to process	traiter
a process	un traitement
powder	poudre
a tablet	un comprimé, une pastille
a pill	une pilule
a capsule	une gélule

The fight against drugs — La lutte contre la drogue

to possess	détenir
possession	la détention
to seize	saisir
a seizure ['si:ʒə]	une saisie
a haul	une prise, une saisie
a street value	une valeur marchande
customs	la douane
a customs officer	un douanier
a drugs test	un contrôle anti-dopage
to detoxify	désintoxiquer
detoxification	la désintoxication
to rehabilitate	réadapter, réhabiliter
rehabilitation	la réhabilitation
to wean	sevrer
to wean oneself off	se détacher de
to get off drugs	abandonner la drogue
to give up sth.	renoncer à qch.
to relapse	rechuter
a relapse	une rechute

Expressions

to be on drugs	se droguer
to experiment with drugs	toucher à la drogue
to spike a drink	verser une drogue dans une boisson
to dabble with drugs	tâter de la drogue
to stay clear of drugs	ne pas toucher à la drogue
to get a fix	se faire une injection
to get high	s'éclater
to get stoned	se défoncer
to be hooked on	être intoxiqué, être accro
to be dependent on	être en état de dépendance
to be strung out on drugs	être sous l'effet de la drogue
to go cold turkey	être en manque
to develop a habit	contracter une habitude
to kick drugs	renoncer à la drogue
to go back on drugs	se remettre à la drogue
to smash a drugs ring	démanteler un réseau de drogue

Vocabulaire complémentaire

Drugs	La drogue
acid	le LSD
pot, grass	l'herbe, la marijuana
hash	le hasch
a reefer	un joint, un pétard
coke	la coca
stuff	la came
amphetamines, speed	les amphétamines
barbiturates	les barbituriques
a hallucinogenic [hælu:sɪnə'dʒənɪk] drug	une drogue hallucinogène
a magic mushroom	un champignon magique/ hallucinogène
paste	la pâte
resin	la résine
to be adulterated with	être coupé avec

Addiction	La dépendance
hypodermic	hypodermique
a disposable syringe	une seringue jetable
[illegible]	[illegible]
to shoot up	se shooter
intravenous	intraveineux
to swallow	avaler, gober
to snort	renifler
withdrawal symptoms	des symptômes de manque
a junkie	un drogué

Drug traffic	Le trafic de drogue
a baron	un baron
a runner, a mule	un passeur
a peddler	un revendeur
to ship, to consign	expédier
a shipment, a consignment	une expédition

Processing	La fabrication
coca	la coca
a substitute	un produit de remplacement
a derivative	un dérivé
a chemical	un produit chimique
a lab	un labo

The fight against drugs	La lutte contre la drogue
to legalise	légaliser
legalisation	la légalisation
to decriminalise	dépénaliser
decriminalisation	la dépénalisation
to declassify	déclasser
relaxation	assouplissement
to confiscate	confisquer
confiscation	la confiscation
a drug bust	une opération anti-drogue
a bigwig, a kingpin	un gros bonnet
a kingfish	un gros poisson
small fry, minnows	le menu fretin
alternative crops	les cultures de substitution
a drugs clinic	un centre de soins aux toxicomanes
a drugs squad	une brigade des stupéfiants

Government told it is losing war on child drug taking

by Celia Hall, Medical Editor

The war on drug taking among children is having little or no impact, with figures released yesterday showing that the problem in England is getting worse. Millions of pounds of government money has been spent in recent years on school programmes to discourage children from drinking, taking drugs and smoking.

The latest survey among 11- to 15-year-olds showed that one in five took drugs in 2003, an increase of one per cent on the previous year. A quarter of these children drank alcohol regularly, also a one per cent increase. Children who drank were taking more than one drink a day. The average amount drunk each week was 9.5 units. Regular smoking was down by one per cent to nine per cent.

The survey of 10,000 children in 321 schools covered a full range of illegal substances, including cannabis, amphetamines, anabolic steroids, cocaine, crack, ecstasy, glue and solvents. Cannabis and "poppers" (amphetamines) were the drugs most likely to have been taken. Eight per cent of children, as young as 11, had taken drugs in 2003 compared with six per cent in 2002. Drug use rose sharply with age. By the time they were 15, 38 per cent had taken drugs compared with 36 per cent in 2002. The number of 11-year-olds offered drugs rose from 16 per cent to 19 per cent.

Martin Barnes, the chief executive of the charity Drugscope, said: "We are particularly concerned about the small but nonetheless disturbing increase in the use of volatile substances. Around eight per cent of young people have used them in the last year." Last year £15.2 million was given to the Education Department for drug education and prevention projects. This has been reduced by £1 million.

Tim Loughton, the shadow health secretary, said: "It is unsurprising that the Government is losing the war against drugs when funding to support drug education and prevention has been cut by almost £1 million."

A Health Department spokesman said: "We are working with the Home Office and the Department for Education and Skills to reduce drug use and are looking to create long-term change of attitude, which will take time."

The Daily Telegraph, 1 April 2004

1 Say whether the following statements are true (T) or false (F).

1. School programmes to discourage children from taking drugs have been effective in recent years.
2. 19 per cent of 11- to 15-year-olds took drugs in 2002.
3. 25% of 11- to 15-year-old children drank alcohol regularly in 2003.
4. Drinking, drug taking and smoking among children were all on the increase in 2003 compared to 2002.
5. The survey showed that the older the children were, the more drugs they used.
6. In 2003, 19% of 11-year-old children offered drugs to other children.
7. Government money given to the Education Department was reduced from £15.2 million to £1 million.
8. The war on drug taking among children is a long-term process according to a Health Department spokesman.

2 Complete the words in the following sentences. Each dash represents one letter.

1. As the successor to Pablo Escobar of the Medellin c _ _ _ _ _ Don Berna is the world's most powerful d _ _ _ _ l _ _ _.
2. One of the reasons for the decision to r _ _ _ _ _ _ _ _ _ cannabis was to give the police more flexibility to focus on serious drugs such as h _ _ _ _ _.
3. A British drug s _ _ _ _ _ _ _ was arrested in Bangkok yesterday with 9,000 e _ _ _ _ _ _ pills in his trousers.
4. A United Nations drug agency urged governments to c _ _ _ _ d _ _ _ on the growth of "Internet pharmacies" illicitly shipping n _ _ _ _ _ _ _ and mood-changing drugs to Britain and other parts of Europe.

3 Fill in the thirteen lines across the grid with translations of the corresponding French words. This will give you the answer to number 14 in column D.

1. aiguille
2. amphétamines
3. stupéfiants
4. manque
5. trafic
6. chanvre
7. pilule
8. blanchiment
9. assouplissement
10. passeur
11. toxicomanie
12. gélule
13. sevrer
14. dépénaliser

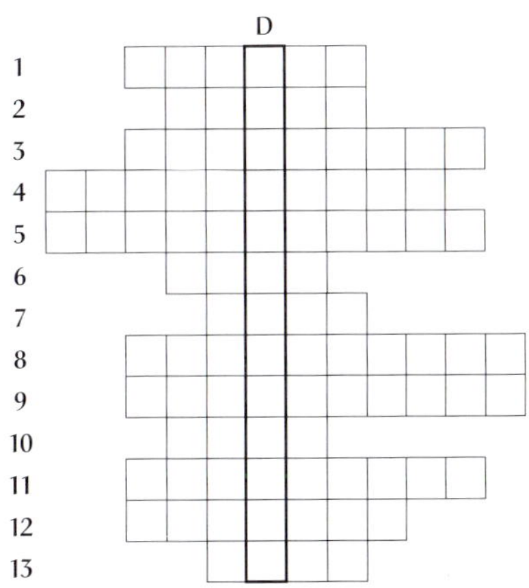

4 **Specific prepositions are used with particular words or phrases. For instance, in the article we find "to discourage from" and "to be concerned about". Suggest a preposition for each of the following verbs.**

1. to consist ...... sth./doing sth.
2. to (dis)approve ...... sth.
3. to rely ...... sth.
4. to concentrate ...... sth./ doing sth.
5. to steal sth. ...... sb.
6. to be interested ...... sth./doing sth.
7. to succeed ...... sth./doing sth.
8. to belong ...... sb.
9. to borrow sth ...... sb.
10. to rob sb ...... sth.

5 **Instead of using the phrase "15-year-olds" as in the article, we can either say "children who are 15 years old" or "15-year-old children" («year» is singular here because it is part of the adjective). Suggest two translations for each of the following phrases.**

1. un livre de 115 pages
2. une marche de 5 miles
3. un trafiquant de 50 ans
4. un poids de 20 kilos

6 **Fill in each blank in the article with the appropriate word from the following list. Use each word only once.**

smuggle	custom	criminals	cocaine
"mules"	cartels	imports	market
detection	traffickers		

Scanners to hunt for drugs in mail

by John Steele, Home Affairs Correspondent

...(1)... drug investigators are to experiment with new scanning devices to search for ...(2)... in letters and packages after a switch by ...(3)... from drug-carrying human ...(4)... to the mail.

New devices, based on "neutron scanning technology" not seen before in Britain, are likely to be used in trial tests of mail bags next year. Neutron "interrogation" of luggage and cargo has been studied and developed in America.

The new technology is to be used against traffickers trying to ...(5)... cocaine from Jamaica into Britain. Jamaican cocaine ...(6)... , though far smaller than cocaine shipped directly to Europe by Colombian ...(7)... , directly feed the crack cocaine ...(8)... in several British towns and cities.

Operation Airbridge, a British attempt to bolster the Jamaican authorities' efforts against traffickers in their country, has led to the increased ...(9)... of human "mules" smuggling cocaine to Britain. But the ...(10)... are known to have switched to packages.

The Daily Telegraph, 19 March 2004

£4m drugs factory found by police in bungalow

by David Sapsted

Chemicals to make millions of pounds of "clubbers' drugs" have been found in the back room of a seaside bungalow.

In an international operation by British and American drug enforcement officers, the raid on the £400,000 detached home in Brighton yielded enough chemicals to produce an estimated £4 million-worth of ecstasy, LSD and amphetamine tablets.

The raid followed the arrest of a 31-year-old American chemist from Idaho in a bar in the town on Wednesday. Officers are now trying to discover how so many chemicals could have been delivered to a quiet residential street without raising suspicions.

British police have been trained in safe search techniques in such operations by their American counterparts at the Drug Enforcement Agency (DEA).

Mike McManamon, DEA attache in London, said his agency had shut 8,000 similar factories in the USA in the past year. He said: "Firefighters are used to dealing with chemicals but these are crime scenes and police need to be taught safety. There is a danger from inhaling or ingesting these chemicals."

The Daily Telegraph, 14 February 2004

DEMONSTRATIONS AND RIOTS

15

LES MANIFESTATIONS ET LES ÉMEUTES

voir Introduction p. 142

Vocabulaire à haute fréquence

Rallies	Les rassemblements
to campaign for	faire campagne pour
a campaign	une campagne
a campaigner, an activist	un militant
to gather, to rally	(se) rassembler
a gathering	un rassemblement
a crowd	une foule
to organise	organiser
to stage, to hold	tenir, organiser
a meeting	une réunion
to demonstrate	manifester
a demonstration	une manifestation
a demonstrator, a protester	un manifestant
to protest [prə'test]	protester
a protest ['prəutest]	une protestation, une manifestation
to march	défiler
to chant	scander
a march	une marche, un défilé
a slogan	un slogan
a placard ['plækɑːd]	une pancarte
a banner	une banderole
a mob	une foule agitée

Security	La sécurité
a precaution	une précaution
a measure	une mesure
security forces	les forces de sécurité
riot police	la police anti-émeutes
to call in	faire appel à
to contain	contenir
to maintain, to keep	maintenir
order	l'ordre
to restore	rétablir
to call/to appeal for calm	appeler au calme
a helmet	un casque
a shield	un bouclier
a baton	une courte matraque
to wield	brandir, manier

Tension and clashes	La tension et les affrontements
an incident	un incident
trouble	des ennuis, des incidents
unrest	l'agitation
to disturb, to disrupt	troubler, perturber
disruption, disturbances	des troubles, des perturbations
to surge	déferler
a surge	un déferlement
to spark, to stir up	déclencher, provoquer
to flare up, to erupt, to break out	se déclencher brusquement
a flare-up, an eruption	une flambée, un accès
to turn violent	devenir violent
to degenerate	dégénérer
to clash with	se heurter à, affronter
a clash, a confrontation	un affrontement
a scuffle	une échauffourée
fierce [fɪəs]	intense, farouche
to drive back, to drive off	repousser
to break up, to disperse	(se) disperser
to chase	poursuivre

Riots	Les émeutes
to riot	manifester avec violence
a rioter	un casseur
to throw	jeter
to pelt	bombarder (projectiles)
to hurl	balancer
a missile	un projectile
a petrol bomb	un cocktail Molotov
to overturn	retourner

chaos ['keɪɒs], mayhem	la pagaille, la confusion
to use force	utiliser la force
tear gas	les gaz lacrymogènes
a water cannon	un canon à eau
to charge	charger
a charge	une charge
to ransack	saccager
an iron bar	une barre d'acier

Expressions

a peaceful demonstration	une manifestation dans le calme
to pass off peacefully	se dérouler sans incident
to call a demonstration	appeler à manifester
to take to the street	descendre dans la rue
law and order	l'ordre public
to keep at bay	tenir en respect
to keep in hand	maîtriser, contrôler
to get out of hand	dégénérer
to be marred by	être gâché par
to force one's way	se frayer un passage
a breach of the peace, a public order offence	une atteinte à la tranquillité publique
an outbreak of violence	une explosion de violence
an outburst/a flare-up of violence	une éruption de violence
fighting broke out	des bagarres ont éclaté
to go on the rampage	se déchaîner
to bring to a standstill	paralyser
to bring chaos	semer la confusion
to open fire (on)	ouvrir le feu (sur)
to condone violence	admettre la violence

Vocabulaire complémentaire

Rallies	Les rassemblements
a sit-in	un sit-in
a counter demonstration	une contre-manifestation
an anti-globalisation campaigner/activist	un alter-mondialiste
to parade	défiler
a parade	un défilé, une parade
the throng	la foule
a route	un parcours, un itinéraire
a steward, a marshal	un membre du service d'ordre des manifestants

a loud hailer	un mégaphone
to muster	rassembler
to hand out	distribuer
a leaflet	un tract
a petition	une pétition
a petitioner	un pétitionnaire

Security — La sécurité

a set-up	un dispositif
a police cordon	un cordon de police
to don	revêtir
gear	une tenue
clad in	revêtu de
a visor ['vaɪzə]	une visière
a truncheon ['trʌntʃən], a club	une longue matraque
to stem	endiguer
to hold off	tenir à distance
to restrain	maîtriser, contenir

Tension and clashes — La tension et les affrontements

a troublemaker	un perturbateur
an agitator	un agitateur
to provoke	provoquer
unprovoked	sans provocation
provocative	provocateur
provocation	la provocation
to daub	barbouiller
to dent	cabosser
to prohibit	interdire
an unlawful assembly, an illegal gathering	un rassemblement interdit
public disorder, disorderly behaviour	trouble de l'ordre public
criminal damage	dégradations volontaires
assault	violences (délit)
to outnumber	déborder
to obstruct	entraver
an obstruction	une entrave
a smoke grenade	une grenade fumigène
a stun grenade	une grenade assourdissante
a tear gas canister	une grenade lacrymogène
a bystander, an onlooker	un badaud
police brutality	les brutalités policières

Riots — Les émeutes

to defy	braver
in defiance of	sans tenir compte de

a catapult	un lance-pierres
to stone	lapider
a hail	une grêle
a Balaclava helmet	un passe-montagne
a pitched battle	une bataille rangée
a running battle	des affrontements incessants
a warning shot	un coup de semonce
to tear up	arracher, desceller
to set up	dresser
to erect [ɪ'rekt]	ériger
a barricade [bærɪ'keɪd]	une barricade

Anti-war demos mark Iraq anniversary

Twenty-five thousand anti-war protesters have marched through London to mark their opposition to the war in Iraq. The demonstrators headed for Trafalgar Square, where they listened to prominent anti-war speakers and released a cloud of black balloons – one for every soldier and civilian who has been killed in the conflict. Hundreds of Scots who opposed the war in Iraq gathered in Glasgow city centre this morning to register their protest to Tony Blair's policy.

Peaceful demonstrations have already taken place in cities around the world, with rallies in Hamburg, Tokyo, Seoul and across Australia. In Sydney, Australia's largest city, more than 3,000 people marched through the city centre chanting "end the occupation, troops out". They were carrying a caged effigy of the head of Australian Prime Minister John Howard, a strong supporter of the war. In Tokyo, several thousand people carrying signs saying "US Go Home" and "World Peace Now", marched to downtown Tokyo, not far from government ministry buildings.

Further demonstrations are expected in a day of world-wide action to mark the first anniversary of the war.

Two Greenpeace demonstrators scaled Big Ben this morning to mark the anniversary of the start of the Iraq war, sparking a security alert. Police were called to Big Ben at about 6.15am after the men were spotted climbing the clock tower. They reached the a ledge just below the clockface at about 9.30am and were intending to <u>unfurl</u> a banner reading Time for Truth, but were prevented from doing so by high winds. Stephen Tindale, Greenpeace executive director said: "It's time we got the truth about why thousands of people had to die in a war that the world did not want. Iraq posed no threat to Britain or the US, but still Tony Blair <u>drove a horse and cart through</u> the international security system – all because he puts his relationship with George Bush above the rule of law and his own electorate." Mr Tindale said it had been "easy" for the protestors to breach security at Big Ben.

The Daily Telegraph, 20 March 2004

1 Choose the right explanation for each of the following words or phrases underlined in the text.

1. to unfurl

A. to enrol
B. to unroll
C. to roll

2. to drive a horse and cart through

A. to force one's way through
B. to ride a horse through
C. to carry something with a horse through

2 Say whether the following statements are true (T) or false (F).

1. The biggest rally seems to have taken place in London.
2. The demonstrators in Glasgow marched to show their opposition to Britain's foreign policy.
3. Prime Minister John Howard was targeted because he backed the war in Iraq.
4. The police prevented two Greenpeace demonstrators from unfurling their banner.
5. According to Stephen Tindale, Tony Blair showed great diplomatic skill in getting round the international security system.

3 The first word in each list is taken from the article. Which of the other three should not be associated with it?

1. protesters, demonstrators, passers-by, campaigners
2. a banner, a placard, a ban, a sign
3. to march, to walk, to demonstrate, to parade
4. to breach, to strengthen, to violate, to break

4 Read the article again and find words which mean the same as the following.

1. to parade
2. to rally
3. gatherings
4. walkouts
5. to stir up

Police fire on Kurds in fifth day of Syria riots

by Robin Gedye, Foreign Affairs Writer

Thousands of Kurds fought pitched battles with paramilitary police across northern Syria yesterday as rioting, in which at least 30 people have died, worsened for the fifth day in a row.

Tanks were reported on the streets of Kameshli, on the Turkish border, where security forces responded with force after rioting broke out last Friday.

The trouble began at a football match at which Kurdish fans waved posters of President George W. Bush while being taunted by Syrian supporters with pictures of Saddam Hussein.

Syrian troops opened fire during a number of demonstrations by ethnic Kurds yesterday, killing at least seven people in the northern cities of Afrin and Aleppo, according to the Turkish state-run news agency.

It said police opened fire after seeking to prevent demonstrations marking the anniversary of Saddam's 1988 chemical weapons attack on Halabja, in the Kurdish region of Iraq, in which 5,000 people died.

A spokesman for the Kurdish Human Rights Project in London said Turkish tanks had been deployed on the border with Syria to prevent Kurds in Turkey crossing over in support. Witnesses reported that hundreds of Kurds had been arrested over the past five days of mounting troubles although Syria has refused to comment other than to reject any suggestion of inter-ethnic incidents.

Kurds comprise almost two million of Syria's 17 million population although about 200,000 of them are not recognised as citizens of the country as a punishment for seeking to establish an autonomous homeland.

Syria and Turkey watched the fall of Saddam with concern, fearing that it would unleash renewed determination among ethnic Kurds, who were brutally suppressed during the Iraqi tyrant's rule, for an autonomous region.

In an attempt to contain the mounting violence, Syria imposed curfews in a number of border towns yesterday. Among them was Ceylanpinar, where five people were killed and 39 injured in earlier fighting. Kurds demonstrated in London, Berlin and Paris, protesting that the situation would deteriorate unless there was outside intervention.

The Daily Telegraph, 18 March 2004

1 Choose the right explanation for each of the following words underlined in the article.

1. to taunt
A. to applaud, to encourage
B. to insult, to mock
C. to praise, to congratulate

2. curfew
A. ceasefire
B. lack of care
C. order prohibiting certain activities after a specific time

2 Say whether the following statements are true (T) or false (F).

1. Tanks were deployed to repress the upsurge of violence which led to running battles in the streets of Kameshli.
2. The Syrian police managed to prevent the demonstrations in commemoration of the 1988 attack in Halabja.
3. The Syrian government described this outburst of violence as inter-ethnic incidents.
4. One tenth of the Kurds living in Syria don't have Syrian citizenship.

3 Choose the appropriate endings for the following sentences.

1. Turkish tanks were deployed on the border with Syria
A. to prevent Kurds in Syria from crossing over.
B. to prevent reinforcements from joining Kurds in Syria.
C. to prevent Kurds from withdrawing from Syria.

2. Syria and Turkey watched the fall of Saddam Hussein with concern because
A. ethnic Kurds were brutally suppressed during the Iraqi tyrant's rule.
B. it could encourage ethnic Kurds to seek to establish an autonomous homeland.
C. ethnic Kurds supported him.

3. Outside intervention is needed
A. to suppress ethnic Kurds in Syria.
B. to impose curfews.
C. to curb the escalation of violence.

4 The first word in each list is taken from the article. Which of the other three should not be associated with it?

1. rioting, rampage, upheaval, revel
2. security forces, police, civilians, troops
3. to break out, to disrupt, to erupt, to flare up
4. trouble, disturbances, disruption, dissent

5 In English when we use a title followed by a name we use no article (no article + title + surname) just as in the article: "ø President George W. Bush". When a title is not followed by a proper name we use an article. Translate the following expressions in English.

1. le Président Chirac
2. le Premier ministre britannique
3. la Reine Elizabeth
4. le Premier ministre John Howard
5. le Capitaine Smith
6. le ministre des Affaires étrangères

TERRORISM AND REVOLUTIONS

16

LE TERRORISME ET LES RÉVOLUTIONS

voir Introduction p. 142

Vocabulaire à haute fréquence

Terrorism	Le terrorisme
war on terror	la guerre contre le terrorisme
a terrorist attack, an act of terror, a terror attack	un attentat
a terrorist	un terroriste
a terror suspect	un terroriste présumé
a target	une cible
to plant	poser, déposer
a car bomb	une voiture piégée
a lorry bomb	un camion piégé
a parcel bomb	un colis piégé
a letter bomb	une lettre piégée
an explosive device	un engin explosif
a bombing, a bomb attack	un attentat à la bombe
a bomber	un poseur de bombe
to blow oneself up	se faire sauter
a suicide bombing	un attentat suicide
a suicide bomber	un(e) kamikaze
a blast	une explosion
a crater	un cratère
bio-terrorism	le terrorisme biologique
a dirty bomb	une bombe radioactive/bactériologique

Hijackings / Les détournements

to hijack	détourner un véhicule
an airspace	un espace aérien
to skyjack, to hijack	détourner un avion
a hijacker	un pirate
a skyjacker, a hijacker	un pirate de l'air
air/sky marshals	policiers embarqués, gardes armés à bord
to divert	dérouter
a false alarm	une fausse alerte
to refuel	refaire le plein
to be grounded	être maintenu au sol

Revolutionary movements / Les mouvements révolutionnaires

a faction	une faction, une fraction
to rise	se soulever
an uprising	un soulèvement
a flashpoint	un point chaud
to rebel [rɪ'bel]	se rebeller
a rebellion	une rébellion
a rebel ['rebəl]	un rebelle
rebellious	rebelle
the armed wing	le bras armé
the political wing	la branche politique
underground	clandestin
an insurrection	une insurrection
a guerrilla	un guérillero
to revolt	se révolter
a revolt	une révolte
to struggle	lutter
an armed struggle	une lutte armée
paramilitary	paramilitaire
a civil war	une guerre civile
an ethnic war	une guerre ethnique
a homeland	une patrie

Seizing power / La prise du pouvoir

to plot	comploter
a plot	un complot
a plotter	un conspirateur
to foment	fomenter
a conspiracy	une conspiration
a separatist	un séparatiste
a coup, a putsch	un coup d'État, un putsch
to topple	faire tomber
to overthrow	renverser
to set up, to establish	établir

Expressions

to resort to violence	avoir recours à la violence
to take up arms/weapons	prendre les armes
to prime a bomb	amorcer une bombe
to be strapped with explosives	porter une ceinture d'explosifs
to carry out a bombing	perpétrer un attentat
to spread chaos	semer la désolation/la destruction
to admit responsibility, to claim responsibility	reconnaître, revendiquer la responsabilité
it was the work of ...	c'était l'œuvre de ...
to be behind sth.	être l'auteur de qch.
to bear the hallmark of	porter le sceau de
to make safe	rendre inoffensif
to meet a demand	satisfaire une exigence
to deal with terrorists	négocier avec les terroristes
to do a deal	passer un marché
to have dealings with	avoir des tractations avec
to condone terrorism	admettre le terrorisme
to sponsor terrorism	soutenir le terrorisme
to keep tabs on sb.	surveiller étroitement qn.
to mount/to organise an operation	monter une opération

Vocabulaire complémentaire

Terrorism	Le terrorisme
to defeat terrorism	vaincre le terrorisme
a commando	un commando
a prime target	une cible de choix
a hit man	un homme de main
a hostage taker	un preneur d'otages
hostage taking	prise d'otage
a captor	un ravisseur
a warlord	un chef de guerre
a reunion	des retrouvailles
debriefing	le déconditionnement psychologique
to harbour	abriter
a hotbed	une pépinière, un terrain fertile
a sanctuary	un sanctuaire
a haven	un havre, un refuge
to sabotage	saboter
a saboteur	un saboteur
a sabotage	un sabotage
an atrocity	une atrocité, une horreur
anthrax	l'anthrax
smallpox	la variole

ricin	la ricine
a death squad	un escadron de la mort
an anti-terrorist squad	une brigade anti-terroriste
an offshoot	une ramification

Bombings / Les attentats à la bombe

the bombsite	le lieu de l'attentat
to perpetrate	perpétrer
an outrage	un attentat
to booby trap	piéger à l'explosif
a booby trap	un dispositif piégé
a home-made bomb	une bombe artisanale
a detonator	un détonateur
a primer, a priming device	un dispositif de mise à feu
a timer	une minuterie
a hoax	un canular
a remote-controlled bomb	une bombe commandée à distance
indiscriminate	aveugle
at random	au hasard
to defuse	désamorcer
to detonate	faire exploser
a bomb disposal expert	un artificier

Revolutionary movements / Les mouvements révolutionnaires

to stand up	se dresser
an upheaval [ʌp'hiːvəl]	un bouleversement
unstable	instable
instability	instabilité
an insurgent	un insurgé
insurgent	insurrectionnel
turmoil	les turbulences
a feud	une lutte interne
the hard core	les irréductibles
intercommunal clashes	les affrontements entre communautés
to mutiny against	se mutiner contre
a mutiny	une mutinerie
a mutineer [mjuːtɪ'nɪə]	un mutin
guerrilla warfare	la lutte de guérilla
a militia [mə'lɪʃə]	une milice
a militiaman	un milicien
a vigilante	une barbouze, un membre d'une milice privée
a mercenary	un mercenaire
to secede, to break away	se séparer, faire sécession
a breakaway/separatist/splinter group	un groupe séparatisite/dissident

a fringe movement	un groupuscule
to break up	éclater, se désintégrer
a break-up	un éclatement, une désintégration
secession	la sécession
partition	la partition
motherland	la mère-patrie
self-determination	l'auto-détermination
self-rule, autonomy	l'autonomie
to disband	renvoyer dans les foyers
to grant	accorder
a status	un statut
independent	indépendant
independence	l'indépendance
sovereignty ['sɒvrɪntɪ]	la souveraineté

Combating rebellion and terrorism / La lutte contre la rébellion et le terrorisme

a checkpoint	un poste de contrôle
to frisk	fouiller corporellement
repression	la répression
covert	en sous-main, clandestin
undercover	clandestin, occulte
a no-go area	une zone de non-droit
an exclusion zone	une zone d'exclusion
to quash, to put down	réprimer, étouffer
to foil	déjouer
to crush	écraser
to storm	prendre d'assaut
to disarm, to decommission	désarmer
disarming, decommissioning	le désarmement
to mop up	nettoyer, ratisser
a mop-up operation	une opération de nettoyage/ratissage
a firing squad	un peloton d'exécution
bloodless	sans effusion de sang
bloody	sanglant

Seizing power / La prise du pouvoir

to depose	déposer
to oust	évincer
an attempted coup, a coup attempt	une tentative de coup d'État
to destabilise	déstabiliser
destabilisation	la déstabilisation
to undermine	saper, ébranler

"At least 50" killed in Iraq car bomb attack

At least 50 people were killed and another 50 injured when a car bomb exploded at a police station south of Baghdad as dozens of would-be recruits lined up to apply for jobs.
Tuesday morning's attack is believed to have been a suicide operation, carried out by a driver who detonated a red pickup as it passed by the station. Most of the victims were Iraqi civilians.
The blast followed warnings from occupation officials that Iraqi insurgents would step up attacks against Iraqis who work with the US-led coalition, especially in the build-up to the planned June 30 transfer of sovereignty to a provisional Iraqi government.
On Monday, US officials said a letter seized last month from an al-Qaida courier asked the terrorist leadership to help foment civil war here to undermine the coalition and the future Iraqi leadership.
The purported author of the letter was Abu Musab al-Zarqawi, a Palestinian-Jordanian suspected of al-Qaida links. The author boasted of having organized 25 suicide attacks in Iraq.
US paratroopers from the 82nd Airborne Division sealed off the area around the station and refused to allow journalists near the blast site about 30 miles south of Baghdad. No US or other coalition forces were killed or injured.
However, hospital director Razaq Jabbar said his facility had received 50 dead and 50 injured – all believed to be Iraqis. He said he had heard that three others died at another hospital. "This figure might increase," he said. "There were some body parts that haven't been identified yet. Some more bodies may be trapped under the rubble."
Hours after the attack, police opened fire in the air to disperse dozens of angry residents who stormed the wrecked police station after hearing rumours that the blast was caused by an American rocket.
Insurgents have mounted a string of car and suicide bombings in recent weeks. The deadliest so far has been in the northern city of Irbil on February 1 when two suicide bombers blew themselves up at two Kurdish party offices celebrating a Muslim holiday, killing at least 109 people.

AP, published in The Independent, 10 February 2004

1 Say whether the following statements are true (T) or false (F).

1. The people who were queuing in front of the police station wanted to work with the US-led coalition.
2. A booby-trapped vehicle was used in this attack.
3. US soldiers from the coalition were the target of this attack.
4. Abu Musab al-Zarquawi is suspected of sending a letter bomb.
5. The blast killed at least 50 Iraqis, injuring another 50.
6. In the police station area the explosion was believed to have been the work of the US Army.
7. So far, this attack has been the deadliest of a string of car and suicide bombings in recent weeks.

2 **Find words in the article which are similar in meaning to the following.**

1. blew up
2. onslaught
3. perpetrated
4. explosion
5. supposed
6. cordoned off
7. devastated
8. a series of

3 **Fill in the 13 lines across the grid with translations of the corresponding French words. This will give you the answer to number 14 in column D.**

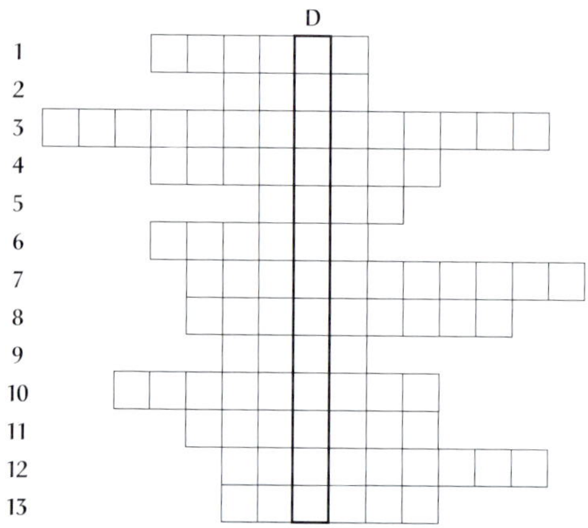

1. désamorcer 2. lutte interne 3. aveugle 4. pirate 5. se soulever 6. sanglant 7. clandestin 8. piéger à l'explosif 9. complot 10. saper, amoindrir 11. abriter 12. renverser 13. cible 14. kamikaze

4 **Read the following phrases taken from the article.**

"Tuesday morning's attack *is believed to have been* a suicide operation..."
"...his facility had received 50 dead and 50 injured – all *believed to be* Iraqis."

This kind of structure is often used in news reports to announce a piece of news believed to be true but not yet checked (translated by a conditional form in French). A number of other verbs are also often used: "thought", "reported", "alleged" and "said".

Translate the following sentences that use this structure.

1. Rebels are reported to have retaken the Town of Dondon. (*The Guardian*, 16 February 2004)
2. The blaze is believed to have started in a temporary storehouse. (*The Guardian*, 16 February 2004)
3. Senator Kerry's credibility is thought to be enhanced (as was John McCain's) because he is a Vietnam hero. (*The Daily Telegraph*, 21 January 2004)

Move to boost crackdown on terrorist finance

by Andrew Parker in Paris

The Financial Action Task Force, the international body that combats money laundering, on Friday unveiled plans to improve information exchange between countries on terrorist financing.

The FATF, at a meeting in Paris, also announced it was removing Egypt and the Ukraine from its blacklist of countries that do not have adequate controls against money laundering.

Better information exchange between countries on methods used by terrorist groups to fund their activities is vital to tackle organisations such as al-Qaeda. One possible reform by the FATF could be exchange of reports about suspected money laundering that are filed by banks to regulators.

The FATF's 31-member countries, mainly from the Americas and western Europe, reached political agreement with 13 non-member countries on the need to develop better mechanisms to collect and share information on terrorist financing. The 13 countries include some previously accused of being important sources of funds for terrorist groups, such as Saudi Arabia and the United Arab Emirates.

The other non-member countries at the FATF meeting were Algeria, Bahrain, China, Egypt, India, Indonesia, Kuwait, Malaysia, Morocco, Pakistan and the Philippines. They participated in a seminar on terrorist financing that focused on the risks posed by underground banking systems, cash couriers, charities and drugs trafficking.

Claes Norgren, FATF president, said: "This seminar played an important role in helping us reach out to key partners in the international effort against the financing of terrorism."

The Financial Times, February 27 2004

1 Read the article and find the following.

1. to support, to encourage
2. clampdown
3. concealing the source of money obtained illegally
4. a list of persons or groups that are under suspicion
5. to finance
6. clandestine
7. mules
8. non-profit organizations concerned with promoting a cause

Haiti rebels kill 14 policemen

Rebels in Haiti have killed 14 policemen in a gun battle with the official forces attempting to recapture a city, opposition leaders claimed. The shooting erupted when police tried to enter Gonaives to take it back from rebels who are demanding the resignation of President Jean-Bertrand Aristide.

The Observer, 8 February 2004

Men charged over Gaza bomb

Four Palestinians were charged yesterday with planting explosives that may have killed three American security guards in the Gaza Strip last October. The bombs were planted on the road leading from the Erez crossing point with Israel. A military prosecutor said the bombs were intended for Israeli tanks, but one may have been to blame for the 15 October blast that ripped apart the US diplomatic car.

The Observer, 8 February 2004

WAR AND ESPIONAGE

17

LA GUERRE ET L'ESPIONNAGE

voir Introduction p. 142

Vocabulaire à haute fréquence

General background	Contexte général
warfare	la guerre
warfighting techniques	les techniques de guerre
military	militaire
a serviceman	un militaire
a civilian	un civil
a soldier ['səuldʒə]	un soldat
a sailor	un marin
an airman	un aviateur
the army	l'armée
the navy	la Marine nationale
the air force	l'armée de l'air
the armed forces	les forces armées
a rapid reaction force	une force de réaction rapide
an officer	un officier
a captain	un capitaine
a veteran	un ancien combattant
a base	une base

Weapons	Les armes
conventional	conventionnel, classique
nuclear	nucléaire

the nuclear weapon	l'arme nucléaire
chemical ['kemɪkl]	chimique
biological	biologique
a weapons programme	un programme d'armement
to reprocess	retraiter
nuclear fuel rods	des barres de combustible nucléaire
deadly	mortel, meurtrier
to test	essayer
a test	un essai
proliferation	la prolifération
to deter	dissuader
a deterrent	une force de dissuasion
deterrence	la dissuasion
a ballistic missile	un missile balistique
intercontinental	intercontinental
strategic	stratégique
range	la portée
medium-range	de moyenne portée
intermediate-range	de portée intermédiaire
a warhead	une ogive, une tête
to site, to install	installer
a site, an installation	un site, une installation
to launch	lancer
Star Wars	la guerre des étoiles
offensive	offensif
defensive	défensif
an arsenal	un arsenal
an arms race	une course aux armements
to build up	renforcer, accumuler
arms build-up	accumulation des armements, le surarmement
to stockpile	constituer des stocks
a stockpile	un stock
a vessel	un vaisseau
a submarine	un sous-marin
a torpedo [tɔ:'pi:dəu]	une torpille
a nerve gas	un gaz neuro-toxique
germ warfare	la guerre bactériologique

Espionage — L'espionnage

to spy on	espionner
a spy	un espion
intelligence	les renseignements
intelligence services, intelligence agencies	les services secrets, les services de renseignements
secret	secret
covert	en sous-main, clandestin

an undercover agent	un agent secret
to infiltrate	infiltrer
an infiltration	une infiltration
to defect	passer dans l'autre camp
a defector	un transfuge
to pass	transmettre, divulguer
classified	classé secret
a file	un dossier
a leak	une fuite
to uncover	mettre à jour, révéler
to expose	démasquer
to betray	trahir
a betrayal	une trahison
a traitor	un traitre
treason	la trahison

Starting a war / L'entrée en guerre

an ally	un allié
to ally with	allier à
a coalition	une coalition
an enemy	un ennemi
a conflict	un conflit
to break out	éclater
to launch a war	déclencher une guerre
to invade	envahir
an invasion	une invasion
to deploy	déployer
deployment	le déploiement
to dispatch	envoyer
a border, a frontier	une frontière
to land	débarquer
a landing	un débarquement
an offensive	une offensive

Combat / Les combats

to drop a bomb	jeter une bombe
to shoot down, to down	abattre (un avion)
to sink	couler
to torpedo	torpiller
to intercept	intercepter
a battle	une bataille
a battlefield	un champ de bataille
a front	un front
an all-out war	une guerre totale
heavy fighting	des combats soutenus
to repel, to beat off	repousser
to overwhelm	submerger

to inflict	infliger
a loss	une perte
a prisoner	un prisonnier
to defeat	vaincre
a defeat	une défaite
a victory	une victoire
to liberate	libérer (un territoire)
liberation	la libération
to pull out, to withdraw	se retirer
a withdrawal, a pull-out	un retrait
a mediator	un médiateur
to sign	signer
a treaty	un traité
peace	la paix
a peace process	un processus de paix
a peace deal	un accord de paix

Expressions

to join the army	s'engager dans l'armée
a chief of staff	un chef d'état-major
to be in command of	avoir le commandement de
the Star Spangled Banner	la Bannière étoilée
the Union Flag/Jack	le drapeau britannique
a shot across the bows	un coup de semonce
to declare war on	déclarer la guerre à
to be at war with	être en guerre avec
a weapon of last resort	une arme de dernier recours
weapons of mass destruction	les armes de destruction massive
Strategic Defense Initiative (SDI)	l'Initiative de défense stratégique
to inflict heavy losses	infliger de lourdes pertes
to sustain heavy losses	subir de lourdes pertes
to strike a mine	heurter une mine
to die in action	mourir au combat
to put out of action	mettre hors de combat
a war of attrition	une guerre d'usure
a scorched earth policy	une politique de la terre brûlée
to decommission weapons	mettre des armes hors service, désarmer
to have access to	avoir accès à
to crack, to break a code	trouver la clé d'un code

Vocabulaire complémentaire

General background	Contexte général
the Admiralty	le ministère de la Marine
a battalion	un bataillon
a platoon	une section

a squadron	un escadron, une escadrille
a seaman	un marin
a convoy	un convoi
a paratrooper	un parachutiste
airborne	aéroporté
marines	l'infanterie de marine
a sentry	une sentinelle
to recruit	recruter
a recruit	une recrue
a child soldier	un enfant soldat
conscription	la conscription
a conscript	un conscrit
to draft *(US)*	appeler
draft *(US)*	la conscription
a draftee *(US)*	un appelé
a draft dodger *(US)*	un insoumis
a pacifist	un pacifiste
a peace movement	un mouvement pacifiste
cannon fodder	la chair à canon
a conscientious objector	un objecteur de conscience
a reservist	un réserviste
to enlist	s'engager
the barracks	la caserne
a garrison	une garnison
a war memorial	un monument aux morts
the national anthem	l'hymne national
a patriot ['peɪtrɪət, 'pætrɪət]	un patriote
patriotic [peɪtrɪ'ɒtɪk, pætrɪ'ɒtɪk]	patriotique
patriotism	le patriotisme
jingoism	le chauvinisme national
jingoistic	chauvin
a graduated/flexible response	une riposte graduée
a task force	une force d'intervention
a no-fly zone	une zone interdite de survol
a buffer zone	une zone tampon
a peacekeeping force	une force d'interposition
combat troops	les troupes de combat
crack troops, elite troops	les troupes d'élite
battle dress	tenue de combat
fatigues	un treillis
logistics	la logistique
a prisoner of war	un prisonnier de guerre
a detainee	un détenu
a detention camp	un camp de détenus

Military personnel | Le personnel militaire

the chain of command	la chaîne de commandement
hierarchy	la hiérarchie
an admiral	un amiral
a commander	un chef militaire
a commander-in-chief, a commanding officer	un commandant en chef
a general	un général
a brigadier-general	un général de brigade
a major-general	un général de division
a lieutenant-general	un général de corps d'armée
a colonel ['kɜ:nl]	un colonel
a major	un commandant
a lieutenant [lef'tenənt, lu:'tenənt]	un lieutenant
a non-commissioned officer	un sous-officier
a sergeant ['sɑ:dʒənt]	un sergent
a private	un simple soldat
a chaplain	un aumônier
a standard bearer	un porte-drapeau
a court martial	une cour martiale
to demote	rétrograder
to discharge	rendre à la vie civile

Weapons | Les armes

a fleet	une flotte
a destroyer	un contre-torpilleur
a frigate	une frégate
an aircraft carrier	un porte-avions
a minesweeper	un dragueur de mines
a flagship	un navire amiral
amphibious	amphibie
anti-aircraft	anti-aérien
a chopper	un hélico
a fighter	un chasseur
a bomber	un bombardier
a stealth bomber	un bombardier furtif
a strike helicopter, a helicopter gunship	un hélicoptère d'attaque
a personnel carrier	un transport de troupes
a first-strike weapon	arme de première frappe
a laser-guided bomb	une bombe guidée au laser
to step up	intensifier
to escalate, to intensify	(s') intensifier
escalation	l'escalade
to wipe out	anéantir
a neutron bomb	une bombe à neutrons
a fuel air bomb	bombe à effet de souffle
to train on	orienter sur

anti-ballistic, anti-missile	anti-missile
a shield	un bouclier
a laser	un laser
a beam	un rayon
a sensor	un capteur
smart weapons	les armes intelligentes
bacteriological	bactériologique
mustard	la moutarde
to scrap	mettre au rebut
armament, weaponry	l'armement
overkill	la surcapacité de destruction
a balance	un équilibre
to disarm	désarmer
disarmament	le désarmement
unilateral	unilatéral
multilateral	multilatéral
a moratorium	un moratoire

Espionage — L'espionnage

counter espionage, counter intelligence	le contre-espionnage
a satellite spy	un satellite espion
a spy plane	un drone
hush-hush	archi-secret
a mole	une taupe
a cipher	un chiffre, un code
to decipher	déchiffrer
to tap	mettre sur écoute
to bug	installer un micro
eavesdropping	l'écoute
to lure	persuader par la ruse
a bait	un appât
to expel	expulser
an expulsion	une expulsion

Starting a war — L'entrée en guerre

to manœuvre [məˈnuːvə]	manœuvrer
a manœuvre	une manœuvre
to concentrate	concentrer
a concentration	une concentration
to reinforce, to beef up	renforcer
a reinforcement	un renforcement
to call up	appeler, rappeler
a call-up, a call-out	un appel, un rappel
an alliance	une alliance
neutral	neutre
neutrality	la neutralité

a warrior	un guerrier
a warmonger	un va-t-en guerre
a hawk	un faucon
a dove	une colombe
to blockade	faire le blocus de
a blockade	un blocus
to intervene |ɪntəˈviːn|	intervenir
an intervention	une intervention
an aggression	une agression
an aggressor	un agresseur
a pre-emptive strike	une attaque préventive

Combat — Les combats

a ground/land offensive	une offensive terrestre
a beachhead, a bridgehead	une tête de pont
to overrun	envahir
a counterattack	une contre-attaque
to strike back	répliquer
to return fire	riposter
an onslaught, an assault	un assaut
a stronghold	un bastion
a bulwark	un rempart, une fortification
to pound	pilonner
to airdrop	parachuter
an airdrop	un parachutage
a dogfight	un combat aérien
to bail/bale out, to eject	s'éjecter
to withstand sth.	résister à qch.
to hold out	tenir bon
to fight off, to repulse	repousser
a trench	une tranchée
to entrench	retrancher
to dig in	se retrancher
a foxhole	un abri individuel
to close in	cerner
to encircle	encercler
to advance	avancer
an advance	une avancée
to scuttle	saborder
to retreat	battre en retraite
a retreat	une retraite
to fall back	se replier
a setback	un revers
to rout |raʊt|	mettre en déroute
a rout	une déroute
to desert	déserter
to capture	capturer

a capture	une capture
unconditional	sans condition
to capitulate	capituler
a capitulation	une capitulation
an armistice	un armistice
peace talks	des pourparlers de paix
reconciliation	la réconciliation
an olive branch	un rameau d'olivier
a safe haven, a security zone	une enclave de sécurité, une zone de protection

Blair Battles to Calm Iraq Bugging Row

by Katherine Baldwin

LONDON - Tony Blair battled on Friday to rise above a row sparked by claims of British subterfuge at the United Nations but the spying furor snowballed as former U.N. officials complained their phones had been tapped.

The Prime Minister was addressing a conference of his Labour Party in Scotland where he was expected to steer clear of the bugging charge and focus on domestic issues in yet another bid to put the controversy over the Iraq war behind him.

But the fallout from the bugging charge – made by former British minister Clare Short – proved relentless as former U.N. Secretary-General Boutros Boutros-Ghali and two former U.N. arms inspectors said they believed they had been spied on. "From the first day I entered my office they told me: beware, your office is bugged, your residence is bugged," Boutros-Ghali told the BBC. "It is a tradition that member states that have the technical capacity to bug will do it without hesitation," he said.

Short, who was in government at the time when London and Washington were seeking U.N. backing to attack Iraq, kicked up a diplomatic storm with her claim Britain had bugged the offices of U.N. Secretary-General Kofi Annan in the run-up to the war. Her claim thwarted Blair's efforts to draw a line under the conflict and focus on the domestic agenda ahead of an expected 2005 general election. British newspapers splashed the "spying scandal" across their front pages. Short, who resigned after the war, said she had seen transcripts of Annan's conversations and that the spying "was being done for some time."

Blair declined to address the charge beyond saying British security services acted within domestic and international law.

Escaping the eavesdroppers

But Richard Butler, a former chief U.N. weapons inspector in Iraq, added his voice to the spying row, saying "there was abundant evidence that we were being constantly monitored."

"I had to go to the basement cafe in the U.N. where there was heaps of noise or I'd go and take a walk in Central Park and keep walking" to avoid eavesdroppers, he told BBC Radio. His successor Hans Blix also said he believed his phone had been tapped, according to media reports from Australia.

The allegations could hinder Blair's efforts to regain the public's trust. His trust ratings plummeted in the wake of the Iraq conflict following the failure to find weapons of mass destruction – the primary Anglo-American reason for the war.

He took a further hit over the suicide of a weapons scientist at the heart of a row between the government and the BBC over allegations Blair's office had deliberately exaggerated the threat from Iraq to support its case for war. An official inquiry cleared Blair of any blame for the suicide but his public image has been damaged. A YouGov poll for The Daily Telegraph on Friday showed that the "trust" factor remains a thorn in Blair's side. Asked whether they thought the government had been honest and trustworthy, 67 percent said "No" while 27 percent said "Yes." Blair, though, was the first choice for Prime Minister over his political rivals, according to the poll.

Reuters, 27 February 27 2004

1 Choose the right explanation for each of the following words underlined in the article.

1. fallout
A. consequence
B. cause
C. reason

2. relentless
A. severe
B. persistent
C. wrong

3. to thwart
A. to encourage
B. to prevent
C. to help

4. to plummet
A. to increase slowly
B. to decrease quickly
C. to remain stable

2 Say whether the following statements are true (T) or false (F).

1. The UN bugging row intensified on Friday.
2. Tony Blair has managed to dispel the bugging charge he has been the target of.
3. Clare Short's claims of UN bugging by British intelligence sparked a diplomatic turmoil.
4. Mr Annan's telephone and fax lines were secure.
5. Any action carried out by British intelligence was legal according to Mr Blair.
6. Mr Butler claimed he was forced to hold confidential talks with contacts during walks in New York's Central Park.

7. Former UN chief weapons inspector Hans Blix could phone safe in the knowledge that any pieces of information he gave would remain confidential.
8. The main reason to go to war against Iraq was Iraq's alleged possession of weapons of mass destruction.
9. Blair's office was found guilty of exaggerating the threat from Iraq.
10. Despite his damaged public image, Mr Blair is the favourite for the expected 2005 general election, according to a recent poll.

3 Which of the four words in each list should not be associated with the others?

1. to bug, to tap, to wire, to lure
2. a row, a dispute, a warning, a controversy
3. to snowball, to increase, to wipe out, to grow
4. to spark, to escalate, to cause, to bring about

4 Complete the missing words. Each dash represents one letter.

1. Sri Lanka's rebels have angrily described a new political alliance as a threat to peace which may provoke e _ _ _ _ _ w _ _.
2. United States _ _ f _ _ _ _ y in southern central Iraq have been engaged in heavy f _ _ _ _ _ _ _ with Iraqi militiamen for control of the strategically important town of Samawah.
3. Security has been tightened at the Guantanamo Bay d _ _ _ _ t _ _ _ c _ _ _.
4. US Secretary of State Colin Powell has conceded that Iraq may not have possessed any stocks of w _ _ _ _ _ _ o _ _ a _ _ d _ _ _ _ _ c _ _ _ _.

Nato sends more troops to Kosovo

by Peter Spiegel in London, Judy Dempsey in Brussels and Eric Jansson in Belgrade

Nato on Thursday began urgently deploying an additional 1,000 troops to Kosovo to quell ethnic violence in the province that has left 31 people dead. The UK will spearhead the force, contributing 600 troops who will be joined by soldiers from the US and Italy.

France announced on Friday that it is to send an additional 400 troops, 200 of which will leave immediately.

The eruption of violence this week between ethnic Albanians and Serbs is the worst in Kosovo since the end of the civil war in 1999, when Nato intervened to expel Serb forces and install a provisional government under the United Nations.

The UK troops, which will be deployed from Britain, will be joined by about 300 US and Italian forces that will move into Kosovo from neighbouring Bosnia, bringing the Nato force in Kosovo to about 20,000. Nato officials said they hope the additional forces would help prevent violence from spiralling out of control. "I think it's clear there has been simmering ethnic tension and these unfortunate incidents have brought that out into the open once again," Geoff Hoon, the UK Defence Secretary, said. "It has occurred in and around [the town of] Mitrovica, but perhaps more disturbingly, that seems to have spilled over into violence in a number of other communities."

Although a large number of troops were already in Kosovo as part of Nato's Kfor operations, an alliance official said the decision was made to call in more troops because "every soldier was now needed in the province to restore calm and prevent further outbursts of unrest".

The official would not say why Nato did not dismantle roadblocks, which had been put up in recent days by ethnic Albanians and Serbs and had added to the tension.

The British troops will be sent to the provincial capital of Pristina, possibly to fill in for Nato forces that have been sent to the Mitrovica area.

The Financial Times, 19 March 2004

18 MISCELLANEOUS TOPICS

SUJETS DIVERS

voir Introduction p. 142

Vocabulaire à haute fréquence

Sexuality	La sexualité
morals	la moralité
sex	le sexe
sex education	l'éducation sexuelle
sexual intercourse	rapport sexuel
a partner	un partenaire
an affair	une liaison
permissive	permissif
permissiveness	la permissivité
contraception	la contraception
contraceptive	contraceptif
a pill	une pilule
a condom	un préservatif
family planning	le planning familial
birth control	la régulation des naissances
a homosexual, a gay	un homosexuel
a metrosexual	un métrosexuel
a lesbian	une lesbienne
heterosexual, straight	hétérosexuel

Abortion and euthanasia / L'avortement et l'euthanasie

pregnant	enceinte
a pregnancy	une grossesse
a single mother	une mère célibataire
unborn	pas encore né
to terminate	interrompre
a termination	une interruption
to abort	avorter
an abortion	un avortement
the morning-after pill	la pilule du lendemain
an unwanted pregnancy	une grossesse non désirée
teenage pregnancy	la grossesse chez les adolescentes
an embryo ['embrɪəʊ]	un embryon
a foetus ['fi:təs]	un foetus
a human being	un être humain
euthanasia [ju:θə'neɪzjə]	l'euthanasie
to legalise	légaliser
legalisation	la légalisation

Women's rights / Les droits de la femme

male	masculin
female	féminin
an object	un objet
sexism	le sexisme
a sexist	un sexiste
a male chauvinist	un phallocrate
male chauvinism	la phallocratie
equality	l'égalité
gender discrimination	la discrimination sexuelle
an opportunity	une chance
to liberate	libérer
to emancipate	émanciper
emancipation	l'émancipation
to stereotype ['sterɪətaɪp]	stéréotyper
a stereotype	un stéréotype
housekeeping	les travaux du ménage
the breadwinner	le soutien de famille

Immigration / L'immigration

a foreigner, an alien ['eiliən]	un étranger
foreign, alien	étranger
to emigrate	émigrer
emigration	l'émigration
an emigrant	un émigrant
immigration	l'immigration
an immigrant	un immigrant

to migrate [maɪ'greɪt]	migrer
a migration	une migration
a migrant	un migrant
to settle	s'installer
a settler	un colon
a settlement	une installation, une colonie de peuplement
to dismantle	démanteler
a permit	un permis
legal	en situation régulière
illegal	clandestin
a citizen	un citoyen
citizenship	la citoyenneté
to naturalise	naturaliser
naturalisation	la naturalisation
to melt	fondre
a melting-pot	un creuset
multi-cultural	multi-culturel
to adapt	s'adapter
adaptation	l'adaptation
to integrate	(s')intégrer
integration	l'intégration
a quota ['kwəʊtə]	un contingent
ethnic	ethnique
a minority	un minorité
a prejudice	un préjugé
racial	racial
a racist	un raciste
racism	le racisme
to discriminate	faire de la discrimination
discrimination	la discrimination
to segregate	faire de la ségrégation
segregation	la ségrégation
a ghetto	un ghetto

Human rights — Les droits de l'homme

to oppress	opprimer
oppression	l'oppression
free	libre
freedom	la liberté
to move	se déplacer
movement	le déplacement
to banish	exiler, bannir
to deport	déporter
deportation	la déportation
ethnic cleansing ['klenzɪŋ]	la purification ethnique
a right	un droit

a charter	une charte
a convention	une convention
to abuse sth. [ə'bju:z]	attenter à qch.
an abuse [ə'bju:s]	une atteinte, un non-respect
to violate	violer
a violation	une violation
to persecute	persécuter
persecution	la persécution
to harass	harceler
harassment	le harcèlement
to pick on sb.	harceler qn.
a dissident	un dissident
to torture	torturer
an ordeal [ɔ:'dɪəl]	une épreuve, un calvaire
to disappear, to vanish	disparaître
a disappearance	une disparition
missing	disparu
to grant	accorder
to deny	refuser
political asylum	l'asile politique
an asylum seeker	un demandeur d'asile
a concentration camp	un camp de concentration
a labour camp	un camp de travail
war crimes	les crimes de guerre
crimes against humanity	les crimes contre l'humanité
a mass grave	un charnier, une fosse commune

Electronics and computers — L'électronique et les ordinateurs

a component	un composant
a chip	une puce
data ['deɪtə, 'dætə]	les données
a data base	une base de données
to process	traiter
processing	le traitement
a processor	un processeur
word processing	le traitement de textes
computing	l'informatique
to computerise	informatiser
computerisation	l'informatisation
a CD-Rom	un CD-Rom
a laptop (computer)	un (ordinateur) portable
a desktop computer	un ordinateur de bureau
a memory	une mémoire
to erase [ɪ'reɪz, ɪ'reɪs], to delete [dɪ'li:t]	effacer

a website	un site internet
dot	point
to download	télécharger
to update	mettre à jour
to upgrade	améliorer
a program	un programme
an operating system	un système d'exploitation
software	le logiciel
hardware	le matériel
to hack	pirater
a hacker	un pirate informatique
a password	un mot de passe
to log on	se connecter
broadband	le haut débit
e-mail	le courrier électronique, courriel
an attachment	un fichier attaché
a file	un fichier
file sharing	le partage de fichiers
a worm, a virus, a bug	un virus
to infect	infecter
to clean up	nettoyer
a cybercafé	un cybercafé
a computer game	un jeu sur PC
a games console	une console de jeux

Expressions

to have sex	avoir des rapports sexuels
sexually transmitted diseases (STD)	les maladies sexuellement transmissibles (MST)
a red-light district	un quartier réservé/chaud
to have an abortion	se faire avorter
to be born out of wedlock	être né hors mariage
a single parent family	une famille monoparentale
to go out to work	prendre un emploi
the right of abode	le droit de s'établir
to be prejudiced against	avoir des préjugés contre
to be detained without trial	être détenu sans jugement
a prisoner of conscience	un prisonnier d'opinion
crime against humanity	crime contre l'humanité
the Data Protection Registrar	la Commission informatique et liberté
computer aided design	la conception assistée par ordinateur
to gain access to	obtenir l'accès à

Vocabulaire complémentaire

Sexuality	La sexualité
promiscuous	de mœurs légères
promiscuity	la promiscuité sexuelle
extra-marital	extra conjugal
to womanise	courir les femmes
casual sex	les rapports sexuels de rencontre
unprotected sex	les relations sexuelles non protégées
sexual harassment	le harcèlement sexuel
a brothel	une maison close
a clinic	un centre médico-social
a French letter	une capote anglaise
a diaphragm	un diaphragme
a coil	un stérilet
a jelly	une gelée
to sterilise	stériliser
sterilisation	la stérilisation
abstinence	l'abstinence

Abortion and euthanasia	L'avortement et l'euthanasie
unwanted	non souhaité
legitimate	légitime
illegitimate	illégitime
a bastard	un bâtard
pro-life	opposé à l'avortement
pro-choice	partisan de l'avortement
mercy killing	l'euthanasie
assisted suicide	le suicide accompagné

Women's rights	Les droits de la femme
motherhood	la maternité
to bring up children	élever des enfants
a day-care centre *(US)*	une halte-garderie
a creche, a day nursery	une crèche
domestic/household appliances	les appareils ménagers
to break up	se briser (mariage)
to divorce	divorcer
a divorce	un divorce
alimony	une pension alimentaire

Immigration	L'immigration
a native	un autochtone
a fellow citizen	un concitoyen

a resident	un habitant
a national	un ressortissant
an expatriate [eks'pætrɪət]	un expatrié
to adjust	(s')adapter
an adjustment	une adaptation
to assimilate	assimiler
an assimilation	une assimilation
a root	une racine
to uproot	déraciner
a way of life	un mode de vie
a lifestyle	un style de vie
an inner city area	un quartier urbain défavorisé
a menial job	un emploi subalteme
to exploit	exploiter
exploitation	l'exploitation
a sweatshop	un atelier clandestin, ou à main-d'oeuvre sous-payée
positive discrimination *(UK)*, affirmative action *(US)*	quotas pour minorités, discrimination positive
xenophobia [zenə'fəubɪə]	la xénophobie
to repatriate	rapatrier
repatriation	le rapatriement

Human rights / Les droits de l'homme

a resolution	une résolution
to comply with sth.	se conformer à qch.
to guarantee [gærən'tiː]	garantir
a guarantee	une garantie
to safeguard	sauvegarder
a safeguard	une sauvegarde
a breach	une infraction, un manquement
to flout	bafouer
to intimidate	intimider
intimidation	l'intimidation
to muzzle	museler
a witch hunt	une chasse aux sorcières
a hunger strike	une grève de la faim
to forcefeed	alimenter de force
to exile ['ekzaɪl]	exiler
exile	l'exil
an exile	un exilé
an exodus	un exode
an influx	un afflux

Electronics and computers	L'électronique et les ordinateurs
to display	afficher
a display	un affichage
to connect	relier
connection	la liaison
a network	un réseau
open-source computing	l'informatique libre, le libre
wi-fi, wireless broadband	le haut débit sans fil
a PDA (Personal Digital Assistant)	un agenda électronique, un organizer

Lib Dems call for assisted suicide and for teenage right to see porn

by Colin Brown, Political Editor

The Liberal Democrats last night voted overwhelmingly to adopt legalising euthanasia as part of its official policy. The three-to-one vote at the party's spring conference in favour of making medically assisted suicide legal caused <u>outrage</u> last night.

Lord Alton, a leading Lib Dem peer and a campaigner for the Society for the Protection of the Unborn Child (SPUC), condemned the policy as a "disaster" for the terminally ill, disabled and the medical profession. He warned: "The right to die will become the duty to die."

The Rev Joanna Jepson, who is taking legal action in the High Court to stop abortion for trivial complaints such as cleft palate*, was shocked by the vote. "I am very surprised at the Liberal Democrats," she said. "It is <u>dreadful</u> news. It is yet another battle that will have to be fought."

The vote also came as an embarrassment to Charles Kennedy, the Lib Dem leader, who last night was distancing himself from his party's own policy. "Charles would not vote for this in the House of Commons," said one of his officials.

The Lib Dems also voted overwhelmingly to reduce the legal age for teenagers to view pornography in sex shops from 18 to 16 years.

Labour and Conservative leaders last night were jubilant that the Lib Dems had made a double blunder. One senior Labour official said: "They are just not a serious party with these policies."

The vote in favour of medically assisted suicide was praised by Dr Evan Harris, the former Lib Dem health spokesman. He said: "It shows the Lib Dems are prepared to debate controversial issues. It doesn't tie the parliamentary party."

The policy would allow doctors legally to provide competent adults with assistance to die in cases of terminal illness or severe incurable illness where patients were without hope of recovery. Requests for medical assistance to die would have to be in writing. Lib Dem MPs will be allowed a free vote on the issue if a Bill is introduced, but it may be difficult to keep out of its election manifesto.

Dr Liam Fox, the joint chairman of the Conservative Party, said of the euthanasia policy: "This is typical of a party that has lost all sense of priorities. It is a moral and intellectual <u>muddle</u>. This is an issue which should be left to individual conscience. It should not form part of party policy." The proposal on pornography would also allow 16-year-olds to appear in porn films.

The Daily Telegraph, 21 March 2004

* fente palatine

1 Choose the right explanation for each of the following words underlined in the article.

1. outrage
A. indifference
B. indignation
C. euthanasia

2. dreadful
A. good
B. terrible
C. pleasant

3. muddle
A. debate
B. confusion
C. issue

2 Say whether the following statements are true (T) or false (F).

1. One third of the Lib Dems voted in favour of euthanasia legalisation.
2. There were discordant voices within the Lib Dem party about the vote on assisted suicide.
3. J. Jepson is against abortion for medical reasons such as birth defects.
4. Charles Kennedy stood by his party's official policy.
5. After this vote the legal age to view pornography in the UK is now 16.
6. The Labour and the Conservative parties don't share the same vision as the Lib Dems on euthanasia.
7. If a Bill on the legalisation of euthanasia is introduced, Lib Dem parliamentarians will have to follow the party's line.
8. Euthanasia should have nothing to do with a party's manifesto, according to Dr Liam Fox.
9. The policy on pornography would allow 16-year-olds to watch and appear in porn films.

3 The first word in each list is taken from the article. Find which of the other three should not be associated with it.

1. euthanasia, assisted suicide, attempted killing, mercy killing
2. duty, obligation, legitimacy, responsibility
3. abortion, promiscuity, termination, miscarriage
4. ill, unhealthy, sick, harmful

4 Complete the words in the following sentences. Each dash represents one letter.

1. The Nepalese National H _ _ _ _ Rights Commission says that thousands of anti-monarchy protesters are held in i _ _ _ _ _ _ conditions, often without access to food or water.
2. Voters in Slovenia have rejected plans to restore rights stripped from e _ _ _ _ _ minorities after the country's independence from Yugoslavia.
3. In 2003, more than 9,000 a _ _ _ _ _ s _ _ _ _ _ _ were refused welfare support under the new rules, which demand that asylum is applied for "as soon as reasonably practicable" after arrival in the UK.
4. A major at the centre of an Army sex tribunal admitted he was a womaniser, but denied s _ _ _ _ _ h _ _ _ _ _ _ _ _ _
5. A special report in Africa asks why people avoid using c _ _ _ _ _ _ even when faced with the risk of HIV infection?

Revolutions in waiting

France has suddenly stolen a march over Britain in the provision of fast "broadband" access to the internet. France Telecom is launching a service enabling it to send as many as 100 TV channels down existing copper wire phone lines. This is done by upgrading the lines to ADSL broadband technology carrying data at nearly 12 times the speed that BT's ADSL lines can currently manage. This is more than enough to provide high-quality television pictures. The service was launched in Paris this week and will be rolled out to other cities later this year.

People used to say of broadband access to the internet: "What's the killer application that will make people want to use it?" To those who already have it, the speed at which information can be accessed and the "always-on" nature of the connection are answer enough. But now other key uses are emerging. If people adopt broadband for multi-channel television, it would boost the take-up of digital television (thereby accelerating the analogue switch-off date), while widening access to the internet which, in turn, could help bridge the threat of a "digital divide" of haves and have-nots.

The prospect of television by phone line coincides with the imminent arrival of another "killer app" for the web. This could be the year when telephone calls via the (broadband) internet start to take off, as they already have in a big way in Japan. Since the cost of the internet part of the telephone call's journey is virtually zero, this could lead to a large rise in poorer people adopting broadband in order to get cheap telephone calls: another way of bridging the digital divide through the back door. If internet telephony takes off in a big way, it will have another consequence – it would make most of the inner-city telephone exchanges largely redundant, providing a property bonanza for BT and liberating a lot of inner-city space that could be turned into houses. And the real moral of all this? It is time Britain started rolling out real broadband and not the 512 kilobits-a-second that masquerades as it at the moment. We are still fighting yesterday's battle, not tomorrow's.

(leader) The Guardian, 27 March 2004

1 Choose the right explanation for each of the following words underlined in the article.

1. take-up

A. development
B. ending
C. fall

2. a "killer app"

A. a great function
B. a great appreciation
C. a great apprehension

3. bonanza

A. anything that brings indignation
B. anything that brings great wealth and prosperity
C. anything that brings problems

2 Say whether the following statements are true (T) or (F).

1. France is one step ahead of Britain with regard to fast broadband access to the internet.
2. Digital TV is now available via broadband access to the internet in France.
3. BT is already able to provide the same access to digital TV as France Telecom.
4. Paris was the first city to be equipped with that new service before it spread across France.
5. People who have broadband access to the internet are still doubtful about its advantages.
6. With broadband access to the internet, people can stay connected to the web with no time limit.
7. Thanks to the internet, analogue TV could disappear earlier than expected.
8. Phoning via the internet is very popular in Japan.
9. Cheap internet telephony could widen the digital gap of haves and have-nots.
10. BT could take advantage of the development of internet telephony by selling part of its downtown property.
11. The speed of 512 kb per second is not real broadband according to the author.
12. Britain is on the right track to be competitive as regards broadband access to the internet.

3 Fill in the blanks in the article with words from the following list.

trial	the web	campaign
freedom	companies	internet
crackdown	pornographic	sexual acts
websites	meeting	

US and UK crack down on web porn

Britain and the United States are to work together to shut down violent sex ...(1)... , it emerged today.

Officials on both sides of the Atlantic will decide how to act against extreme ...(2)... sites, which were implicated in the ...(3)... of the man who killed Brighton teacher Jane Longhurst.

Initial steps were agreed by the home secretary, David Blunkett, during a ...(4)... with the US deputy attorney general, Jim Comey, at the department of justice in Washington DC.

Longhurst's family met Mr Blunkett in London last week as part of their ...(5)... to ban sites that feature necrophilia and other extreme ...(6)... .

Mr Blunkett's official spokesman [...] noted the legal implications of a ...(7)... were "more complicated" than banning child pornography, for example, because of the first amendment in the US, which establishes ...(8)... of expression.

But possible action could involve work with ...(9)... service providers and credit card ...(10)..., whose services enable users to pay to access porn on ...(11)... , he added.

Press Association, 9 March 2004

Computer virus arrest

Belgian police have arrested a 19-year-old technology student who gained international notoriety for creating computer viruses. The woman, identified only by her nickname "Gigabyte", was charged with computer data sabotage under legislation introduced in 2000 to deal with cyber-crime, the daily *La Libre Belgique* reported.

19

ACCIDENTS

LES ACCIDENTS

voir Introduction p. 142

Vocabulaire à haute fréquence

Road crashes	Les accidents de la route
a vehicle	un véhicule
a lorry, a truck *(US)*	un camion
a tanker	un camion-citerne
a coach	un car
a van	une camionnette
a caravan	une caravane
a camper (van)	un camping car
a seat belt	une ceinture de sécurité
a pedestrian	un piéton
a motorist	un automobiliste
a motorcyclist	un motard
a micro-scooter	un trottinette
a (motor) scooter	un scooter
an eye witness	un témoin oculaire
a crash helmet	un casque
a bend, a corner	un virage, un tournant
to overtake	doubler
to brake	freiner
a brake	un frein
to slow down	ralentir
to pull up	s'arrêter
to pull out	déboîter

a pile-up	un carambolage
to skid	déraper

Rail crashes — Les accidents de chemin de fer

a station	une gare
the rail network	le réseau ferroviaire
the railway, the railroad *(US)*	le chemin de fer
the locomotive, the engine	la locomotive
a carriage	un wagon
a passenger train	un train de voyageurs
a goods train, a freight train	un train de marchandises
a commuter train	un train de banlieue
a level crossing	un passage à niveau
a track	une voie
a line	une ligne
a rail	un rail
to derail	dérailler
a derailment	un déraillement

Air crashes — Les accidents d'avion

an aircraft	un appareil
an airliner	un avion de ligne
a jumbo jet	un gros porteur
a jet engine	un réacteur
a flight	un vol
an air show	un meeting aérien
to land	atterrir
to take off	décoller
take-off	le décollage
an airport	un aéroport
the runway, the tarmac	la piste
a control tower	une tour de contrôle
a pilot	un pilote
a hostess, a stewardess	une hôtesse
to crash	s'abîmer, s'écraser
a crash landing	un atterrissage forcé
the flight (data) recorder	l'enregistreur de vol
the black box	la boîte noire
to retrieve data	récupérer des données

Shipwrecks — Les naufrages

a vessel	un vaisseau
a trawler	un chalutier
a ferry	un ferry
a cargo ship, a freighter	un cargo
a merchant vessel	un navire marchand

an oil tanker	un pétrolier
a captain	un commandant
to sail	naviguer
a sailor	un marin
a fisherman	un marin-pêcheur
shipping	la navigation
to register	immatriculer
to run aground	s'échouer
a hull	une coque
a hold	une soute, une cale
to sink	sombrer
to abandon	évacuer
to drift	dériver
a lifeboat	un canot de sauvetage
to pick up	recueillir
a tug	un remorqueur
a salvage ship	un bateau d'assistance
to tow	remorquer
a wreck	une épave
to drown	se noyer

Mining accidents / Les accidents de mine

a coal-mine, a coalpit, a colliery	une mine de charbon
a miner	un mineur
a pitman, a colliery worker	un mineur de charbon
a shaft	un puits
a gallery	une galerie
a (coal) seam	un filon (de charbon)
fire damp	le grisou
to seep from	fuir
dust	la poussière
to drill, to bore	creuser, forer

Fires / Les incendies

a bushfire	un feu de brousse
a blaze	un incendie, un brasier
ablaze	en flammes
arson	incendie criminel/volontaire
an arsonist	un incendiaire, un pyromane
to catch fire	prendre feu
to burn, to blaze	brûler
a burn	une brûlure
a firefighter, a fireman	un pompier
a fire engine, a firetruck *(US)*	une pompe à incendie
to pour	déverser
a ladder	une échelle

to put out, to extinguish	éteindre
to burn out	calciner
ashes	les cendres
sparks	des étincelles

Climbing accidents — Les accidents de montagne

a peak	un pic
to climb, to scale	grimper, escalader
to abseil down	descendre en rappel
ascent	l'ascension
a rope	une corde
rock climbing	l'escalade, la varappe
a rock climber	un varappeur
a cliff	une falaise
the rock face	la paroi
an avalanche	une avalanche

Common vocabulary — Vocabulaire commun

safety	la sécurité
an inquest	une enquête
a passenger	un passager
a crew	un équipage
to carry, to transport	transporter
on board, aboard	à bord
an engine failure	une panne de moteur
to steer	piloter, diriger, gouverner
to overturn	se retourner
to hit	heurter
to bump into, to run into, to crash into	percuter
to knock down	renverser
to run over	écraser
to collide with	entrer en collision avec
a collision	une collision
a head-on collision	une collision de front
to involve	impliquer, comprendre
a shock	un choc, une commotion
to bruise [bru:z]	meurtrir
a bruise	une meurtrissure
a stitch	un point de suture
a distress signal	un signal de détresse
May Day, an SOS message	un SOS
to locate	localiser

Expressions

a hit-and-run driver	un chauffard (avec délit de fuite)
to appeal for witnesses	lancer un appel à témoins

to come off the rails	quitter les rails
an unmanned level crossing	un passage à niveau non gardé
to be bound for	être à destination de
to be on one's way to, to be en route to	faire route vers
to be due to land at	dont l'atterrissage est prévu à
to ditch in the sea	faire un amerrissage forcé
to lose control	perdre le contrôle
to be cut free	être désincarcéré
to get out of control	échapper au contrôle
to bring under control	maîtriser, circonscrire
to winch to safety	hélitreuiller
to be airlifted to hospital	être évacué par les airs vers l'hôpital
to be detained in hospital	être hospitalisé
to be discharged from hospital	sortir de l'hôpital

Vocabulaire complémentaire

Road crashes — Les accidents de la route

an estate car, a station wagon *(US)*	un break
a roadworthy car	une voiture en bon état
an articulated lorry	un semi-remorque
a trailer	une remorque
to jacknife	se mettre en travers
winding	sinueux
to veer, to swerve	faire une embardée
an MOT (= Ministry of Transport) test	un contrôle obligatoire

Rail crashes — Les accidents de chemin de fer

rolling stock	le matériel roulant
a truck, a wagon	un wagon de marchandises
an embankment	une levée de terre, un remblai
a driver	un mécanicien
a guard	un chef de train
a buffer	un butoir

Air crashes — Les accidents aériens

a freight plane	un avion cargo
a wide-body jet	un avion gros-porteur
the body	la carlingue
to pressurise	pressuriser
pressurisation	la pressurisation
the fuselage	le fuselage
the landing gear, the undercarriage	le train d'atterrissage
an escape chute	un toboggan
an airstrip	une piste sommaire

airworthy	en état de vol
to ground	clouer au sol
a balloon [bə'lu:n]	un ballon
an airship	un dirigeable
a glider	un planeur
a hang glider	un deltaplane
a paraglider	un parapente
a descent	une descente
to disintegrate	se désintégrer
disintegration	la désintégration
to scatter	(se) disperser
a mid-air collision	une collision en vol

Shipwrecks / Les naufrages

a flag of convenience	un pavillon de complaisance
a trawl net	un chalut
a shipping lane	un couloir de navigation
a sailing ship	un voilier
a sailing dinghy	un dériveur
a bulk carrier	un vraquier
a container vessel	un porte-conteneurs
crippled	désemparé
stricken	en détresse
a (sunken) ship	un bateau (immergé)
the bridge	la passerelle
the deck	le pont
a rudder	un gouvernail
a line	un câble
to list	gîter
overloaded, overcrowded	surchargé
to capsize	chavirer
to bail out	écoper
a distress beacon	une balise de détresse
a flare	une fusée de détresse
a coastguard	un garde-côte
a life-raft	un radeau de survie
adrift	à la dérive
to refloat	renflouer

Fires / Les incendies

a fire brigade	un corps de pompiers
a water-bombing aircraft	un Canadair
a breathing apparatus	un appareil respiratoire
an inferno	une fournaise
to shroud	envelopper
plumes of smoke	des colonnes de fumée

a conflagration	un sinistre
a seat of fire	un foyer d'incendie
to ignite	(s')allumer
embers	des braises
a short-circuit	un court-circuit
fumes	les émanations
asphyxiated	asphyxié
to smoulder	couver
to fan	attiser
to rage	faire rage
to douse	noyer en arrosant
foam	la mousse
to spray	pulvériser
to smother	étouffer
remains	les restes

Climbing accidents / Les accidents de montagne

a mountaineer [maʊntɪ'nɪə]	un alpiniste
a potholer	un spéléologue
an expedition	une expédition
a ledge	une corniche
a ridge	une crête
a gully	un couloir
a crevasse [krɪ'væs]	une crevasse
frostbite	des gelures

Common vocabulary / Vocabulaire commun

to career	aller à toute vitesse
to cartwheel	faire des tonneaux
hypothermia [haɪpə'θɜːmɪə]	l'hypothermie
to topple	(se) renverser
to ram	emboutir
to plough into	s'encastrer dans
concussion	commotion
to hamper, to hinder	gêner, entraver
a near miss	une quasi collision
to maintain, to service	entretenir
maintenance, servicing	l'entretien
negligence, carelessness	la négligence

At least 13 dead as pool roof collapses

By Steve Bloomfield

At least 13 people died, nearly 100 were injured and many others trapped when a giant glass roof covering a water park collapsed in Moscow last night. Emergency service officials feared the number of dead could rise as those trapped were exposed to temperatures nearing -20C. As midnight approached, rescuers reported that voices could still be heard from under the rubble. Clouds of steam billowed up from the site and rescuers used heating machines to pump warm air into the complex to prevent the water from freezing around those still stuck.

The collapse happened at around 7.30pm at the Transvaal water park, a five-storey leisure centre in south-west Moscow. There were around 1,300 people in the complex, and more than 400 in the pool area, all basking in its heat while temperatures outside hovered around -15C.

An eyewitness told Russia's Channel One television: "Suddenly, there was a loud noise. Everybody started to run. All of the roof over the zone of water collapsed." Panicking swimmers, some in bathing suits, rushed outside into below freezing temperatures. Roman Yazymin, 29, was sun-tanning in a solarium on the upper floors of the complex when he heard a loud noise and the crash of shattering glass. "It wasn't an explosion, but the noise of metal collapsing," he said. "Everything was covered in blood."

Scores of people, many of them children, were rushed to hospital with fractures, concussion and bruises. The latest casualty reports said that three children were among those who died.

The water park is one of several new entertainment facilities that have opened over the past couple of years on the city's outskirts. It includes a large pool, an artificial river and a lengthy water slide. Initial reports of the cause of the collapse being terrorism were swiftly discounted, and emergency service officials said that the building's roof had caved in under the weight of several days' heavy snow falls. [...]

The Independent, 15 February 2004

1 Choose the right explanation for the following words underlined in the article.

1. to billow up
A. to spread upwards
B. to hiss
C. to illuminate the sky

2. storey
A. fable
B. floor
C. pool

3. to cave in
A. to resist
B. to collapse
C. to repair

2 Say whether the following statements are true (T) or false (F).

1. Rescue workers feared that some survivors could die because of sub-zero temperatures.
2. Warm air was pumped into the building to prevent survivors in the pool area from being trapped by ice.
3. It was a giant glass roof over the pool area which collapsed.
4. The accident caused widespread panic among the swimmers.
5. It was an explosion which caused the roof structure to collapse.
6. The leisure centre is an ageing entertainment facility.
7. It is feared that terrorism is to blame.
8. The roof gave way because of the snow which had accumulated on it.

3 Fill in the nine lines across the grid with translations of the corresponding French words. This will give you the answer to number 10 in column D.

1. car
2. emboutir
3. envelopper
4. point de suture
5. faire une embardée
6. feu de brousse
7. piloter, diriger
8. filon
9. en flammes
10. faire des tonneaux

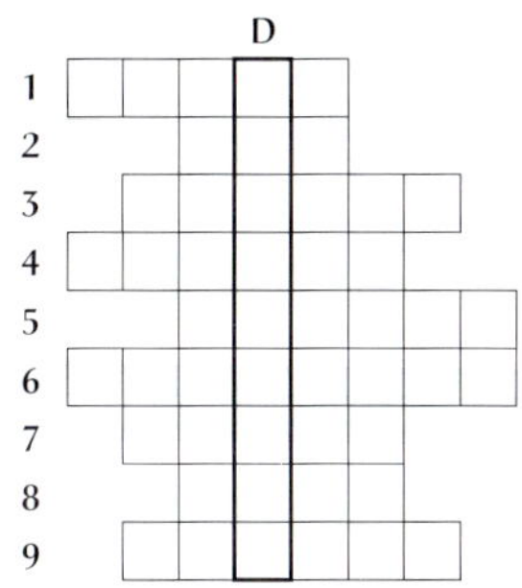

24 teenagers killed in bus crash

by Matti Huuhtanen

A bus carrying mostly teenagers crashed into a truck in icy conditions in southern Finland early today, killing 24 and injuring 15 in one of the worst accidents in the country's history.

The accident occurred soon after 2am (midnight GMT) when the truck's trailer, loaded with heavy paper rolls, swung into the middle of the slippery road and hit the oncoming bus, Senior Constable Jari Tikanoja said.

About 40 passengers were on the <u>chartered</u> bus travelling to ski resorts in Lapland, northern Finland, he said. "Large paper rolls in the truck's trailer crashed through the windscreen of the bus," Constable Tikanoja said.

Several injured were in critical condition. "We are treating 14 young patients here. Four are in critical condition," said Jukka Puolakka, the head physician at the Central Finland Hospital nearby. "Many of them have head injuries and injuries to the upper body."

"The driver said the icy road had caused the trailer to suddenly start swerving, and he was unable to control it," Constable Tikanoja said. Roads in Finland froze overnight after a day of mild temperatures nationwide.

A government-appointed commission began an investigation into the accident near Aanekoski, some 190 miles north of Helsinki. It was one of Finland's most deadly accidents to date. In 1979, 27 people died in a fire in an old people's home. In 1940, 17 people were killed when a bus crashed into the sea.

The Cabinet met in emergency session and recommended that <u>flags be flown at half-mast</u> Friday to commemorate the victims.

AP, 19 March 2004

1 Choose the right explanation for the following words underlined in the article.

1. chartered

A. stolen
B. hired
C. seized

2. to fly a flag at half-mast

A. to remove a flag from a mast to pay respect to victims
B. to fly a flag midway up a mast as a symbol of mourning
C. to fly a half flag on a mast to commemorate victims

2 Choose the appropriate endings for the following sentences.

1. The bus

A. was trailing the truck.
B. was pulling out.
C. was coming in the oppos' direction.

2. The truck driver could not control the trailer when it started

A. veering.
B. braking.
C. overtaking.

3. *The crash has been the worst accident*
A. in the country's history.
B. since 1940.
C. since 1979.

3 Say whether the following statements are true (T) or false (F).
1. Black ice is at the root of this crash.
2. The collision occurred when heavy paper rolls skidded into the path of the oncoming bus.
3. Some children sustained life-threatening injuries in the crash.
4. The truck driver was killed in the accident.

4 Read the article again and find words synonymous with the following.
1. a lorry
2. to strike
3. to veer
4. an inquest
5. fatal
6. a blaze

Skier survives blizzard ordeal

A British skier has told how he cheated death when he was forced to spend the night on a freezing mountain in blizzard conditions. Father-of-three Nigel Magson, 38, became lost after skiing off-piste on Mount Rosa in the Italian Alps and was forced to seek shelter in an isolated shepherd's hut after the weather took a dramatic turn. With temperatures dipping to minus 15C, he battled through thick snow to reach the shelter, where he lit a stove to keep warm.

The Observer, 22 February 2004

32 killed by gas blast in Russian tower block

Daniel McLaughlin, Moscow

At least 32 people were killed and dozens injured and buried under rubble yesterday when a gas explosion razed a block of flats in Arkhangelsk, northern Russia. A government spokesman said three of the dead were children.

Hundreds of rescuers with sniffer dogs pulled 23 people alive from the ruins and were combing the mass of twisted metal and shattered concrete for about 20 missing people last night. Police were looking for two men who they believe removed brass safety valves from the heating system of the nine-storey block shortly before it exploded. Poor Russians regularly steal metal piping, wiring and even railway tracks to sell for scrap. Earlier, it was feared that sabotage or terrorism was to blame.

The Daily Telegraph, 17 March 2004

20 NATURAL DISASTERS

LES CATASTROPHES NATURELLES

voir Introduction p. 142

Vocabulaire à haute fréquence

Earthquakes	**Les tremblements de terre**
a tremor	une secousse (tellurique)
a shock wave	une onde de choc
a quake	un séisme
an earthquake	un tremblement de terre
to register, to measure	mesurer
the Richter scale	l'échelle de Richter
magnitude	l'amplitude, la magnitude
an epicentre ['epɪsentə]	un épicentre
an aftershock	une réplique, une secousse résiduelle
to rock	ébranler
a crack	une fissure
a fault line	une ligne de fracture
a landslide, a landslip	un glissement de terrain
a landfall	un éboulement de terrain
sniffer dogs	des chiens renifleurs
Wind, water and rain	**Le vent, l'eau et la pluie**
a gale	un coup de vent, une tempête
a storm	une forte tempête
a hurricane ['hʌrɪkən]	un ouragan
a tornado [tɔː'neɪdəu]	une tornade
a cyclone ['saɪkləun]	un cyclone

the path	le trajet, la trajectoire
a typhoon [taɪ'fu:n]	un typhon
torrential	diluvien
to rip off, to blow off	arracher
to blow down, to tear down	abattre
to be downed	être abattu
to sweep across/trough	balayer
a flood	une inondation
floodwaters	les eaux en crue
flash flooding	inondation éclair
to inundate, to flood	inonder
to swell	(se) gonfler
a surge	un gonflement, une montée des eaux
swell	la houle
the tide	la marée
a tidal wave	un raz de marée
to overflow	déborder
waterlogged	détrempé, gorgé d'eau
a bank	une rive
to sandbag	protéger avec des sacs de sable
a sandbag	un sac de sable
a dyke	une digue
mud	la boue
a mudslide	une coulée de boue
a dam	un barrage
to burst	se rompre
to wash away	emporter
to drown, to submerge	submerger, noyer
to pump	pomper
to drain	drainer
drought [draʊt]	la sécheresse

Volcanoes — Les volcans

a volcano [vɒl'keɪnəʊ]	un volcan
a crater ['kreɪtə]	un cratère
to erupt	entrer en éruption
an eruption	une éruption
to steam	dégager de la vapeur
steam	la vapeur
to spit	cracher
to spew out	vomir
lava ['lɑ:və]	la lave
ash	la cendre
to blanket	recouvrir
to be coated with	être recouvert de
a slope	une pente
a flow, an outflow	une coulée

Common vocabulary — Vocabulaire commun

Common vocabulary	Vocabulaire commun
to brace oneself (up) for	se préparer à faire face
damage	les dégâts matériels
to hit, to strike, to pound	frapper, atteindre
to affect	toucher
to disrupt	perturber
a disruption	une perturbation
to be cut off	être coupé du reste
to be stranded, marooned	être bloqué, coincé
to subside	baisser, décroître
homeless	sans abri
to re-house	reloger
makeshift	de fortune
to warn	avertir
a warning	une alerte, un avis d'alerte
power lines	les lignes électriques
power supply	l'alimentation en courant
a power failure	une panne de courant
a power cut	une coupure de courant
to wipe out	anéantir
to crush	écraser, détruire

Expressions

to overflow its banks	déborder
to burst its banks	sortir de son lit
to bring chaos	semer la confusion
to wreak havoc, to leave a trail of devastation/destruction	provoquer de gros dégâts, tout détruire sur son passage
to cut a swathe (through)	décimer, dévaster
to take shelter/refuge	s'abriter
overhead power lines	les lignes électriques aériennes
a stricken area	une zone sinistrée
to wipe off the map	rayer de la carte
to post a warning	émettre un bulletin d'alerte

Vocabulaire complémentaire

Earthquakes — Les tremblements de terre

Earthquakes	Les tremblements de terre
a tectonic plate	une plaque tectonique
a foundation	une fondation
concrete	le béton
to slip off	glisser
to crumble	s'effriter
seismological [saɪzmə'lɒdʒɪkəl]	sismologique
a seismologist [saɪz'mɒlədʒɪst]	un sismologue

Wind and rain	Le vent et la pluie
a whirlwind	un tourbillon
to unleash	déclencher, déchaîner
to roar	rugir
to batter	battre, assaillir
to lash	fouetter, cingler
a groundswell	une lame de fond
a tsunami	un tsunami
a wall of water	un mur d'eau
to swamp	submerger
to whip up	soulever, faire monter
to flatten	aplatir
to toss	ballotter
to board up	obstruer avec des planches
a levee	une levée, une digue

Volcanoes	Les volcans
dormant	en sommeil
extinct	éteint
volcanic	volcanique
to rumble	gronder
molten	en fusion, liquide
a layer	une couche

Common vocabulary	Vocabulaire commun
structural damage	dégâts aux installations
to engulf	engloutir
to uproot	déraciner
to seal	colmater

Bam aid workers step up relief efforts

Aid workers in the earthquake-hit Iranian city of Bam were today increasing efforts to bring relief to survivors and prevent the outbreak of diseases caused by poor sanitation and cold weather.

The moves came as 80 US aid workers and a team from British agency Oxfam arrived in the devastated city, bringing water and medical supplies. Workers rushed blankets and medical supplies to survivors, with a US team of 60 doctors treating patients at a field hospital.

At least 12,000 inhabitants of the city, in south-eastern Iran, were injured in last Friday's earthquake. The official death toll is now more than 28,000, although unnamed Iranian sources have said that it could be as high as 50,000.

Aid workers fear that the lack of sanitation could lead to a disease epidemic. "We are very concerned about the situation in Bam. We know that thousands of people have lost their homes and do not have access to clean water," Oxfam's Mhairi Hearle told the Press Association. "Restoring this access and providing adequate sanitation facilities is essential if we are to help prevent the spread of diseases like typhoid and cholera."

Talks between US aid officials and Iranian ministers have been taking place amid UK reports that the US is softening its line towards Iran. The US president, George Bush, had previously described the country as being part of the "axis of evil". Yesterday, he said that there was "a chance for Iran to step forward" after the earthquake.

Bill Garvelink, the head of the US agency for international development team, yesterday met Iranian ministers in what he said was probably the first official meeting between US and Iranian officials since Washington cut diplomatic links following the 1979 Iran hostage crisis.

Mr Garvellink insisted the meeting had not focused on political issues. The Iranian president, Mohammad Khatami yesterday thanked Washington for US assistance, but downplayed its significance to the political relationship between the two countries.

Iranian health officials say that they have almost abandoned hope of finding survivors buried under the rubble of Bam, which the health ministry has divided up into 10 zones. "There's no hope of finding people alive," ministry official Mohammad Nickam told the Associated Press.

Aid is arriving from more than 20 countries. An Australian air force plane carrying blankets, water purification tablets, heaters and other equipment has unloaded its supplies in the provincial capital of Kerman, 120 miles northwest of Bam, a defence spokesman said.

China has pledged 10 million yuan (£600,000) in additional aid, the Chinese Foreign Ministry yesterday said on its website.

The Guardian, 31 December 31, 2003

1 Choose the appropriate ending for the following sentences.

1. There could be an outbreak of disease because
A. of the lack of food and shelter.
B. of inadequate health care and sanitation facilities.
C. there is almost no hope of finding survivors buried under the rubble.

2. The final death toll
A. is around 28,000.
B. is impossible to say.
C. is 50,000.

3. The US sent a relief team to Bam
A. because Iran stepped forward.
B. because the political relationship between the two countries has been renewed.
C. despite long-severed diplomatic relations with Iran.

4. The Iranian health ministry
A. has been divided up into 10 zones.
B. has split the earthquake zone in 10.
C. has hope of finding more survivors.

5. Aid workers' main task is to
A. treat the injured and homeless.
B. unload supplies arriving from more than 20 countries.
C. find survivors buried under the rubble of Bam.

2 Reorder the following statements to fit the order of the article.

A. There is little hope of finding any more survivors under the city's rubble.
B. The injured are being treated in a temporary medical centre.
C. The Iranian government have welcomed the US rescue team sent to Bam despite US President G. W. Bush's naming of Iran as part of an "axis of evil".
D. The relief operation is backed by more than a dozen countries sending planes carrying humanitarian aid.
E. Rescuers try to help survivors who have to face sub-zero temperatures.
F. The number of dead could be almost double the official death toll.

3 Read the article again and find equivalents for the following.

1. rescue
2. preservation of clean and healthy living conditions
3. food, equipment and other essential things people need
4. to take sth. quickly to a place
5. a temporary medical centre
6. expansion
7. to minimize
8. to cover with soil, earth, bricks…
9. debris

4 Name the natural disaster described by each of the following statements.

1. a sudden release of energy from the earth's crust.
2. normally dry land covered with water because a river has overflowed.
3. a severe, often destructive storm.
4. a large, often destructive sea wave.
5. the falling of a large mass of soil down the side of a mountain or cliff.
6. the violent ejection of lava.
7. a strong, bitterly cold wind accompanied by a heavy snowfall.

25 hurricane deaths

A total of 25 deaths and estimated damage of £300 million were recorded as Hurricane Isabel petered out over Canada early yesterday after lashing America's eastern seaboard.

The Daily Telegraph, 21 September 2003

83 killed in Philippine landslides

Rescuers fought their way through rain, mud and floodwaters yesterday in search of survivors after landslides and huge waves devastated villages in the eastern Philippines.

At least 83 people were killed, including 61 in the province of Southern Leyte, and 123 were missing. Officials feared more deaths as bad weather, blocked roads and toppled power and telephone lines hampered rescue workers.

The Daily Telegraph, 22 December 2003

1 **Choose the right explanation for each of the words underlined in the first article.**

1. to peter out	*2. to lash*	*3. the seaboard*
A. to die down	A. to hit gently	A. overseas
B. to strengthen	B. to hit with force	B. the area along the coast
C. to rush	C. to hit mildly	C. off the coast

2 **Read the second article and find equivalents for the following.**

1. relief workers	3. enormous	5. to blow down
2. a landslip	4. to wreck	6. to hinder

Floods hit West as 5in of rain falls in 18 hours

Homes were flooded and motorists stranded yesterday as storms battered the west of Britain.

Worst hit were the North West, Midlands and Wales, where more than five inches of rain fell over 18 hours. Forecasters predict more deluges today, with no sign of a respite before tomorrow.

At Kendal in the Lake District, the Kent reached its highest point for 30 years, while the Cocker at Cockermouth and the Derwent at Keswick also burst their banks.

At Llanwrst, near Conwy, North Wales, two breakdown mechanics had to be winched to safety by helicopter, along with the motorist they were attempting to rescue, when they were trapped in five feet of floodwater.

At 6pm yesterday there were 42 flood warnings in Wales, 15 in the Midlands, 10 in the North East and five in the North West.

Temperatures reached record levels for Feb 3 in Church Fenton, North Yorks, (62F), Lossiemouth, Scotland, and Hawarden, north Wales (both 61F).

The Daily Telegraph, 4 February 2004

21 THE WEATHER

LE TEMPS

Vocabulaire à haute fréquence

Common features	Traits communs
fine, fair	beau
unsettled, unstable	instable
changeable	variable
dull	maussade
clear	clair
sunny, bright	ensoleillé
to brighten up, to clear	s'éclaircir, se dégager
to spread (across)	s'étendre
sunshine	l'ensoleillement
mist	la brume
fog	le brouillard
slight, light	léger
thick	épais
dense	dense
to form, to develop	se former
to lift	se lever
a patch	une nappe, une plaque
patchy	en nappes
an anticyclone	un anticyclone
a depression	une dépression
pressure	la pression
a ridge	une dorsale
a trough [trɒf]	une zone (basse pression)
a front	un front
widespread	répandu, général

a spell, a period ['pɪəriəd]	une période
to range from ... to	aller de ... à (températures)
a range	une gamme
a prospect	une perspective
an outlook	une prévision
a weather forecast	un bulletin météorologique
a weather forecaster	un présentateur météo
full five-day forecast	les prévisions à cinq jours
Celsius	Celsius, centigrade
bad weather	les intempéries
a weather warning	un bulletin d'alerte météo
an area ['ɛərɪə]	une zone

Wind — Le vent

calm	calme
windy	venteux, agité
windswept	balayé par le vent
wind speed	la force du vent
moderate	modéré
fresh	frais
to freshen	fraîchir
strong, high, heavy	fort, violent
a breeze	une brise
to gust	souffler en rafales
a gust	une rafale
to turn	tourner
to veer	remonter (sens des aiguilles)
to back	descendre (sens inverse)
prevailing	dominant
a gale	un coup de vent, une tempête
severe [sɪ'vɪə]	fort
a storm	une forte tempête
stormy	très agité, orageux
to let up	se calmer
a let-up, a lull	une accalmie, un répit
to blow over	se calmer, s'apaiser
to die down	tomber
southerly	du sud
southwards	vers le sud

Rain — La pluie

rainfall	les précipitations
rainy	pluvieux
wet, damp	humide
cloudy	nuageux
to cloud over	se couvrir
drizzle	la bruine

light rain	le crachin
heavy rain	de fortes pluies
a shower	une averse
showery rain	pluie en averses
an outbreak of rain	une ondée
a cloudburst	une violente averse
to pour	tomber à flots
to dry up	devenir plus sec
to clear away	se dégager
a thunderstorm	un orage
thunder	le tonnerre
thundery	orageux
to brew	couver
to break out	éclater
lightning	la foudre
hail	la grêle
a rainbow	un arc-en-ciel

Heat — La chaleur

mild	doux
warm	chaud
warmth	la chaleur modérée
hot	très chaud
a heat wave	la canicule
to swelter	étouffer de chaleur
dry	sec
drought [draʊt]	la sécheresse
the sun index	l'indice UV
the air pollution index	l'indice de pollution

Cold — Le froid

to cool	se rafraîchir
cool	frais
chilly	très frais
to freeze	geler
freeze	le gel
a frost	une gelée
a sharp frost	une forte gelée
freezing-point	zéro degré centigrade
minus 6	moins 6
hoar frost, white frost	la gelée blanche
ice	la glace
icy	glacé, glacial
sleet	le grésil
to snow	neiger
snowy	neigeux
a blizzard	un blizzard
to melt	fondre

Expressions

a trough of low pressure	une zone dépressionnaire
a ridge of high pressure	une ligne de hautes pressions
a breath of wind	un souffle de vent
a gale warning in force	un avis de grand frais en cours
it's pouring with rain	il pleut à verse
a clap of thunder	un coup de tonnerre
a flash/bolt of lightning	un éclair
torrents of rain	des trombes d'eau
a burst of rain	une averse
the thaw sets in	le dégel s'installe
to bask in the sun	se dorer au soleil

Vocabulaire complémentaire

Common features	Traits communs
settled	stable
set fair	beau fixe
to break through	percer
haze	la brume légère
smog	le smog
to thicken (up)	s'épaissir
to hang around, to linger	traîner
to persist	persister
to prevail	l'emporter
to extend	s'étendre
to establish	s'établir
prolonged	prolongé
to wear off, to weaken	s'affaiblir
to fill	se combler
the met office	les services de la météo
a weatherman	un météorologue
a meteorologist	un météorologiste
the shipping forecast	la météo marine
a synopsis	un résumé de la situation
to predict, to forecast	prévoir
overnight	pendant la nuit
coastal	côtier
inland	à l'intérieur (du pays)

Wind	Le vent
brisk	vif
an airflow, an airstream	un flux d'air
breezy	avec de la brise
to whip up	activer

to strengthen, to pick up	se renforcer
a squall	une bourrasque
a whirlwind	un tourbillon
to ease off	s'atténuer, mollir
to abate, to subside	s'apaiser, se calmer
a shift	une saute
south-westerly	du sud-ouest

Rain — La pluie

the damp, moisture, humidity	l'humidité
overcast	couvert
a blustery shower	une giboulée
thundery showers	ondées orageuses
a squally shower	un grain
torrential	torrentiel, diluvien
a downpour, a deluge	un déluge
patchy rain, scattered showers	pluies éparses
persistent	persistant
to break up	se disperser
a bright/sunny interval	une éclaircie
to peter out	s'effilocher
to die away, to die out	s'affaiblir, cesser
a hailstone	un grêlon

Heat — La chaleur

sultry	étouffant
close	lourd
to pick up	remonter (températures)
sun-tanned	bronzé
sun-stroke	une insolation

Cold — Le froid

wintry	hivernal
frosty	glacial
groundfrost	gelée au sol
raw	rigoureux
the ice cap	la calotte glaciaire
a flurry	une rafale (neige)
to thaw	dégeler
a thaw	un dégel
slush	la neige fondue, la gadoue
a cold snap	un coup de froid

Weather records continue to tumble in year of the sun

by Graham Tibbetts

Another weather record tumbled yesterday when it was confirmed that January to October was the sunniest period documented. The Meteorological Office said it was also likely to be the driest 10-month stretch since records began in 1873.

Unparalleled levels of warm sunshine have already earned this year a place in the annals of weather history for the highest temperature, warmest summer nights and the sunniest September.

Previously, the brightest January to October in England and Wales occurred in 1995 – 34 years after these records began – with 1,604.8 hours of sunlight. But 2003 has comfortably surpassed that with 1,618 hours and the final figure will be even higher once statistics for the last two days of October are assimilated. The record for the driest January-to-October period is also expected to fall. In 1964, 540.7 millimetres (21in) of rain fell during those months in England and Wales but this year there has been only 514.6mm (20in) so far. "It will be a close thing," said a Met Office spokesman. "This is perhaps because we have had warm weather from the south hanging around. The cold, wet weather from the north usually arrives earlier."

According to the Climatic Research Unit at the University of East Anglia, if temperatures remain slightly above average until the end of December, 2003 will also become the warmest year since statistics were first compiled in 1659. The record was set in 1990 and equalled four years ago, with an average temperature of 10.63C (51.1F). But Tim Osborn, a senior research associate at the unit, said it was difficult to link the recent temperature rise with global warming. "The changes are consistent with what we expect due to man-made climate change, but they are not necessarily proof on their own," he said.

The unit predicts that rainfall will increase during winters and decrease during summers. "We think there will be more extremes - more frequent summer droughts but possibly more frequent winter flooding," Dr Osborn said.

The Daily Telegraph, 1 November 2003

Measurements

Several measurements are mentioned in the text. Here are their equivalents.

Length

Inch (abbreviated to "in" or «). One inch = 2.54 cm

Temperature

°Fahrenheit (abbreviated to °F). 1°F = 1°C x 9/5 + 32.

°Celsius (abbreviated to °C). 1°C = 1°F x 5/9 - 32.

1 Choose the right explanation for each of the following words underlined in the text.

1. to tumble
A. to stabilise
B. to unsettle
C. to fall

2. to compile
A. to put out
B. to put together
C. to put aside

3. senior
A. old
B. retired
C. experienced

2 Say whether the following statements are true (T) or false (F).

1. It was announced that January to October might be the driest period documented.
2. The highest temperature since records began in 1873 was reached in 2003.
3. The first records for the January-to-October period were kept in 1961.
4. Damp weather bringing increased rainfall usually comes from the south.
5. 1999 was one of the warmest years since statistics were first compiled in 1659.
6. Tim Osborn asserts that the impact of human activity on climate accounts for the weather changes.
7. The Climatic Research Unit forecasts that weather patterns will return to normal in the future.

3 Reorder the following words from the lowest to the highest temperature.

warm, cold, hot, freezing, cool, mild, chilly

4 Use the definitions to find the corresponding words. Each dash represents one letter.

1. a sudden, heavy rainstorm — c _ _ _ _ _ _ _ _ _
2. to be afflicted by oppressive heat — to s _ _ _ _ _ _
3. future prospect — o _ _ _ _ _ _
4. to predict — to f _ _ _ _ _ _ _
5. with high cloud cover, very cloudy — o _ _ _ _ _ _ _
6. a light, continuous rain — d _ _ _ _ _ _
7. unsettled — u _ _ _ _ _ _ _

75mph gales to sweep South

Severe weather warnings were issued last night with predictions of further snow and winds of almost hurricane force this weekend. The Met Office forecast gales with 75mph gusts in the Midlands and South. Blizzards are expected in Scotland. A spokesman said: "The strong winds in the South should be kicking off about lunchtime, going across the country to the South East. We are looking at some prolonged heavy rain in the North of England."

The Daily Telegraph, 31 January 2004

22 TRAVEL AND TRAFFIC

LES VOYAGES ET LA CIRCULATION

Vocabulaire à haute fréquence

The weather	Le temps
poor visibility	mauvaise visibilité
(black) ice	le verglas
icy	verglacé
a patch	une plaque, une nappe
treacherous ['tretʃərəs]	plein d'embûches, traître
hazardous	dangereux, risqué
slippery	glissant
a snowdrift	une congère
snowbound	enneigé
flooded	inondé
to be stranded	être bloqué
to close	barrer
a closure	une fermeture
to block	bloquer
to abandon	abandonner
to re-open	ouvrir de nouveau
care	la prudence
a crossing	une traversée
smooth	calme
choppy	légèrement agitée
rough	agitée

Incidents	Les incidents
to disrupt	perturber
a disruption	une perturbation

chaos ['keɪɒs]	la confusion, le chaos
road works	les travaux routiers
to break down	tomber en panne
a breakdown	une panne

Traffic flow — La circulation

a trip, a journey	un voyage
to travel	voyager
busy	animé
heavy	dense
crowded	chargé
overloaded	surchargé
congested	encombré
congestion	encombrement
a tailback	une retenue
a jam	un embouteillage
to crawl	avancer au pas
gridlock	embouteillage
stationary	immobile
eastbound	vers l'est
southbound	vers le sud
speed	la vitesse
a limit	une limitation
a restriction	une restriction
to avoid	éviter
to divert	dévier
a diversion	une déviation
an alternative route	un itinéraire de remplacement
rush hours, peak hours	les heures de pointe
to commute	faire la navette entre son domicile et son travail
a commuter	un banlieusard
suburban traffic	la circulation en banlieue
car-sharing	le co-voiturage

Road traffic — La circulation routière

the Highway Code	le code de la route
a driving licence	un permis de conduire
a driving test	un examen d'obtention du permis
a road hump, a sleeping policeman	un ralentisseur, une bande rugueuse
a chicane	une chicane
a cycle lane	une piste cyclable
a built-up area	une agglomération
a thoroughfare, an arterial road	une artère
main	principal
a carriageway	une chaussée

a dual carriageway	une quatre-voies
a motorway, a freeway *(US)*	une autoroute
a highway	une route nationale
a lane	un couloir, une voie
the hard shoulder	la bande d'arrêt d'urgence
a junction	une bretelle d'accès et/ou de sortie, un échangeur
a turn-off	une sortie
a bypass	une route de contournement
a ring road	une rocade
a beltway *(US)*	un périphérique
a rest area	une aire de repos
a service area	une aire de services
a filling station	une station-service
petrol, gasoline *(US)*, gas *(US)*	l'essence
diesel (oil)	le gazole
a roundabout	un rond-point
a toll	un péage
congestion charging	la taxe embouteillage
the car number plate	le numéro d'immatriculation
fee, charge	tarif, prix
to park	garer, stationner
a car park, a parking lot *(US)*	un parking
drink driving	la conduite en état d'alcoolémie
careless	imprudent
reckless	dangereux
to speed	commettre un excès de vitesse

Public transport / Les transports publics

the underground, the Tube, the subway *(US)*	le métro
a high-speed train	un train à grande vitesse
a tilting train	un train pendulaire
a ferry	un ferry
a ferry terminal	une gare maritime
to board, to get on board	monter à bord
to sail	naviguer, partir
a sailing	un départ de bateau
a harbour, a port	un port
to run	fonctionner
to delay	retarder
a delay	un retard
a schedule ['ʃedju:l, 'skedju:l]	un horaire
on schedule	à l'heure
a scheduled flight	un vol régulier
domestic	intérieur
nonstop	sans escale

to charter	affréter
a charter plane	un avion charter
a low-cost company	une compagnie à bas prix
an air traffic controller	un contrôleur de la navigation aérienne, un aiguilleur du ciel
to depart	partir
a departure	un départ
an arrival	une arrivée
incoming traffic	le trafic à l'arrivée
outgoing traffic	le trafic au départ
to cancel	annuler
a cancellation	une annulation
to enquire [ɪn'kwaɪə]	se renseigner
an enquiry	une demande de renseignements
information	des renseignements

Holidays / Les vacances

a vacation *(US)*	un congé
a bank holiday	un jour férié
a holidaymaker	un vacancier
a package holiday	un séjour à forfait
a holiday resort	une station de vacances
to rent	louer
to book, to reserve	réserver
a reservation	une réservation
a berth	une couchette
a travel agent	un agent de voyages
a travel agency	une agence de voyages
a tour operator	un voyagiste, un organisateur de voyages
accommodation	le logement
a boarding-house, a guest-house	une pension de famille
board and lodging	la pension
to put sb. up	loger qn.
self-catering accommodation	une location meublée
an en suite bedroom	une chambre avec w.c. et salle d'eau privés
no vacancies	complet

Expressions

visibility down to 20 yards	visibilité réduite à 20 mètres
closed to traffic	interdit à la circulation
to drive with extra care	conduire avec une extrême prudence
to set out on a journey	se mettre en route
to go dead slow, to go at a crawl	avancer au pas

to jump the lights	griller les feux
bumper to bumper	pare-chocs contre pare-chocs
a one-way street	une rue à sens unique
to do/make a U-turn	faire demi-tour
to ban sb. from driving	suspendre le permis de qn.
fully booked up	complet (à la réservation)
back to normal	retour à la normale
to enquire with somebody	se renseigner auprès de qn.
to be a good sailor	avoir le pied marin
to blow in the bag	souffler dans le ballon

Vocabulaire complémentaire

The weather	Le temps
fogbound	noyé dans le brouillard
to grit	sabler
to salt	saler
to drift	accumuler
impassable	impraticable
unusable	inutilisable, impraticable
marooned	bloqué, isolé

Incidents	Les incidents
to shed	répandre
a load	un chargement
to leak	s'échapper (liquide, gaz)
a leak, a leakage	une fuite
to burst	éclater, se rompre
a burst	une rupture (canalisation)
a main	une canalisation
maintenance	l'entretien
a repair	une réparation
to dig up roads	effectuer des travaux
re-surfacing	la réfection du revêtement
a recovery vehicle	une dépanneuse
a hotspot, a troublespot	un point chaud

Traffic flow	La circulation
packed	comble, bondé
to slow down	ralentir
a slow-down	un ralentissement
to hold up	retarder
a traffic warden	un contractuel
a ticket	un ticket
a fine	une amende

a clamp, a Denver boot	un sabot de blocage
a major road, a trunk road *(UK)*	une route principale
a minor road, a B-road	une route secondaire
a country lane	un chemin rural
signage	le fléchage
an access	un accès
a slip road	un voie d'accès ou de sortie
a stretch	une portion, une section
a lay-by	une bande de stationnement
an interchange	un échangeur
a turnpike *(US)*	une autoroute à péage
a breathaliser, a drunkometer *(US)*	un éthylomètre
a breath test	un passage à l'éthylomètre
intoxicated	en état d'ébriété
to disqualify	frapper d'une suspension
a disqualification	une suspension, un retrait
to take away	retirer
an endorsement	une mention sur le permis
an underground walkway	un passage piéton souterrain
a pedestrian crossing	un passage piéton

Public transport — Les transports publics

a wharf, a quay [ki:]	un quai
to dock	accoster
a hovercraft	un aéroglisseur
a taxiway	une piste de dégagement
jet lag	l'effet du décalage horaire

12-lane freeways to ease crisis on roads

Darling to announce spending of £6bn to widen motorways

Juliette Jowit

Britain's first 12-lane superhighway, modelled on America's freeways, is set to be built in Britain as part of expansion plan costing up to £6bn to cope with the crisis on the country's roads.

Faced with growing public discontent over traffic jams amid warnings that the roads system is <u>overloaded</u>, the Government is considering plans to introduce tolls on the extra "hot" lanes, which would be faster and freer of traffic.

Transport Secretary Alistair Darling will announce details of the <u>scheme</u>, which is likely to include widening part of the M42 in the Midlands to a 12-lane motorway; parts of the M25 round London and several stretches of the M1.

Following a series of studies into congestion hotspots across the country, Darling is considering funding the projects by private toll road companies, which would charge drivers to use the extra lanes – another idea imported from America.

The package of widening, bypasses and new junctions would be the biggest single road-building announcement since Labour came to power.

However, it is likely to prompt a <u>backlash</u> from environmental campaigners worried about the effects on sensitive areas and noise pollution, while motoring groups fear the plans will not cope with the rising scale of the congestion problem.

Darling, who last week signalled plans for satellite charging of motorists in congested inner-city routes at peak periods, hopes he can head off criticism that he is building new roads without planning longer-term measures to manage demand. […]

The Observer, 15 June 2003

1 **Choose the right explanation for the following words underlined in the article.**

1. overloaded
A. too heavy
B. congested
C. too expensive

2. scheme
A. plan
B. road work
C. widening

3. a backlash
A. a come-back
B. an agreement
C. a revolt

2 **Choose the appropriate endings for the following sentences.**

1. Britain's first 12-lane superhighway is going to be built because
A. it's modelled on America's freeways.
B. Britain's roads are congested.
C. the expansion plan is expensive.

2. The Government is considering plans to

A. introduce extra tolls on the 12 lanes.
B. introduce a levy to enter the 12-lane freeway.
C. tax only a few lanes.

3. The roads under consideration in the scheme were chosen

A. because they have bypasses and junctions.
B. because they are around London.
C. because they are congestion blackspots.

4. The road-building plan will be funded by

A. money imported from America.
B. a tax levied on drivers willing to use the extra lanes.
C. money from the Labour Government.

5. The road-building plan is likely to

A. anger environmentalists but satisfy motorists.
B. enrage environmentalists and worry motorists.
C. gain the backing of both environmentalists and motorists.

3 Fill in the ten lines across the grid with translations of the corresponding French words. This will give you the answer to number 11 in column D.

1. dangereux
2. point chaud
3. annuler
4. fléchage
5. chaussée
6. perturber
7. train pendulaire
8. embouteillage
9. surchargé
10. amende
11. encombrement

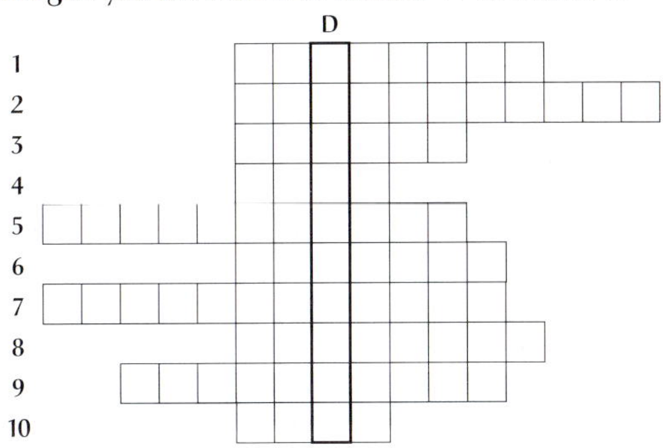

4 Complete the words in the following sentences. Each dash represents one letter.

1. Drifting snow and i _ _ caused a number of m _ _ _ _ r _ _ _ _ to remain closed, but main routes had mostly opened.
2. The City Council's plan to replace a r _ _ _ _ _ _ _ _ _ with t _ _ _ _ _ _ lights would make cycling safer.
3. A Derbyshire bus station is campaigning to encourage more people to use p _ _ _ _ _ t _ _ _ _ _ _ _ _.
4. The Travel Plan Co-ordinator wants to create a c _ _ - s _ _ _ _ _ _ _ database to reduce the number of single occupied cars.
5. Roadside barriers along with more p _ _ _ _ _ _ _ _ _ crossings and u _ _ _ _ _ _ _ _ _ _ _ _ w _ _ _ _ _ _ _ will be installed to increase walkers' safety.

Congestion charge deters third of cars on Day 1

by Paul Marston, Transport Correspondent

The number of cars entering central London slumped by about 30 per cent yesterday as a result of the launch of the congestion charge and fears of jams on routes outside the toll zone.

Ken Livingstone, the London mayor, was careful not to claim success, saying that the first tentative conclusions were not likely to be reached before Easter. Despite intermittent problems, the system for payment of the £5-a-day toll appeared to function well, with more than 75,000 drivers paying the charge by last night.

The number of motorists to be issued with £80 fines for forgetting or trying to evade the levy will be issued today.

More than 200 delivery firms said that mistakes by the administrators, Transport for London (TfL), had left them not knowing whether their vehicles were registered for the charge. TfL said that total traffic in the eight square mile toll area was down by 25 per cent on a normal weekday. The drop in cars, which usually account for nearly half the zone's movements, was greater.

Motoring organisations said the fall, which was twice as big as the expected half-term holiday dip, largely reflected the "hassle factor" involved in paying the charge and a fear of displaced traffic causing jams on routes skirting the zone.

The mayor's frequent predictions of a "bloody day" were thought to have deterred many drivers.

Vehicle flows proved so light that TfL did not have to re-phase traffic lights on the edge of the zone in favour of vehicles travelling round it. But traffic engineers expect this to be necessary by next week. Normal congestion blackspots on the zone perimeter, such as Elephant and Castle and Vauxhall Cross, were described by the RAC Foundation as "deserted, like 5am on a Sunday". Alistair Darling, the Transport Secretary, welcomed the "apparent smoothness" of the launch. "It is not in anyone's interest for it to fail," he said.

The Daily Telegraph, 18 February 2003

1 Choose the right explanation for each of the following words underlined in the article.

1. to slump
A. to decrease
B. to stagnate
C. to increase

2. hassle
A. convenience
B. ease
C. trouble

3. to skirt
A. to go into
B. to go round
C. to go through

4. to deter
A. to discourage
B. to encourage
C. to determine

2 Say whether the following statements are true (T) or false (F).

1. The number of cars dropped by one third inside the toll zone on the first day of the congestion charge.
2. The payment system encountered no problem at all.
3. Drivers entering the toll zone without paying the £5-a-day levy are fined £80.
4. The drop in cars in the toll area surpassed all expectations.
5. Traffic was displaced and caused jams on routes outside the toll zone.
6. Heavier traffic in the coming days could lead to the necessity of re-phasing traffic lights on the edge of the zone.

3 Read the article again and find the following.

1. three nouns synonymous with a fee
2. two nouns which refer to the blocking of places with traffic
3. two nouns which refer to all the vehicles that are moving along the roads in a particular area
4. two nouns which refer to people who drive cars

23

SPORT
LE SPORT

Vocabulaire à haute fréquence

General background	Contexte général
to play	jouer, disputer
an event	une rencontre, une épreuve
a game	une partie
a tie	une rencontre éliminatoire
a qualifier	un match de qualification
the trials	les qualifications
a friendly match	une rencontre amicale
away	à l'extérieur
at home	à domicile
a team	une équipe
a squad	un groupe
a champion	un champion
reigning, defending	en titre
a championship	un championnat
a substitute	un remplaçant
a coach, a manager, a trainer	un entraîneur
to train	s'entraîner
to practice	pratiquer
practice	la pratique
a referee [refə'riː]	un arbitre
a ball	un ballon
shape, fitness	la forme
fit	en forme
to race	participer à une course
a race	une course

a tournament	un tournoi
Olympic	olympique
the Olympics	les jeux olympiques
to attempt	tenter
a bid, an attempt	une tentative
to compete (in)	participer (à)
a competition	une compétition
a competitor	un concurrent
an opponent	un adversaire
a stage/a leg	une étape
a cup	une coupe
a round	un tour
a final	une finale

Sports results / Les résultats sportifs

to score	marquer
a goal	un but
a try	un essai
a point	un point
to lead	mener
to equalise, to level	égaliser
a lead	une avance
a penalty	une pénalité
to win	gagner
a win, a victory	une victoire
to defeat	vaincre
a defeat	une défaite
to lose	perdre
to draw, to tie	faire match nul
a draw	un match nul
to qualify, to be through	(se) qualifier
to knock out, to eliminate	éliminer
elimination	l'élimination
to retain	conserver
a title	un titre
to set up/to break a record	établir/battre un record
a performance	une performance
to finish	terminer

Spectators and facilities / Les spectateurs et les installations

a stadium	un stade
a ground	un terrain
the pitch	l'aire de jeu, le terrain
a stand	une tribune
the terraces	les gradins

a spectator	un spectateur
to watch	regarder
to attend sth.	assister à qch.
attendance	le public, le nombre de spectateurs
a track	une piste
a lap	un tour (de piste)
to support	encourager
support	le soutien
a supporter, a fan	un supporter
to behave	se conduire
behaviour	la conduite
to cheer	acclamer
to hiss at sb.	siffler qn.
to jeer at sb.	railler, huer
to boo	conspuer, huer
a hooligan	un casseur, un voyou
hooliganism	le vandalisme

Expressions

short of practice	à court d'entraînement
in fine form	en bonne forme
to turn professional	devenir professionnel
Arsenal versus Chelsea	Arsenal contre Chelsea
the first round of the Cup	le premier tour de la Coupe
to win/to lose the toss	gagner/perdre le tirage au sort
with one game in hand	avec un match de retard
to be held to a draw	être tenu en échec, devoir se contenter du match nul
to extend one's lead	augmenter son avance
to clinch/to claim/to wrap up a title	décrocher un titre
to take a battering	subir une déroute
to drop one's serve	perdre son service
to break sb.'s serve	prendre le service de qn.
against all odds	contre toute attente
to be the odds-on favourite	être le grand favori
to be in contention for medals	être en course pour une médaille
to cross the finishing line	franchir la ligne d'arrivée
to carry shoulder high	porter en triomphe
to play for time	jouer la montre
to score an own goal	marquer contre son camp
to disallow a goal	refuser un but
to clock under 4 minutes	être chronométré à moins de 4 minutes
top of the table	en tête du classement
bottom of the table	en queue de classement
to fail a drugs test, to test positive	subir un contrôle positif

Vocabulaire complémentaire

General background	Contexte général
a fixture	une rencontre
the first leg	la rencontre aller
the second leg	la rencontre retour
to contest, to contend	disputer
a contest	une rencontre
a contestant, a contender	un concurrent
the title holder	le tenant du titre
a heat	un éliminatoire, une série
a dead-heat	un résultat ex-aequo
to field	aligner (une équipe)
a field	l'ensemble des concurrents
a side	une formation
a team mate	un coéquipier
a runner-up	un deuxième (classement)
amateur	amateur
professional	professionnel
a rookie	un débutant chez les professionnels
to select	sélectionner
a selector	un sélectionneur
to be capped	être sélectionné
a cap/a selection	une selection
a fitness test	un dernier essai (pour voir si le joueur peut jouer)
warm-up	l'échauffement
kick-off	le coup d'envoi
to shoot	tirer
a shot	un tir
a foul	une faute, une irrégularité
to book	avertir
a booking	un avertissement
a yellow card	un carton jaune
to send off	expulser
a send-off	une expulsion
to suspend	suspendre
a suspension	une suspension
to substitute for sb.	remplacer qn.
a tracksuit	un survêtement
an umpire	un juge, un arbitre
a linesman	un arbitre assistant
a post	un poteau
half-time	la mi-temps
a quarter	un quart-temps
injury time, stoppage time	les arrêts de jeu
extra time	les prolongations

a quarter-final	un quart de finale
a semi-final	une demi-finale
the play-offs	les phases finales
on aggregate	sur l'ensemble des deux rencontres
the Grand Slam	le Grand Chelem
to transfer	transférer
a transfer	un transfert
a transfer fee	le montant d'un transfert
to sign sb.	faire signer qn.
to be traded to	être vendu à

Football / Le football

soccer *(US & fam. UK)* ['sɒkə]	le football
a midfielder	un milieu de terrain
a striker	un avant de pointe, un buteur
a sweeper	un libéro
a keeper	un gardien de but
the penalty area, the box	la surface de réparation
a free kick	un coup franc
the crossbar	la barre transversale
an equaliser	une égalisation
to save	parer, sauver
a save	une parade
to dribble	dribbler
to tackle	tacler
a cross	un centre
a header	une tête
to volley	reprendre de volée
a volley	une volée
to clear	dégager
a clearance	un dégagement
a throw-in	une remise de touche
a penalty kick	un pénalty
a penalty shootout	la séance de tirs au but
on penalties	aux tirs au but
the football pools	le loto sportif

Rugby football / Le rugby

rugby union	le jeu à quinze
rugby league	le jeu à treize
a scrum	une mêlée
a loose scrum	une mêlée ouverte
a scrum half	un demi de mêlée
a fly half, a stand-off (half)	un demi d'ouverture
a three-quarter (back)	un trois-quart
a prop	un pilier

a hooker	un talonneur
the backline	la ligne d'arrières
a ruck	un regroupement
a line-out	une remise à la touche
a drop goal	un drop
a try, a touchdown	un essai
a penalty	une pénalité
the conversion	la transformation

Tennis — Le tennis

(the) lawn	le gazon
clay	la terre battue
the baseline	la ligne de fond
a singles match	un simple
a doubles match	un double
to serve	servir
a serve	un service
an ace	un ace
a double fault	une double faute
a service return	un retour de service
a forehand	un coup droit
a backhand	un revers
a net	un filet
a net approach	une montée au filet
a seeded player	une tête de série
the seeds	les têtes de série
30-love	30-zéro
an unforced error	une faute directe
deuce	égalité
advantage	avantage
a tie-break	un jeu décisif
a match point	une balle de match
in straight sets	sans concéder un set

Athletics — L'athlétisme

an athlete ['æθli:t]	un athlète
high jump	le saut en hauteur
long jump	le saut en longueur
pole vault	le saut à la perche
triple jump	le triple saut
discus	le disque
shot put	le lancer de poids
javelin	le javelot
hammer	le marteau
a runner	un coureur
a hurdle	une haie

a hurdler	un coureur de haies
the finishing straight	la dernière ligne droite
a relay	un relais
the baton	le témoin

Miscellaneous sports — Sports divers

boxing	la boxe
to outpoint	surclasser
on points	aux points
to knock out	mettre KO
a bout, a fight	un combat
cricket	le cricket
baseball	le baseball
to bat	être à la batte
to bowl	lancer la balle
the wicket	le guichet
inning *(US)*, innings *(UK)*	tour de batte
cycling	le cyclisme
a jersey	un maillot
the polka dot jersey	le maillot à pois
a breakaway	une échappée
a time trial	un contre la montre
fencing	l'escrime
golf	le golf
to card	rendre une carte de
to par	faire le par
a shot/a stroke	un coup
hiking, rambling	la randonnée
horse racing	les courses hippiques
a race course	un champ de courses
show jumping	le saut d'obstacles
judo	le judo
a judoka	un judoka
motorsport	les sports mécaniques
motor-racing	la course automobile
a racing car	une voiture de course
a racing driver	un pilote de course
Formula One	la Formule 1
a Grand Prix	un Grand prix
a rider	un pilote moto
the grid	la grille (de départ)
the pole	la pôle position
practice	les essais
the pits	les stands
to retire	abandonner
rowing	l'aviron
coxless	sans barreur

sailing	la voile
windsurfing, sailboarding	la planche à voile
a sailboard	une planche à voile
a skipper	un capitaine
a yachtsman/woman	un navigateur, une navigatrice
a crew	un équipage
multihull	multicoque
a trimaran ['traɪmərӕn]	un trimaran
a catamaran ['kӕtəmərӕn]	un catamaran
to dismast	démâter
a regatta	une régate
a single-handed race	une course en solitaire
skating	le patinage
figure skating	le patinage artistique
skiing	le ski
downhill	la descente
snooker	le snooker
a frame	une partie
swimming	la natation
a pool	une piscine
freestyle	la nage libre
breaststroke	la brasse
butterfly	le papillon
backstroke	le dos crawlé
medley	les quatre nages
diving	le plongeon
wrestling	la lutte

Sports results — Les résultats sportifs

to outplay	surclasser
to overwhelm, to crush	écraser
to thrash	battre à plate couture
to trounce	rosser
a rout, a drubbing	une déroute, une raclée
to abandon	abandonner
to triumph	triompher
a triumph	un triomphe
a success	un succès
a showing	une prestation
a goalless draw	un match nul 0 à 0
two-nil	deux à zéro
the final whistle	le coup de sifflet final
a trophy	un trophée
a medal	une médaille
a medallist	un médaillé
a podium	un podium
to dethrone	détrôner

to draw	tirer au sort
a draw	un tirage au sort
to relegate	reléguer
relegation	la relégation
a table	un classement
an overall leader	un leader au classement général
the overall standings	le classement général
the scoreline	le score
a division	une division
to cheat	tricher
a drugs test	un contrôle anti-dopage
anabolic steroids	les stéroïdes anabolisants
random testing	les contrôles inopinés
a performance enhancing drug	un produit dopant

Spectators and facilities — Les spectateurs et les installations

a gate	une grille,une porte, une assistance, une foule
a capacity crowd	un stade/une salle comble
a turnstile	un tourniquet
a grandstand	une tribune d'honneur
the Mexican wave	la ola
a dressing-room	un vestiaire
the venue ['venju:]	le lieu de déroulement
a ticket tout	un revendeur de billets
to gamble	jouer de l'argent
to bet	parier
a bet, a wager	un pari
a punter	un parieur

Federer finally proves fallible

by Alix Ramsay in Miami

It is hard work, this perfection business. In the four months and five tournaments that Roger Federer, the world No 1, had played coming into the Nasdaq-100 Open, he had lost just one match.

The champion of the Masters Cup, the Australian Open, Dubai and Indian Wells was seemingly untouchable. Or he was until he ran into Rafael Nadal, 17, Spain's latest, greatest hope, and was thumped 6-3, 6-3 on Sunday night.

Nadal first announced his arrival on the ATP tour back in April last year when, as a qualifier, he pushed past Karol Kucera and Albert Costa to reach the third round of the Masters Series event in Monte Carlo. It was clear that the boy from Majorca had a big forehand and an even bigger future.

It was not that Federer did not know what to expect from Nadal, it was just that he was in no fit state to cope with him. Suffering from the after effects of sunstroke, a legacy of his two weeks in the scorching sun of the Californian desert, he was exhausted and Nadal's cool head and ferocious ground strokes were too much for him. "I felt it were the reactions that were missing," Federer said. "I had pain in my whole body from my match yesterday because I couldn't prepare the way I wanted to."

Unable to mount a counter offensive against the young Spaniard and given the run around by Nadal's game plan and sheer nerve, Federer made his excuses and left. "I don't think this is a surprise for anybody," Federer said. "I think he's enjoying his tennis and that's exactly what he should do. We'll see how strong he is in two years. But the start to his career so far has been incredible."

The Daily Telegraph, 30 March 2004

1 Choose the right explanation for each of the following words underlined in the article.

1. thumped
A. narrowly defeated
B. outplayed
C. slightly dominated

2. scorching
A. burning
B. cooling
C. warming

3. sheer
A. pure
B. incomplete
C. gradual

4. nerve
A. anger
B. audacity
C. nervousness

2 Choose the appropriate endings for the following sentences.

1. In the four months Roger Federer had played coming into the Nasdaq-100 Open
A. he had lost just one set.
B. he had won four tournaments.
C. he had been undefeated.

2. Federer couldn't match Nadal in the Nasdaq-100 Open final

A. because he suffered from Nadal's big forehand stroke.
B. because of the consequences of overexposure to the sun.
C. because of the scorching sun during the match.

3. Nadal's strokes were

A. very dangerous.
B. very powerful.
C. very hazardous.

3 Say whether the following statements are true (T) or false (F).

1. Roger Federer seemed unbeatable when coming into the Nasdaq-100 Open.
2. Rafael Nadal, 17, Spain's latest, greatest hope, was thumped 6-3, 6-3 in the Open final.
3. Nadal had to qualify to play in Monte Carlo.
4. Federer was not fit enough to compete with Nadal.
5. Federer was not surprised by Nadal's performance.

Swimming: Thorpe atones for blunder

by Oliver Clive in Sydney

Ian Thorpe qualified for Australia's Olympic team yesterday with victory in the final of the 200 metres freestyle at the Australian Championships, two days after he was disqualified in the 400m freestyle.

An Olympic silver medallist behind Dutchman Pieter van den Hoogenband in the 200m freestyle at the Sydney 2000 Games, Thorpe won Monday's final in a time of 1min 45.07sec, ahead of Grant Hackett in 1-45.61. "I'm really relieved after that swim," said Thorpe, who is also likely to qualify for the team with a top-two finish in tomorrow's 100m freestyle final. "I swam the race to make sure I got on the team, not to swim as fast as I could," added Thorpe, who raised his right arm to acknowledge the crowd's applause immediately after the race and breathed a big sigh of relief.

Thorpe, the 200m and 400m world record holder, will be unable to defend his Olympic 400m title in Athens. The 21-year-old overbalanced on the blocks and fell into the water before the start of his heat in Sydney on Saturday and was disqualified under the one false-start rule. Hackett and Craig Stevens finished first and second in the 400m freestyle final to secure their places in that event for Athens.

Shane Gould, Australia's three-times gold medallist from the 1972 Munich Games, led calls for Australian Swimming officials to find a way to include Thorpe in the 400m event for Athens.

However, while radio and television stations conduct polls on whether Thorpe should be given another opportunity to qualify for the 400m freestyle, the Olympic champion has told the nation to get over it. "I've accepted that I won't swim it. I think now everyone else has to accept that as well," Thorpe said.

The Daily Telegraph, 30 March 2004

1 **Choose the right explanation for each of the following words underlined in the text.**

1. to atone
A. to swim
B. to compensate
C. to qualify

2. blunder
A. a swimming event
B. an embarrassing mistake
C. a resounding success

3. to overbalance
A. to cause imbalance
B. to go too fast
C. to slip

2 **Say whether the following statements are true (T) or false (F).**

1. Peter van den Hoogenband is both the 400m freestyle reigning Olympic champion and world record holder.
2. Ian Thorpe was runner-up in the 200m freestyle in Sydney in 2000.
3. Thorpe finished over half a second ahead of Hackett in the 200m freestyle.
4. Thorpe is likely to qualify for the relay.
5. The crowd was pleased with Thorpe's performance in the 200m freestyle.
6. Thorpe was disqualified because he made a false start.
7. The first two swimmers in the 400m freestyle qualified for Athens.
8. Shane Gould won three gold medals in Munich in 1972.
9. Shane Gould thinks Thorpe should be given a second chance to defend his Olympic 400m title in Athens.
10. Ian Thorpe is still unable to come to terms with his disqualification.

3 **The letters of the names of various swimming strokes have been scrambled (1-5). Put the letters back into the right order and match the strokes with their corresponding definitions (A-E).**

1. emyeld
2. tsabekrcok
3. rulefttyb
4. obkertrestas
5. tfeyersle

A. The arms are extended together in front of the head and swept back on either side accompanied by a frog kick.
B. The arms are thrown forward together out of the water while the feet kick up and down.
C. The swimmer uses a different stroke for each of several equivalent distances.
D. The arms are moved alternately overhead accompanied by a flutter kick.
E. A stroke that resembles the crawl except the swimmer lies on his or her back.

4 **The prefix "over-" is to be found in the verb "overbalance". Match the similarly-constructed verbs (1-6) with their explanations (A-F).**

1. to overthrow
2. to overdo
3. to overweigh
4. to overtake
5. to overcome
6. to overdraw

A. to pass after catching up with
B. to exceed in importance
C. to exceed appropriate limits; to exaggerate
D. to take out money in excess of available funds
E. to conquer after a struggle with
F. to cause the fall or collapse of

Sports round-up

Athletics

Double world cross-country champion Kenenisa Bekele will start his build-up for the Athens Olympics with a possible attempt on fellow-Ethiopian Haile Gebrselassie's world 5,000 metres record in the Dutch town of Hengelo on May 31.
Twice Olympic 10,000m champion Gebrselassie is the current world record holder over the 5,000m, clocking 12min 39.36sec in Helsinki six years ago.
Brazilian long jumper Maurren Maggi may miss the Olympics after the Court of Arbitration for Sport (CAS) was called in yesterday to overturn her acquittal by her own national authority for a doping offence.

The Daily Telegraph, 23 March 2004

Yachting

Steve Fossett said this week that he hoped Cheyenne's impressive 58 days, 9 hours round-the-world record would be «difficult to beat,» but Olivier de Kersauson in Geronimo is steaming up the south Atlantic and only some 500 miles behind Cheyenne's pace. Geronimo rounded Cape Horn early on Thursday after a torrid 10 days facing the worst the Southern Ocean can dish out. «Never again, whatever happens,» said De Kersauson, a veteran of eight round-the-world attempts.

The Daily Telegraph, 10 April 2004

Skiing: Super-G win for Maier

by Astrid Andersson in Garmisch-Partenkirchen

Hermann Maier won the super-giant World Cup and took the lead in the overall standings after victory on his favourite piste yesterday.
The Austrian, who burst onto the scene with a super-G win in this Bavarian Alps resort in 1997, knocked compatriot Benjamin Raich off the top of the standings with his third win of the season. Raich suffered concussion after crashing out on the lower section of a tricky, icy Kandahar course, losing his balance sliding into the safety netting.
Maier, 31, in his first full season since he nearly lost a leg in a motorcycle accident in 2001, clocked a winning time of 1min 18.09sec. He also won the World Cup title for the discipline for the fifth time with only two races remaining.

The Daily Telegraph, 2 February 2004

24

COUNTRIES AND PEOPLE

LES PAYS ET LES GENS

A-C

Afghanistan	l'Afghanistan
Afghan	afghan
an Afghan, an Afghani	un Afghan
Albania	l'Albanie
Albanian	albanais
Algeria	l'Algérie
Algerian	algérien
Andorra	Andorre
Andorran	andorran
Angola	l'Angola
Angolan	angolais
Argentina	l'Argentine
Argentinian	argentin
Armenia	l'Arménie
Armenian	arménien
Australia	l'Australie
Australian	australien
Austria	l'Autriche
Austrian	autrichien
Azerbaijan	l'Azerbaïdjan
Azerbaidjani	azeri
an Azeri, an Azerbaijani	un Azerbaïdjanais
Bahamas	les Bahamas
Bahamian	bahaméen
Bahrain	Bahreïn
Bahraini	bahreini
Bangladesh	le Bangladesh

Bangladeshi	bengalais
B(y)elarus, B(y)elorussia	le Bélarus, la Biélorussie
B(y)elorussian	biélorusse
Belgium	la Belgique
Belgian	belge
Benin	le Bénin
Beninese	béninois
Bhutan	le Bhoutan
Bhutani	bhoutanais
Bolivia	la Bolivie
Bolivian	bolivien
Bosnia-Herzegovina	la Bosnie-Herzégovine
Bosnian	bosniaque
Botswana	le Botswana
Botswanan	botswanais
Brazil	le Brésil
Brazilian	brésilien
Brunei	Brunei
Bruneian	bruneien
Bulgaria	la Bulgarie
Bulgarian	bulgare
Burkina Faso	le Burkina Faso
Burkinese	burkinabais
Burma	la Birmanie
Burmese	birman
Burundi	le Burundi
Burundi	burundais
a Burundian	un Burundais
Cambodia	le Cambodge
Cambodian	cambodgien
Cameroon	le Cameroun
Cameroonian	camerounais
Canada	le Canada
Canadian	canadien
Cape Verde	le Cap Vert
Cape Verdian	cap verdien
(the) Central African Republic	la République Centre Africaine
Chad	le Tchad
Chadian	tchadien
Chile	le Chili
Chilean	chilien
China	la Chine
Chinese	chinois
Colombia	la Colombie
Colombian	colombien
Comoros	les Comores
Comoran	comorien

the Congo	le Congo
Congolese	congolais
Costa Rica	le Costa Rica
Costa Rican	costaricain
Côte d'Ivoire, Ivory Coast	la Côte d'Ivoire
Ivorian	ivoirien
Croatia	la Croatie
Croatian	croate
a Croat	un Croate
Cuba	Cuba
Cuban	cubain
Cyprus	Chypre
a Cypriot	un Chypriote
the Czech Republic	la République tchèque
Czech	tchèque

D-I

Denmark	le Danemark
Danish	danois
a Dane	un Danois
Djibouti	Djibouti
Djiboutian	djiboutien
Ecuador	l'Equateur
Ecuadorian	équatorien
Egypt	l'Egypte
Egyptian	égyptien
El Salvador	le Salvador
Salvadorian	salvadorien
England	l'Angleterre
English	anglais
an Englishman	un Anglais
Eritrea	l'Erythrée
Eritrean	érythréen
Estonia	l'Estonie
Estonian	estonien
Ethiopia	l'Ethiopie
Ethiopian	éthiopien
Fiji	Fidji
Fijian	fidjien
Finland	la Finlande
Finnish	finlandais
a Finn	un Finlandais
France	la France
French	français
Gabon	le Gabon
Gabonese	gabonais
the Gambia	la Gambie

Gambian	gambien
Germany	l'Allemagne
German	allemand
Georgia	la Géorgie
Georgian	géorgien
Ghana	le Ghana
Ghanaian	ghanéen
Great Britain	la Grande-Bretagne
British	britannique
a Briton	un Britannique
Greece	la Grèce
Greek	grec
Grenada	la Grenade
Grenadian	grenadien
Guatemala	le Guatemala
Guatemaltan	guatémaltèque
Guinea	la Guinée
Guinean	guinéen
Guyana	la Guyane
Guyanese	guyanais
Haiti	Haïti
Haitian	haïtien
Holland	la Hollande
Dutch	hollandais
a Dutchman	un Hollandais
Honduras	le Honduras
Honduran	hondurien
Hungary	la Hongrie
Hungarian	hongrois
Iceland	l'Islande
Icelandic	islandais
an Icelander	un Islandais
India	l'Inde
Indian	indien
Indonesia	l'Indonésie
Indonesian	indonésien
Iran	l'Iran
Iranian	iranien
Iraq	l'Irak
Iraqi	irakien
Ireland	l'Irlande
Irish	irlandais
an Irishman	un Irlandais
Israel	Israël
Israeli	israélien
Italy	l'Italie
Italian	italien

J-N

Jamaica	la Jamaïque
Jamaican	jamaïcain
Japan	le Japon
Japanese	japonais
Java	Java
Javanese	javanais
Jordan	la Jordanie
Jordanian	jordanien
Kazakhstan	le Kazakhstan
Kazakh	kazakh
Kenya	le Kenya
Kenyan	kenyan
Korea	la Corée
Korean	coréen
Kuwait	le Koweït
Kuwaiti	koweïtien, koweïti
Kirghizstan	le Kirghizstan
Kirghiz	kirghiz
Laos	le Laos
Laotian	laotien
Latvia	la Lettonie
Latvian	letton
Lebanon	le Liban
Lebanese	libanais
Lesotho	le Lésotho
Sotho	lesothan, lesothien
Liberia	le Libéria
Liberian	libérien
Libya	la Libye
Libyan	libyen
Liechtenstein	le Liechtenstein
Liechtensteiner	liechtensteinien
Lithuania	la Lituanie
Lithuanian	lituanien
Luxembourg, Luxemburg	le Luxembourg
Luxemburger	luxembourgeois
Macedonia, Former Yugoslav Republic of	Macédoine, Ex-République yougoslave de
Macedonian	macédonien
Madagascar	Madagascar
Madagascan/Malagasy	malgache
Malaysia	la Malaisie
Malaysian	malais
Mali	le Mali
Malian	malien
Malta	Malte

Maltese	maltais
Mauritania	la Mauritanie
Mauritanian	mauritanien
Mauritius	Maurice
Mauritian	mauricien
Mexico	le Mexique
Mexican	mexicain
Moldova	la Moldavie
Moldovan	moldave
Morocco	le Maroc
Moroccan	marocain
Mozambique	le Mozambique
Mozambican	mozambicain
Namibia	la Namibie
Namibian	namibien
Nepal	le Népal
Nepalese	népalais
the Netherlands	les Pays-Bas
New Zealand	la Nouvelle-Zélande
a New Zealander	un Néo-zélandais
Nicaragua	le Nicaragua
Nicaraguan	nicaraguayen
Niger	le Niger
Nigeria	le Nigéria
Nigerian	nigérian
Norway	la Norvège
Norwegian	norvégien

O-Z

Oman	Oman
Omani	omanais
Pakistan	le Pakistan
Pakistani	pakistanais
Palestine	la Palestine
Palestinian	palestinien
Panama	le Panama
Panamanian	panaméen
Paraguay	le Paraguay
Paraguayan	paraguayen
Peru	le Pérou
Peruvian	péruvien
the Philippines	les Philippines
Phillipine, Filipino	philippin
a Filipino	un Philippin
Poland	la Pologne
Polish	polonais
a Pole	un Polonais

Portugal	le Portugal
Portuguese	portugais
Qatar	le Qatar
Qatari	qatarien
Romania, Roumania	la Roumanie
Romanian, Roumanian	roumain
Russia	la Russie
Russian	russe
Rwanda	le Rwanda
Rwandan	rwandais
Samoa	Samoa
Samoan	samoan
Saudi Arabia	l'Arabie saoudite
Saudi	saoudien
Scotland	l'Écosse
Scottish, Scots	écossais
a Scot, a Scotsman	un Écossais
Senegal	le Sénégal
Senegalese	sénégalais
Serbia and Montenegro	la Serbie Monténégro
Serbian	serbe
a Serb	un Serbe
Montenegrin	monténégrin
Sierra Leone	la Sierra Léone
Sierra Leonean	sierra léonais
Singapore	Singapour
Singaporean	singapourien
Slovakia	la Slovaquie
Slovakian	slovaque
a Slovak	un Slovaque
Slovenia	la Slovénie
Slovenian	slovène
a Slovene	un Slovène
Somalia	la Somalie
Somalian, Somali	somalien
a Somali	un Somalien
South Africa	l'Afrique du Sud
South African	sud-africain
Spain	l'Espagne
Spanish	espagnol
a Spaniard	un Espagnol
Sri Lanka	le Sri Lanka
Sri Lankan	sri lankais
Sudan	le Soudan
Sudanese	soudanais
Surinam	le Surinam
Surinamese	surinamais

Swaziland	le Swaziland
Swazi	swazilandais
Sweden	la Suède
Swedish	suédois
a Swede	un Suédois
Switzerland	la Suisse
Swiss	suisse
Syria	la Syrie
Syrian	syrien
Taiwan	Taiwan
Taiwanese	taiwanais
Tajikistan, Tadzhikistan	le Tadjikistan
Tajiki, Tadzhiki	tadjik
a Tajik, a Tadzhik	un Tadjik
Tanzania	la Tanzanie
Tanzanian	tanzanien
Thailand	la Thaïlande
Thai	thaïlandais
Tibet	le Tibet
Tibetan	tibétain
Togo	le Togo
Togolese	togolais
Tunisia	la Tunisie
Tunisian	tunisien
Turkey	la Turquie
Turkish	turc
a Turk	un Turc
Turkmenistan	le Turkménistan
Turkmen	turkmène
Uganda	l'Ouganda
Ugandan	ougandais
The Ukraine	l'Ukraine
Ukrainian	ukrainien
the United Arab Emirates (UAE)	les Emirats Arabes Unis
the United Kingdom (UK)	le Royaume-Uni
the United States of America (USA)	les États-Unis d'Amérique
American	américain
Uruguay	l'Uruguay
Uruguayan	uruguayen
Uzbekistan	l'Ouzbekistan
Uzbek	ouzbek
Venezuela	le Venezuela
Venezuelan	vénézuélien
Vietnam	le Vietnam
Vietnamese	vietnamien
Wales	le Pays de Galles
Welsh	gallois

a Welshman	un Gallois
the West Indies	les Antilles
West Indian	antillais
Yemen	le Yemen
Yemeni	yéménite
Yugoslavia	la Yougoslavie
Yugoslavian	yougoslave
a Yugoslav	un Yougoslave
Zambia	la Zambie
Zambian	zambien
Zimbabwe	le Zimbabwe
Zimbabwean	du Zimbabwe

KEY
Corrigé

Les références de page correspondent aux pages où vous trouverez les articles sur lesquels portent les exercices.

1 The environment

page 16

1 1/A, 2/C, 3/B

2 1/F, 2/T, 3/T, 4/F, 5/F, 6/F, 7/T

3 organic, carcinogenic, chemical, historically, ecological, biological, catalytic, philosophically

4 1. waste, 2. sustainable, 3. fertiliser, 4. lead, 5. slick, 6. noxious, 7. harmful, 8. spread, 9. wildlife

page 18

1 1/A, 2/C, 3/A, 4/B, 5/B, 6/A, 7/C, 8/C

2 1/F, 2/T, 3/F, 4/T, 5/T, 6/F, 7/F, 8/T

3 1. untested, 2. to trouble, 3. to train

4 1. children, 2. mice, 3. lives, 4. phenomena, 5. knives, 6. leaves, 7. criteria, 8. thieves, 9. women, 10. men, 11. fungi, 12. feet, 13. wives, 14. halves, 15. calves, 16. teeth, 17. sheep, 18. bacteria

2 The economy I

page 30

1 1. an activist, 2. to march, 3. global, 4. to highlight, 5. businesses, 6. to thrive

2 1. in favour of, 2. huge, 3. success, 4. to widen, 5. inequities, 6. previous

3 1/F, 2/T, 3/T, 4/F, 5/F, 6/T, 7/T, 8/T

4 1/D, 2/C, 3/A, 4/E, 5/B

5 1. to march, 2. regional, 3. to undermine, 4. agenda

3 The economy II

page 42

1 1/E, 2/D, 3/B, 4/F, 5/C, 6/A

2 1/T, 2/T, 3/T, 4/F, 5/T, 6/T, 7/T, 8/F, 9/T

3 Assessment: plunges into the red, restructuring, crashed into the red, debt-laden, cash crisis, refinancing, capital repayments, the shares fell, to buy back debt, a fall in operating revenues, a drop in operating profits, the loss swelled. All these expressions express a downtrend.

4 1/B, 2/C, 3/C

5 FTSE 100: London, UK stock index; Dow Jones: New York, US stock index; Nasdaq: New York, US stock index (new technologies); Cac 40: Paris, French stock index; Dax: Frankfurt, German stock index; Hang Seng: Hong Kong, Hong Kong stock index; Nikkei: Tokyo, Japanese stock index.

6 1. board, 2. company, 3. hostile bid, 4. rival, 5. value, 6. drugs giant, 7. global, 8. launch, 9. fevered, 10. shares, 11. investors, 12. cost-cutting, 13. comment, 14. fight, 15. hired, 16. government, 17. deal, 18. merger

4 The Third World

page 51

1 1/A, 2/B, 3/C, 4/B

2 1. leaking, 2. to rely on, 3. a shortage, 4. sanitation

3 1. underground, 2. supplies, 3. to decrease, to diminish, 4. liquid, 5. heavily, 6. safe

4 1/F, 2/T, 3/T, 4/F, 5/T, 6/T, 7/T, 8/T

5 The world population has increased more than twofold in the past 60 years./The world population has multiplied by more than two in the past 60 years.

6 1. one tenth, 2. one fourth/one quarter, 3. two-fifths, 4. four-fifths, 5. 33%, 6. 60%, 7. 66%, 8. 5%

5 Employment

page 58

1 1/B, 2/B, 3/C

2 1/F, 2/ T, 3/F, 4/T, 5/T, 6/T, 7/T

3 1. redundancy/trade unions, 2. losses/voluntary, 3. axing/workforce, 4. out of work/benefit, 5. relocated/developing, 6. unemployment

page 60

1 1/B, 2/A, 3/C, 4/A, 5/B, 6/A, 7/B

2 1. wages, 2. to retrain, 3. to vet, 4. plant, 5. to gauge

3 1. work sharing, 2. unemployment, 3. claimant, 4. gridlock or deadlock, 5. shed, 6. redundant, 7. pensioner, 8. register, 9. competitive, 10. retrain, D. head hunter

4 slashing, business, workforce, cuts, money, lay off, company, shares

6 Disputes and tension

page 70

1 1/B, 2/A, 3/B

2 1/F, 2/T, 3/T, 4/T, 5/F, 6/T

3 1. proposal, 2. mediation, 3. a claim, 4. partner

4 1. thaw, 2. resolution, watchdog, 3. walk out, 4. hammer out, 5. trade unions, all-out

page 72

1 1/B, 2/A

2 1/F, 2/T, 3/F, 4/T, 5/F, 6/T, 7/F

3 1. bargain, 2. strained, 3. failure, 4. extradite, 5. backlash, 6. blockade, 7. official, 8. breakthrough, 9. gridlock

7 Medicine

page 84

1 1/T, 2/F, 3/T, 4/T, 5/T, 6/T, 7/T, 8/T

2 B, E, A, C, F, D

3 1. to forgive, 2. to cancel, 3. unfit, 4. to oppose

4 1. Therapeutic cloning consists in growing embryos in a test tube to supply stem cells that can grow into any tissue.

2. Dolly the sheep, who became the first cloned mammal when she was born on 5 July 1996, was euthanised aged 6.

5 1. narrow, 2. virtual, 3. absolute, 4. scientifically, 5. completely, 6. reproductively, 7. therapeutically, 8. genetically, 9. ethically, 10. remarkably, 11. medically, 12. originally, 13. global, 14. individually, 15. angrily, 16. confidently

8 Space

page 91

1 1/B, 2/A, 3/C, 4/B, 5/C, 6/C

2 1. grinding, 2. delay, 3. grief, 4. to identify, 5. ordinary, 6. sent, 7. trivial

3 1/F, 2/F, 3/T, 4/F, 5/T, 6/T, 7/T, 8/T, 9/T, 10/T

4 1. touchdown, 2. crew, 3. probe, 4. weightlessness, 5. setback, 6. gravity, 7. launch, 8. crash, 9. steer, 10. interplanetary, 11. scuttle, 12. glide, 13. ignition, 14. training, 15. orbit insertion

5 Mercury, Venus, Earth, Mars, Jupiter, Saturn, Uranus, Neptune, Pluto

9 Politics I

page 101

1 1/E, 2/F, 3/A, 4/H, 5/C, 6/G, 7/B, 8/I, 9/D

2 1/T, 2/T, 3/T, 4/F, 5/T, 6/T, 7/T, 8/T, 9/F

3 1. challenge, 2. polls, election, 3. delegates, 4. nomination, 5. vice president

4 1. close, 2. voter, 3. deputy, 4. grassroots, 5. swing, 6. challenger, 7. defeat, 8. leadership, 9. nomination, 10. activist, 11. funding, 12. pledge, 13. overwhelming

10 Politics II

page 113

1 1/ B, 2/C, 3/A, 4/B

2 1/T, 2/T, 3/F, 4/T, 5/T

3 1/C, 2/C, 3/B

4 1. passion, 2. qualified, 3. loss, 4. to promote

5 1. lengthen, 2. widen or broaden, 3. deepen, 4. shorten, 5. strengthen, 6. tighten, 7. loosen, 8. heighten, 9. deaden

page 116

1 1/B, 2/A, 3/C, 4/A, 5/A, 6/B

11 Religion

page 124

1 1/B, 2/A, 3/A

2 1/A, 2/C, 3/B

3 1/T, 2/T, 3/T, 4/F

4 1. churchgoing, 2. devout, 3. a religious affiliation, 4. evangelists, 5. faith, 6. secularists

5 1/D, 2/F, 3/A, 4/B, 5/E, 6/C

page 126

1 1/C, 2/C, 3/A, 4/B, 5/B, 6/C

2 1. a sect, 2. evangelism, 3. red tape, 4. a bishop, the Right Rev., a minister, a cleric, an archbishop, a cardinal

3 1. A leading academic has warned that education is the only way to tackle religious extremism and hatred.

2. Only one in 10 people in Scotland go to church on a Sunday according to the latest figures.

3. A mosque is going to be built for the town's Muslim community to have somewhere quiet to worship.

12 Entertainment and the mass media

page 138

1 1/B, 2/A, 3/C, 4/A, 5/B

2 1/F, 2/T, 3/T, 4/F, 5/T, 6/F, 7/T, 8/T, 9/F, 10/T, 11/T, 12/F, 13/T, 14/F

3 1. familiarity, 2. gig, 3. to edit, 4. awards, 5. a score

4 1. fantasy, 2. reality, 3. censorship, 4. album, charts, 5. newspaper, daily, broadsheet

5 1. downloaded, 2. albums, 3. singles (2 and 3 can be reversed), 4. play, 5. websites, 6. music, 7. Internet, 8. legal, 9. CDs, 10. success, 11. worldwide

13 Crime and punishment

page 161

1 1/F, 2/T, 3/F, 4/T, 5/F, 6/T, 7/T, 8/F

2 1. indicted, 2. mob, 3. sentence, 4. case, 5. innocently

3 1. plea-bargaining, 2. a supergrass, 3. to smuggle, 4. a sentence

4 1. photographer, 2. player, 3. offender, 4. donor, 5. writer, 6. supervisor, 7. poacher, 8. sailor, 9. worker, 10. shoplifter, 11. trespasser, 12. prosecutor, 13. murderer, 14. robber, 15. smuggler, 16. actor, 17. operator, 18. shopper

page 162

1 1/A, 2/C, 3/A

2 1/B, 2/C, 3/A, 4/B

3 A. 1. bloodless, 2. homeless, 3. hopeful, hopeless, 4. jobless, 5. lawful, lawless, 6. useful, useless, 7. forgetful, 8. harmful, harmless, 9. cloudless, 10. dreadful

B. 1. goodness, 2. readiness, 3. forgetfulness, 4. happiness, 5. sadness, 6. weakness, 7. joblessness, 8. seriousness

C. 1. penalise, 2. modernise, 3. industrialise, 4. legalise, 5. commercialise, 6. centralise

4 1. hunt, 2. abducted, 3. knifepoint, 4. missing, 5. officers, 6. arrested, 7. questioning, 8. searched, 9. treatment

14 Drugs

page 170

1 1/F, 2/T, 3/T, 4/F, 5/T, 6/F, 7/F, 8/T

2 1. cartel, drugs lord, 2. reclassify,

heroin, 3. smuggler, ecstasy, 4. crack down, narcotic

3 1. needle, 2. speed, 3. narcotics, 4. withdrawal, 5. trafficking, 6. hemp, 7. pill, 8. laundering, 9. relaxation, 10. mule, 11. addiction, 12. capsule, 13. wean 14. decriminalise

4 1. in, 2. of, 3. on, 4. on, 5. from, 6. in, 7. in, 8. to, 9. from, 10. of

5 1. a book of 115 pages/a 115-page book, 2. a walk of 5 miles/a 5-mile walk, 3. a trafficker who is 50 years old/a 50-year-old trafficker, 4. a weight of 20 kilos/a 20-kilo weight

6 1. customs, 2. cocaine, 3. traffickers, 4. "mules", 5. smuggle, 6. imports, 7. cartels, 8. market, 9. detection, 10. criminals

15 Demonstrations and riots

page 178

1 1/B, 2/A

2 1/T, 2/T, 3/T, 4/F, 5/F

3 1. passers-by, 2. a ban, 3. to walk, 4. to strengthen

4 1. to march, 2. to gather, 3. rallies, 4. demonstrations, 5. to spark

page 180

1 1/B, 2/C

2 1/T, 2/F, 3/F, 4/T

3 1/B, 2/B, 3/C

4 1. revel, 2. civilians, 3. to disrupt, 4. dissent

5 1. President Chirac, 2. the British Prime Minister, 3. Queen Elizabeth, 4. Prime Minister John Howard, 5. Captain Smith, 6. the Foreign Secretary

16 Terrorism and revolutions

page 187

1 1/T, 2/T, 3/F, 4/F, 5/T, 6/T, 7/F

2 1. exploded, 2. attack, 3. carried out, 4 blast, 5. purported, 6. sealed off, 7. wrecked, 8. a string of

3 1. defuse, 2. feud, 3. indiscriminate, 4. hijacker, 5. rise, 6. bloody, 7. underground, 8. booby trap, 9. plot, 10. undermine, 11. harbour, 12. overthrow, 13. target, 14. suicide bomber

4 1. Les rebelles auraient repris la ville de Dondon.

2. L'incendie se serait déclaré dans un entrepôt temporaire.

3. On pense que le sénateur Kerry pourrait gagner en crédibilité (comme ce fut le cas pour John McCain) grâce à son statut de héros du Vietnam.

page 189

1 1. to boost, 2. crackdown, 3. money laundering, 4. a blacklist, 5. to fund, 6. underground, 7. couriers, 8. charities

17 War and espionage

page 200

1 1/A, 2/B, 3/B, 4/B

2 1/T, 2/F, 3/T, 4/F, 5/T, 6/T, 7/F, 8/T, 9/F, 10/T

3 1. to lure, 2. a warning, 3. to wipe out, 4. to escalate

4 1. ethnic war, 2. infantry, fighting, 3. detention camp, 4. weapons of mass destruction

18 Miscellaneous topics

page 212

1 1/B, 2/B, 3/B

2 1/T, 2/T, 3/T, 4/F, 5/F, 6/T, 7/F, 8/T, 9/T

3 1. attempted killing, 2. legitimacy, 3. promiscuity, 4. harmful

4 1. human, inhuman, 2. ethnic, 3. asylum seekers, 4. sexual harassment, 5. condoms

page 214

1 1/A, 2/A, 3/B

2 1/T, 2/T, 3/F, 4/T, 5/F, 6/T, 7/T, 8/T, 9/F, 10/T, 11/T, 12/F

3 1. websites, 2. pornographic, 3. trial, 4. meeting, 5. campaign, 6. sexual acts, 7. crackdown, 8. freedom, 9. internet, 10. companies, 11. the web

19 Accidents

page 224

1 1/A, 2/B, 3/B

2 1/T, 2/T, 3/T, 4/T, 5/F, 6/F, 7/F, 8/T

3 1. coach, 2. ram, 3. shroud, 4. stitch, 5. swerve, 6. bushfire, 7. steer, 8. seam, 9. ablaze, 10. cartwheel

page 226

1 1/B, 2/B

2 1/C, 2/B, 3/C

3 1/T, 2/T, 3/T, 4/F

4 1. a truck, 2. to hit, 3. to swerve, 4. an investigation, 5. deadly, 6. a fire

20 Natural disasters

page 232

1 1/B, 2/B, 3/C, 4/B, 5/A

2 E, B, F, C, A, D

3 1. relief/aid, 2. sanitation, 3. supplies, 4. to rush, 5. a field hospital, 6. spread, 7. to downplay, 8. to bury, 9. rubble

4 1. an earthquake, 2. flood, 3. a hurricane, 4. a tsunami/a tidal wave, 5. a landslide/a landslip, 6. an eruption, 7. a blizzard

page 234

1 1/A, 2/B, 3/B

2 1. rescuers/rescue workers, 2. a landslide, 3. huge, 4. to devastate, 5. to topple, 6. to hamper

21 The weather

page 240

1 1/C, 2/B, 3/C

2 1/T, 2/T, 3/T, 4/F, 5/T, 6/F, 7/F

3 freezing, cold, chilly, cool, mild, warm, hot

4 1. cloudburst, 2. to swelter, 3. outlook, 4. to forecast, 5. overcast, 6. drizzle, 7. unstable

22 Travel and traffic

page 248

1 1/B, 2/A, 3/C

2 1/B, 2/C, 3/C, 4/B, 5/B

3 1. reckless, 2. troublespot, 3. cancel, 4. sign, 5. carriageway, 6. disrupt, 7. tilting train, 8. gridlock, 9. overloaded, 10. fine, 11. congestion

4 1. ice, minor roads
2. roundabout, traffic
3. public transport
4. car-sharing,
5. pedestrian, underground walkways

page 250

1 1/A, 2/C, 3/B, 4/A

2 1/T, 2/F, 3/T, 4/T, 5/F, 6/T

3 1. toll, levy, charge
2. congestion, jam
3. traffic, vehicle flows
4. drivers, motorists

23 Sport

page 261

1 1/B, 2/A, 3/A, 4/B

2 1/B, 2/B, 3/B

3 1/T, 2/F, 3/T, 4/T, 5/T

page 262

1 1/B, 2/B, 3/A

2 1/F, 2/T, 3/T, 4/T, 5/T, 6/T, 7/T, 8/T, 9/T, 10/F

3 1. medley/C, 2. backstroke/E, 3. butterfly/B, 4. breaststroke/A, 5. freestyle/D

4 1/F, 2/C, 3/B, 4/A, 5/E, 6/D

Sources

The Financial Times (FT) http://www.ft.com

460 000 ex., Royaume-Uni, quotidien. Journal économique reconnaissable entre tous à sa couleur rose saumon, il dispose également d'un vaste réseau de correspondants internationaux couvrant l'actualité. Bien que basé à Londres, la plus grande partie de son lectorat se situe à l'étranger. Il n'a aucun lien avec *The Times* malgré son nom.

New Scientist http://www.newscientist.co.uk

140 000 ex., Royaume-Uni, hebdomadaire. Magazine scientifique généraliste et bon vulgarisateur, ses articles servent souvent de base aux rubriques scientifiques de la presse quotidienne. Créé en 1956, il réalise un tiers de ses ventes à l'étranger.

The Daily Telegraph http://www.telegraph.co.uk

920 000 ex., Royaume-Uni, quotidien. Grand journal conservateur de référence fondé en 1855, il partage la même rédaction avec sa version dominicale *The Sunday Telegraph* qui apparaît en 1961 (886 300 ex.).

The Guardian http://www.guardian.co.uk

400 000 ex., Royaume-Uni, quotidien. Fondé en 1821 à Manchester sous le nom de *The Manchester Guardian,* il devient *The Guardian* en 1959 et quitte sa base du nord de l'Angleterre pour Londres à partir 1964 revendiquant toujours une ligne éditoriale indépendante.

The Independent http://www.independent.co.uk

230 000 ex., Royaume-Uni, quotidien. Fondé en 1986, c'est le journal de presse sérieuse le plus récent de Grande-Bretagne. Depuis 2003 le journal est publié à la fois en grand format et en format tabloïd avec le même contenu dans chaque édition suivant une ligne éditoriale proche de celle du *Guardian*.

The Observer http://www.guardian.co.uk

460 000 ex., Royaume-Uni, journal du dimanche. Édition dominicale la plus ancienne de la presse mondiale (publiée pour la première fois en 1791) elle est publiée depuis juin 1993 par le même groupe de presse qui possède *The Guardian.*

The Times http://www.timesonline.co.uk

620 000 ex., Royaume-Uni, quotidien. Créé en 1785 sous le nom de *The Daily Universal Register* c'est en 1788 qu'il devient *The Times*. Premier quotidien à

avoir des envoyés spéciaux à l'étranger et des correspondants couvrant des événements particuliers, il fut longtemps considéré comme sans rival et joua ainsi un rôle très important dans la vie politique britannique.

AFP **(Agence France Presse) http://www.afp.com**

Fondée en 1835 par Charles-Louis Havas, l'AFP est l'agence de presse la plus ancienne au monde. Installée à Paris, elle n'a depuis lors cessé de développer ses activités de couverture médiatique grâce à ses antennes installées dans 165 capitales à travers le monde.

AP **(Associated Press) http://www.ap.org**

Née en 1848 d'une entente entre 6 journaux new-yorkais réunis autour des enjeux du télégraphe, *The Associated Press* est aujourd'hui une organisation diffusant dans 112 pays à destination de plus de 15 000 organismes.

Reuters **http://www.reuters.com**

D'abord confinée aux informations boursières entre Paris et Londres, l'agence *Reuters* créée en 1851 se fit rapidement un nom à travers la Grande-Bretagne avant d'étendre ses activités à l'Europe puis au monde entier.

Imprimé en France par Mame à Tours
N° d'imprimeur : 07072146 - N° d'édition : 003933-03
Dépôt légal : juillet 2007